The Stamp Act Congress

The Stamp Act Congress

WITH AN EXACT COPY OF THE COMPLETE JOURNAL

C. A. Weslager

A UNIVERSITY OF DELAWARE BICENTENNIAL BOOK

Newark
University of Delaware Press
London: Associated University Presses

© 1976 by Associated University Presses, Inc.

Associated University Presses, Inc.
Cranbury, New Jersey 08512

Associated University Presses
108 New Bond Street
London W1Y OQX, England

Library of Congress Cataloging in Publication Data

Weslager, Clinton Alfred date
    The Stamp Act Congress.

    "A University of Delaware bicentennial book."
    Bibliography: p.
    Includes index.
    1. Stamp Act Congress, New York, 1765.
E215.2.W47   973.3'111   75-21514
ISBN 0-87413-111-1

PRINTED IN THE UNITED STATES OF AMERICA

Contents

Abbreviations
Frequently Used in Notes

Adams Diary *Diary And Autobiography Of John Adams,*
ed. L. H. Butterfield. 4 vols. Cambridge, 1961.

Adams Works Charles Francis Adams, *The Works Of
John Adams.* 10 vols. Boston, 1850–1856.

Appletons' Cyc. *Appletons' Cyclopedia of American Biography,* ed. James Grant Wilson and John Fisk. New
York, 1888. (This work is not fully trustworthy, and
entries must be checked with other sources.)

Conn. Recs. *The Public Records of the Colony of Connecticut.* 15 vols. Hartford, 1850–1890.

Conn. Hist. Colls. *Connecticut Historical Collections.* 31
vols. Hartford, 1860–1867.

Crisis Edmund S. Morgan and Helen M. Morgan, *The
Stamp Act Crisis.* Chapel Hill, 1965.

Dickinson *The Writings of John Dickinson,* ed. Paul
Leicester Ford. Historical Society of Pennsylvania,
Memoirs 14. Philadelphia, 1895.

Dict. Amer. Biog. *Dictionary Of American Biography,*
ed. Allen Johnson. New York, 1964.

Gibbes R. W. Gibbes, *Documentary History of the American Revolution.* 3 vols. New York, 1853–1857.

Gipson, 1961 Lawrence Henry Gipson, *The British
Empire before the American Revolution,* 15 vols. New
York, 1961–1970.

Knollenberg Bernhard Knollenberg, *Origin of the American Revolution, 1759–1766.* rev. ed. New York, 1965.

7

Lovejoy, 1958   David S. Lovejoy, *Rhode Island Politics and the American Revolution, 1760–1776.* Providence, 1958.

Mass. Hist. Colls.   *Massachusetts Historical Society Collections.* 10 vols. Boston, 1852–1871.

Mass. Journals   *Journals of the House of Representatives of Massachusetts, 1765–1766,* vol. 42. Boston, 1972.

Minutes Lower Counties   *Minutes of House of Representatives of the Government of the Counties of New Castle, Kent and Sussex Upon Delaware at Sessions Held at New Castle in the Years 1765–1770.* Wilmington, 1931. (Printed for the Public Archives Commission.)

Nat'l. Cyc.   *The National Cyclopedia of American Biography.* New York, 1892. (Entries must also be carefully checked.)

N.H. Recs.   *Provincial Papers: Documents and Records Relating to the Province of New Hampshire, 1623-1800.* 39 vols. Concord, N.H., 1867–1941.

NJCD   *Archives of the State of New Jersey: Documents Relating to the Colonial History of the State of New Jersey, 1631–1800.* 47 vols. Newark, N.J., 1880–1949.

NYCD   *Documents Relative to the Colonial History of the State of New York.* 15 vols. Albany, N.Y., 1856–1887.

Pitkin   Timothy Pitkin, *A Political and Civil History of the United States of America.* 2 vols. New Haven, Conn. 1828.

Prologue   *Prologue to Revolution,* ed. Edmund S. Morgan. Chapel Hill, 1959.

R.I. Recs.   *Records of the Colony of Rhode Island and Providence Plantations in New England.* 10 vols. Providence, R.I., 1856–1865.

Preface

Historians may disagree about the cause of the American Revolution, but there can be little doubt that the decision made by colonial leaders to unify the efforts of the thirteen mainland colonies, instead of allowing them to continue to act separately in their relations with England, was necessary to attain independence. Intercolonial unity was not hastily conceived, nor speedily achieved; it was by no means universally accepted in the beginning, and its initial objective had nothing to do with seeking independence from the mother country. Unification was in the making during the long and painful decade before the signers of the Declaration of Independence resolved their differences and cast the die by mutually pledging to each other their lives, fortunes, and sacred honor.

The resurgence of interest in the First and Second Continental Congresses during the Bicentennial has tended to obscure the significance of an earlier, self-initiating step to bring the colonies together—the Stamp Act Congress. That term was invented by historians of a later era, not by those who attended what might be termed an *ad hoc* meeting, but the Congress must be seen in its proper perspective. It was an outgrowth of the grievances, principally, but not exclusively, resulting from the passage of the Stamp Act, and none of the participants expected that it would be necessary for them to meet together again nine years later in what is now known as the First Continental Congress.

Although the Stamp Act and its attendant crisis have been

9

treated in books and numerous papers (see Bibliography), there has never been a book published about the Congress; in fact, there has not been a single paper on the subject published in any of the "learned journals." Owing to this lack of information, writers of history texts have misconstrued the purpose of the Congress; some have confused the dates it was held and where it took place, others have erred in naming the delegates, and practically all of them are vague about precisely what the Congress accomplished.

The American Revolution was germinating in the tumult and riots that occurred during the Stamp Act crisis, but few colonial leaders, including the delegates to the Congress, were then cognizant of it. Colonial historians are well aware that even the most radical and violent agitators, the Sons of Liberty, did not instigate street riots in 1765 for the purpose of encouraging rebellion and the severance of political ties with Great Britain. What they wanted was unmistakably expressed by members of the New York City organization in the January 13, 1766, edition of the *New York Mercury:*

> Resolved, That we will go to the last Extremity and venture our Lives and Fortunes effectually to prevent the Stamp Act from ever taking Place in this City and Province.

Other sections of their resolution might be considered equally revolutionary in tone, although the document did not contain one word about revolt or independence. The authors held the mother country in such high regard that they emphasized "their firm Adherence to the English Constitution [and] their unshaken Loyalty and Affection to his Majesty King George the Third, and his Royal House. . . ."

The Sons of Liberty in Norfolk, Virginia, who also protested violently against the Stamp Act, acknowledged George III as their "rightful and lawful King," and their rioting brethren in New London, Connecticut, declared an "unshaken faith and true Allegiance to George III" (*Prologue,* pp. 116–17).

When the delegates to the Stamp Act Congress assembled, the idea of a break with England was as far from their thoughts as it was from the minds of the members of the Sons of Liberty. The Congress was not a body of revolutionists determined to unify colonial strength for the purpose of shaking off British rule. To the contrary, the records are clear that the delegates believed that a firm union between Great Britain and her New World colonies was best politically and economically for all of them. Their concept of acting in concert did not mean that they were taking a deliberate step to bring them closer to independence. They believed that by meeting together they would be able to express their opposition effectively, but nonetheless respectfully, as they sought redress for their mutual grievances. What they hoped to achieve more than anything else by their joint action was a restoration of the harmonious and prosperous relations they had formerly enjoyed as a ward of the mother country.

There were no firebrands in the Stamp Act Congress. Sam Adams, who had not yet risen to power in Massachusetts, was not a delegate; neither was John Adams nor John Hancock. Richard Henry Lee was not present, nor was Patrick Henry; his "Liberty or Death" speech was not delivered until almost ten years later. John Dickinson, one of the delegates, wrote to William Pitt on December 21, 1765, that he regarded "with inexpressible Detestation and Abhorrence the Notion of the Colonies becoming independent." James Otis, another delegate, wrote passionately about the deep loyalty he felt toward the mother country and his beloved King. Thomas McKean, Caesar Rodney, Christopher Gadsden, Thomas Lynch, John Rutledge, John Morton, and other delegates who were destined to become leaders in the revolt against the mother country had no rebellious fervor in 1765. All they wanted was the privilege of continuing to enjoy their legal rights as Englishmen. The transformation in their

thoughts and attitudes came slowly, and like most patriot
leaders, they were extremely tardy in recognizing the need
for independence. A revolution in mind and spirit preceded
the bold decision to fight for independence. The Stamp Act
Congress was the forum where, after much debate, intel-
lectual opposition first crystallized.

None of the delegates then had any serious doubt that King
and Parliament, acting together, had the right to govern the
colonies by legislation, supervision, royal veto, the appointment of royal governors and other officials, or by other legal
means. The prime issue they denied was Parliament's right
to levy taxes on them, for the purpose of raising revenue,
without their consent. They were also deeply concerned about
their loss of the right of trial by jury in the Vice-Admiralty
Courts, and they worried about the initial scarcity of English
specie, which was needed to pay the taxes as specified in the
texts of both the Sugar Act and the Stamp Act. Some of them
seriously believed that this restriction would render them
unable to purchase English goods in the same quantity in the
future as they had in the past. Unknowingly, the delegates
were actors in the first scene of a drama, whose last act, to be
written at a later date, would find the colonists claiming that
they were not subject at all to King and Parliament.

Because this is the first published book dealing with the
Stamp Act Congress, it seemed not only desirable, but necessary, to discuss briefly the reactions of the Colonial Assemblies
when the Massachusetts letter was received inviting deputies
to attend the Congress. This was all part of the unifying process that took place very slowly amid the political stresses and
strains in each colony. To learn how these thirteen component
parts were eventually welded together is important in understanding the beginning of the American nation.

It also seemed that the first published book on the subject
should include verbatim the significant references from primary sources, instead of merely footnote citations that a
majority of readers will never take the time to consult.

These quotations should add authority, as well as interest, to the narration.

Brief biographical data have been included about each of the delegates to the Congress. Admittedly this information is incomplete; the reader should understand that this is an attempt, in broad strokes, to characterize the makeup of the delegates without going into complete biographical detail.

Finally, this volume is principally intended for general readers seeking information about this great country. At the same time historians may find much in it that is new, and hopefully the information will contribute to an enlarged understanding of the events leading up to the Revolution and the birth of the nation.

C. A. W.

Brandywine College
Wilmington, Delaware

Acknowledgments

Grateful acknowledgment is made for assistance given by the following institutions located within the thirteen original colonies, either on personal visits, through correspondence, or both. Where individuals have been especially helpful their names are included in parentheses as evidence of appreciation. The omission of personal names, however, is by no means a reflection on the institutions and the quality of their cooperation.

CONNECTICUT
>Connecticut Historical Society (Thompson R. Harlow)
>Connecticut Archives, History and Genealogy Unit (Linda S. Winters)

GEORGIA
>Historical Society of Georgia (Lilla M. Hawes)
>Department of Archives and History

LOWER COUNTIES (DELAWARE)
>State Archives (Ronald Finch, Elizabeth Moyne)
>Morris Library, University of Delaware (John Dawson)
>Brandywine College Library (Jane Hukill)
>Wilmington Institute Free Library
>Historical Society of Delaware (Dale Fields, Gladys M. Coghlan)
>Winterthur Museum Library (Helen Belknap)
>Eleutherian Mills Library, Hagley Foundation (Betty-Bright P. Low, Carol B. Hallman)

MARYLAND

Maryland Historical Society (Richard J. Cox, William B. Marye)

Hall of Records (Gust Skordas)

MASSACHUSETTS

Houghton Library, Harvard University (Deborah B. Kelley)

Massachusetts Historical Society (John D. Cushing)

State Archives Division (Leo Flaherty)

NEW HAMPSHIRE

New Hampshire Historical Society (Robinson Murray III)

New Hampshire State Archives (Robert A. Lauze)

NEW JERSEY

New Jersey Historical Society (Robert M. Lunny, E. Richard McKinstry, Don Skemer)

Savitz Learning Resource Center (Magdalena Houlroyd)

State Archives (Kenneth W. Richards)

NEW YORK

Long Island Historical Society (Anthony M. Cucchiara)

New York Historical Society (James J. Heslin)

New York Public Library (Faye Simkin, John D. Stinson, Jean R. McNiece)

Manuscript Memorial Library, State Education Department (James Corsaro)

Columbia University (Alice H. Bonnell, Kenneth A. Lohf)

NORTH CAROLINA

University of North Carolina Library (Carolyn Wallace)

State Department of Archives and History

PENNSYLVANIA

Pennsylvania Historical and Library Commission (William A. Hunter)

Historical Society of Pennsylvania (Nicholas B. Wainright, Peter J. Parker)

Library Company of Philadelphia (Edwin Wolf, 2nd)

Free Library of Philadelphia (Howell J. Heaney)
American Philosophical Society (Murphy D. Smith)
Haverford College Library (Elizabeth Tritle)
RHODE ISLAND
Rhode Island Historical Society (Nancy F. Chudacoff)
John Carter Brown Library (Thomas R. Adams)
Rhode Island State Archives (Phyllis Peloquin)
SOUTH CAROLINA
South Caroliniana Library, University of South Carolina (Allen H. Stokes)
South Carolina Historical Society (Mary B. Prior)
South Carolina Department of Archives and History
VIRGINIA
Virginia Historical Society (Howson F. Cole)
Archives Division, Virginia State Library (John W. Dudley)
William & Mary College Library
I also want to acknowledge the assistance of the following institutions:

Henry E. Huntington Library
San Marino, Calif.

Public Archives
Halifax, Nova Scotia

Public Records Office
London, England

Manuscript Room
British Museum

Tennessee State Library & Archives
Nashville, Tenn.

Library of Congress
Washington, D. C.

West India Reference Library
Institute of Jamaica
Kingston, W. I.

St. James Parish Library
Montego Bay, Jamaica

I would also like to express my appreciation to the following persons for their help and cooperation: William Baldwin, Herbert Bernstein, J. Caleb Boggs, John M. Coleman, Jere R. Daniell, Bruce Finnie, Harold B. Hancock, Francis P. Jennings, Adolph Koeppel, David S. Lovejoy, Edmund S. Morgan, Wm. B. Marye, Ernest J. Moyne, John A. Munroe, Arthur G. Volkman, and G. S. Rowe.

Harry W. Pfanz, Chief Historian, National Park Service, U.S. Department of the Interior, kindly provided me with photocopies of a research study made in 1963, and a supplement written in 1964, by Alfred Mongin, then an employee of the Park Service. Entitled "The Stamp Act Congress," these reports dealt with the Federal Hall National Memorial. Although these reports did not contain data unfamiliar to me, I found them very interesting in corroborating information that I had independently uncovered.

None of the persons or institutions named above are answerable for anything appearing in this volume, and their assistance in no way relieves me of full responsibility for the contents.

The Stamp Act Congress

1

Introduction

(A) EVENTS LEADING UP TO THE STAMP ACT

Following the defeat of the French in the French and Indian War (1754–1763), not only were the whole of Canada and the eastern Mississippi Valley ceded to Great Britain by France, but also the thirteen mainland colonies were rid of an enemy who had blocked their westward expansion. The colonists were elated by the defeat of the French, which removed a threat to their security, allowed them to control the Indian trade, and gave them the opportunity to move into the trans-Appalachian region. The victory contributed to their pride in being English subjects having coequal political rights with other Englishmen under the British constitution. It also strengthened their emotional ties with the mother country, with whom they had a sense of family kinship, speaking the same language, having the same legal system, and a common sovereign, George III, then aged 24, who was widely admired in the colonies as well as in England.

No feeling of American nationalism had yet matured, nor was there any movement to separate from England.[1] The colonists did not feel mistreated nor in any way abused, and there was no reason to consider consolidating the thirteen separate colonial governments into a new, independent nation. British finances and her military forces were largely responsible for the victory over the French, and the colonists felt that they were fortunate to be subjects of a loving king in a great and growing British Empire.

Under British rule the colonies had grown and prospered, and the economic opportunities found in America were unparalleled in the Old World. Yet, within a few years after the close of the war, these same colonial subjects were bitterly opposing the policies of Parliament, and within a period of twelve years they were at war with England, accusing their former beloved monarch of being "a tyrant unfit to be ruler of a free people." To understand what caused this about-face, it is necessary to bring into perspective some of the events that took place following the peace treaty with France which preceded the Stamp Act Congress.

One of the measures that antagonized the colonists was a Royal Proclamation issued October 7, 1763, prohibiting settlement in the territory west of "the Heads of Sources of any of the Rivers which fall into the Atlantic Ocean from the West and Northwest."² This had the effect of excluding the colonists from the land won from the French in the Ohio Valley, and in the vast territory stretching from the Ohio to the Mississippi. The King intended the measure as an expedient to allay the fears of the Indians that his subjects would move west and drive them away from their hunting grounds. The colonists opposed the proclamation as an unnecessary obstacle to western expansion. Some saw it as a move on the King's part to keep them pinned down along the Atlantic seaboard, where they could be more readily controlled, and this may, in fact, also have been in the King's mind.

King and Parliament realized that the American colonies were rapidly achieving economic maturity. The problem was that the Crown was going into debt in supporting and protecting England's investment in the New World. With the war ended and a vastly larger area to defend and regulate, there was no question that the expenses would increase. The British national debt had gone up at an alarming rate, and about half of the increase had been incurred in defending the colonies during the war with the French.[3] The annual interest to retire the national debt, added to the cost of meeting current expenses, weighed heavily on taxpayers in England. English land taxes had been augmented with a tax on ownership of silver plate, a tax on public houses of entertainment, as well as taxes on malt, cider, and beer. The stamp taxes in England had been increased, and in 1761 a new tax was imposed on all windows or lights of glass in English houses.[4] There was a limit beyond which no ministry could raise taxes and continue to remain in power, and many members of Parliament believed that this limit had been reached.

The North American colonies, numbering 2,000,000 to 2,500,000 people and growing steadily, gave Parliament a new place to look for added revenue. The New World possessions included not only the thirteen mainland colonies, but also Quebec, Bermuda, Barbados, Jamaica, the Bahamas, Nova Scotia, East Florida, West Florida, and the four Leeward Islands of Antigua, St. Kitts (as St. Christopher was called), Nevis, and Montserrat. These colonies were all capable of contributing taxes to the kingdom, and English squires assessed with heavy land taxes were convinced that revenue collected from the colonies would reduce their own tax burdens.

The administrator who undertook the difficult task of balancing the budget was Lord George Grenville, who became First Lord of the Treasury and Chancellor of the Exchequer in the summer of 1763. When he came into office there were already in force a number of trade regulations that required payment of customs duties on certain products delivered to American ports. These duties, intended for regulation of trade and not as a source of revenue, were an outgrowth of the Acts of Trade and Navigation designed to strengthen the commerce of the British Empire.[5] There had never been any serious doubt in British North America that it was the mother country's prerogative to regulate the commerce of the British colonies. Trade relations with foreign nations were involved, and there was no practical way for each colony to handle the trade that would serve the best interests of the empire. The customs duties were a vital part of regulating and protecting the commerce, and the resulting revenue was a collateral benefit. These duties were termed indirect or external taxes, and although they might eventually have been reflected in price levels, the colonial consumer did not consider that he was being taxed by the mother country.

There was another factor having an important bearing on the situation: payment of the custom duties was widely evaded. Customs officials were bribed to allow taxable products to be unloaded in American ports at a tax rate less than the legal one, or entirely free of taxes. The English customs service was inefficient and corrupt, and some of the officials themselves were engaged in smuggling and illicit trading. In a memorial to the Privy Council in 1763, Grenville stated that the customs revenue from America amounted to less than one-quarter of the cost of collecting it.[6]

Since Grenville's responsibility was to effect economies and raise sufficient revenue to balance the budget, he recommended strict enforcement of the existing trade laws. Parliament supported him by stationing warships in American waters with orders to seize all vessels violating the law and confiscate their cargoes.[7] Officers in the Royal Navy had previously been given authority to perform as customs officials, and they were permitted the use of "writs of assistance," general search warrants that allowed them to board vessels in search of contraband goods. Notice was also given to all customs officials in North America that they must discharge their duty and obligations without failure and collect in full the taxes specified by the law or risk instant dismissal.

Needless to say, colonial merchants were not overjoyed at these measures to enforce the laws.

On April 5, 1764, Parliament passed a modified version of the Molasses Act (enacted in 1733 and later amended), which was about to expire. According to the 1733 statute, colonial merchants were required to pay a customs duty of six pence per gallon on the importation of foreign molasses. Molasses was especially important to the business in Massachusetts and it was the cornerstone of the economy in Rhode Island.[8] Molasses was a sweetener used in cooking Boston baked beans, baking Boston brown bread, making puddings and pies, curing meat, pickling fish, and home-brewing "small beer," a beverage with a low alcoholic content. It was also distilled to make rum, used principally for domestic consumption and in the Indian trade, although the surplus was exported to the Southern colonies, Nova Scotia, Newfoundland, and Africa.[9]

The importation of molasses gave the New England colonies a market for their surplus lumber, cheese, flour, and farm products. Income from the sale of rum also provided the specie for buying manufactured goods from England. Molasses made from sugar cane had been imported in very large quantities from the French West Indies colonies of Guadeloupe, Martinique, and Santo Domingo (present Haiti). Since the duty had been evaded at American ports, and French molasses was cheaper and more plentiful to begin with, the New England distillers bought molasses at a low price, which enabled them to maintain a strong competitive position with cheap rum. Molasses was also made in the islands of the British West Indies, where it was distilled into rum that was shipped to England in large volume. English distillers in the West Indies had not been able to compete in the colonies with the cheaper rum made in New England. The tax was intended to restrict the colonial importation of molasses from the French islands, thus forcing the New England distillers to turn to the British West Indies for their molasses where the supply was limited. If the objective of the original molasses taxes was to put the New England distillers out of the rum business and switch colonial customers to English-made rum, English merchants failed to attain that end. American-made rum continued to dominate the colonial market.

The new legislation entitled the American Revenue Act of 1764, also known as the Sugar Act, reduced the duty on imported molasses from six pence to three pence per gallon. This might have been considered a welcome reduction if colonial importers had been paying six pence per gallon as required by the 1733 statute, but they were not. They had either been paying less or nothing at all, and now Grenville insisted that the new statute must be vigorously enforced. In addition to the tax on molasses, the Revenue Act of 1764 also levied duties on the colonial importation of foreign sugar, certain wines, coffee, pimiento, cambric, printed calico, and other products. It also contained provisions governing the exportation of lumber and iron. Under Lord Grenville's policies the import duties specified in the Act were not only intended to regulate the trade, but were designed *"for improving the revenue of this kingdom."*[10]

The result of enforcing the three-pence tax on molasses increased the price of rum, which made the New England distillers uncompetitive, and their business declined. As rum sales fell off it had a depressing effect on other phases of colonial commerce that affected the other colonies. The increased duties on wine discouraged the trade between the colonies and Madeira, the Azores, and the Canary Islands, because it drove upward the price of imported wines, which were popular beverages in the colonies. In short, the Act of 1764 upset the colonial economy, although this was certainly not Grenville's intention. The Act also left the impression with colonial merchants that this was the first step on Parliament's part to force the New World colonies to share the increasing tax burdens of the British Empire.

(B) THE VICE-ADMIRALTY COURTS

The Vice-Admiralty Courts played a significant role in the enforcement of the trade laws, and their function must be understood to appreciate why they became of concern during the period of the Stamp Act crisis. At the close of the French and Indian War there were eleven Vice-Admiralty Courts in North America. Each court served a distinct territory, often consisting of two or three colonies. There were also colonies having their own Vice-Admiralty Courts, such as Pennsylvania, whose court also had jurisdiction over the Three Lower Counties, New Castle, Kent, and Sussex, later to become the state of Delaware.

The original function of the Vice-Admiralty Courts in America, as in England, was to adjudicate disagreements and problems arising among merchants and seamen. Sometimes they were referred to as "salt water courts," although they were not held on vessels, but were all land-based. Their jurisdiction in America was later extended to include enforcement of the Trade and Navigation Acts, and in wartime the courts were given authority to condemn captured enemy vessels and dispose of their cargoes.

Each court had its own judge, who heard and tried the cases and then rendered his decision. There was no jury, in contrast to the Common-law Courts where the defendant had the right to be judged by his peers. In certain trade and revenue matters there was overlapping jurisdiction, and customs officials and merchants could bring action either in a Common-law Court or a local Vice-Admiralty Court, wherever they felt that their interests would best be served. For instance, the Molasses Act of 1733 gave Vice-Admiralty Courts concurrent jurisdiction with Common-law Courts for its enforcement.

Following passage of the Sugar Act of 1764, colonial merchants took the position that, as a measure to raise tax money, the Act was a clear departure from previous laws enacted to regulate the trade. They maintained that if England sought tax revenue in America (and there was strong opposition to the principle of England's levying taxes for revenue purposes), a person accused of violating the revenue laws was entitled to trial by jury. They claimed that it infringed their legal rights to be tried in Vice-Admiralty Courts.[11]

The situation was aggravated when Great Britain created a new Vice-Admiralty Court in Halifax, the headquarters of the North American fleet. Because the colonial Vice-Admiralty Courts, like the Common-law Courts, usually favored American shippers and merchants, the new court was established to provide a more effective method of condemning vessels seized in colonial waters for illicit trading. The court at Halifax was not intended to replace the other Vice-Admiralty Courts, but was a sort of supercourt whose jurisdiction extended from Florida to Newfoundland. Whereas most of the judges of the other Vice-Admiralty Courts were native born colonists, a judge was sent from England to preside over the new court.

Officers of the Royal Navy, customs officials, and other Crown officers could bring action against a ship's master, or owner of a vessel, anywhere in American waters, and then compel the defendant to make the long trip to Halifax to be tried in a court that was unsympathetic to him. To make matters worse, the legal concept in the Vice-Admiralty Court was that a defendant was assumed to be guilty until he proved his innocence. The creation of this new supercourt in Halifax further fanned the flame of resentment among American merchants.

(C) THE CURRENCY ACT

The Currency Act passed by Parliament, to become effective on September 1, 1764, was fully supported by Lord

Grenville, and it, too, caused considerable opposition in the colonies.

The thirteen colonies were without gold or silver mines, and their specie was obtained principally from England or the West Indies in payment for exported products such as tobacco, rum, indigo, furs, lumber, and others. The quantity of manufactured goods shipped from England to America created a trade imbalance, which tended to drain the colonies of their specie. Facing a chronic shortage of cash, colonial merchants were forced to resort to the use of paper currency, or bills of credit, as legal tender.

To meet their fiscal needs some of the colonies established land banks, or loan offices, which issued paper currency backed by mortgages on land. Several other different kinds of paper currency were issued, but they all lacked an intercolonial standard of value, which tended to complicate business dealings. Some of the paper notes bore interest while others did not; some were accepted as legal tender for the payment of all sorts of debts, whereas some could be used only for future obligations and could not be used to pay past debts. Some could be used for public debts, but not for private transactions between individuals; some were payable on demand, and others were not. In addition to this paper currency colonial businessmen also used a system of book credits, which was equally important in conducting commerce both at home and abroad.

The Currency Act of 1764 forbade the colonies to issue any new paper currency, or to reissue any of the paper notes in circulation on the theory that it was "false in its principles, unjust in its foundations, and manifestly fraudulent in its operations."[12] The Act applied to all paper tender used in the colonies, or in the international trade, which meant that the mother country was taking over control of the colonial currency system.

Many British merchant-creditors strongly favored the Currency Act because of the depreciation of colonial paper currency, especially the paper notes that Virginia and North Carolina merchants used to pay their bills. London mercantile houses reached a point where they demanded that the government protect them against the fluctuation in the rate of paper exchange, which depreciated the paper notes to amounts far less than their face value.

Although the passage of the Currency Act served the purposes of the English merchants, Parliament's response was not solely due to the pressures exerted by the business firms. As a result of the financial crisis in England at the close of the French and Indian War, the Board of Trade favored a hard money policy, and the Grenville ministry was determined to reform the colonial currency system as part of a larger postwar fiscal program. The ministry even went so far as to consider inaugurating a colonial paper currency system under the full control of the mother country, although the plan was finally rejected. As the Revolution approached, the antagonism between England and the American colonies over parliamentary taxation tended to magnify the objections to the fiscal policies of the mother country. But even as early as 1764 this opposition was developing, because the colonies wanted to control their own currency system, but Parliament was determined to assert its authority in fiscal matters.

A provision in the Sugar Act stated that all customs duties had to be paid in the "sterling money of Great Britain," and this same restriction was written into the Stamp Act (see below). Even though the revenues from the stamp taxes were intended to remain in America to be spent there for the support of British troops, this did not satisfy the colonies. Colonial merchants argued that since the colonies were forbidden by the Currency Act to issue paper notes, and having an inadequate supply of specie with which to pay their taxes, it was inevitable that they would suffer hardships, and even recession, in their commerce. This was probably an exaggeration, but in 1766 Benjamin Franklin informed British leaders in London, in well-rehearsed answers to their questions, that one of the reasons for American ill feeling toward the mother country was the passage of the Currency Act of 1764.

(D) THE STAMP ACT

None of this prior legislation, restrictive and unpopular though it was, caused so much indignation and widespread resentment as the Stamp Act, although the cumulative effect of the former statutes made the situation far worse than it might otherwise have been.

The acquisition of Canada, and the elimination of the French from the trans-Appalachian area, added a new dimension to the problem of administering a growing English empire. There was now vastly more territory in North America to be protected against possible incursions of French, Spanish, and Indian foes. The King's Proclamation of 1763 prohibited colonial occupation of lands west of the Appalachians, which were reserved as hunting territory for the Indian tribes. The proclamation was not popular in the colonies, because after the defeat of the French the colonists fully expected to be able to move west of the Alleghenies.

Before Lord Grenville took office Parliament had decided that it would be desirable to increase English military forces in North America over their prewar strength. The decision was made to maintain an army in the colonies of no less than 10,000 regulars, and the announced purpose was for the defense of the colonies, but the troops were also to conduct certain police actions that were not widely publicized.

In the western areas from which the colonists were excluded from settling were located the important fur-trading posts, and it was necessary to garrison them with English troops to protect the traders. Parliament was well aware that the colonists might choose to ignore the Proclamation of 1763 (as some actually did), and start unauthorized settlements on the lands reserved for the Indians, which would lead to opposition by the natives, who had been assured by the King that they would suffer no interference from the colonists. The presence of British troops at the interior trading posts was expected to keep the colonial settlers and the Indians from confrontations that could result in war and bloodshed.[13]

It seemed reasonable to the Grenville ministry, and to Parliament, that the Americans should be willing to support the cost of troops sent from England to defend them. The only alternative was for each colony to contribute manpower to an army that would be commanded by British officers, which would have to be supported by colonial taxes. Even if Parliament approved this plan, which was extremely unlikely, it was an alternative that would be next to impossible to implement. Each of the colonies was a separate entity with its own economic and social problems, and with a social structure and cultural life peculiar to itself. There were jealousies among the colonies—even antagonisms—and the Americans would have to resolve these differences before there was any hope of their acting together successfully in their common interest.

A Confederation of the United Colonies of New England had been formed as early as 1643, and there were subsequent joint meetings of certain of the colonial representatives to negotiate peace treaties with the Indian tribes. At the opening of the French and Indian War an attempt had been made at a conference, held in June of 1754 in Albany, New York, with the Six Nations Iroquois to form a confederacy of the mainland colonies for their common defense. The representatives from New York, Connecticut, Massachusetts Bay, New Hampshire, Rhode Island, Pennsylvania, and Maryland who attended the meeting, voted unanimously in favor of the plan. Whether the British government would have consented to the formation of a colonial union is debatable, but the issue never reached the point where the mother country was called upon to act on it. When the delegates returned to their homes not a single one of the Colonial Assemblies would ratify the Albany plan.[14]

Now—ten years later—the colonies were facing another military problem, different from and less critical than the earlier ones, to be sure, but there was still no practical way for the Assemblies to meet it in concert. Parliament estimated that the annual cost of supplying, feeding, and housing troops sent to America from England ostensibly for the common defense of the colonies would amount to more than £220,000. As long as England bore the cost of maintaining these troops, as she had done in the past, the colonies had no reason to object. Moreover, England set a precedent during the French and Indian War by partially reimbursing the individual colonies for their assistance in supplying men and food.[15] The colonies expected the mother country to continue to pay for their defense, if such defense were needed. Some American merchants took the position that England had long enjoyed immense profits through the sale of manufactured goods exported to the colonies, and the mother country had the obligation of protecting these loyal customers. Others said that if England was burdened with an increased national debt it was due to her own extravagances, and it was unfair and improper to try to shift any of the financial burden on to the colonies. After all, she had engaged in a war for her own selfish interests, and having tasted victory, she should not object to paying for it.

Colonial leaders believed that it was unreasonable to ask the colonies to pay for the upkeep of English troops, because they had not been consulted about the number, composition, and where they would be distributed and stationed. Commissions in the British army had not been offered to colonial officers, many of whom had distinguished themselves in the French and Indian War. Furthermore, the troops to be sent to America may have been adequately trained for European combat, but they knew nothing about fighting savage Indians.

Some believed that although English troops were supposedly to be sent to defend the colonies, they were really being organized for the purpose of keeping the colonists in check should the need arise.

Regardless of colonial opposition, the decision had been made, and it was Grenville's responsibility to develop tax measures to pay for the upkeep of the troops. Not long after he took office he offered a resolution in Parliament to the effect that it might be proper, in due course, to enact a stamp tax, whereby the colonies could help pay for their own defense. It was not an original idea with him—others had suggested it before.[16] Stamp taxes, which had been inaugurated in England as far back as 1694, proved effective as a source of revenue, and had been accepted by the public.[17] In America two of the colonies, Massachusetts and New York, had imitated the mother country by imposing their own stamp taxes for a limited time.[18] Grenville did not ask for immediate action on his resolution, and it was almost a year later that Parliament passed the Stamp Act.

The Stamp Act, a lengthy and complicated piece of legislation having sixty-three sections, was approved by the House of Commons on February 27, 1765, by a vote of 205 to 49. It was then engrossed and sent to the House of Lords, which approved it unanimously on March 8 without debate or protest. Due to the illness of George III, it was given royal assent by a special commission on March 22, at which time it became a statute of the realm. As specified in the Act, it did not become effective until November 1, 1765, a lapse of seven months. This time was allowed for due and proper notice to reach the colonies, and also to make plans for the production and shipment of stamped paper and the appointment of Stamp Distributors. There was nothing sudden or unexpected about its passage; there had been lengthy discussions about its enactment in England and in the colonies after Grenville introduced the resolution.

The political significance of the Stamp Act was that it

imposed the first direct, internal tax ever to be laid on the colonists by Parliament.[19] The members of Parliament, as well as Lord Grenville, realized that the colonists would object to it, but they did not expect that it would create such a storm. After all, Grenville hoped to raise only about £60,000 from the tax, which was less than one-third of the estimated cost of supporting English troops in America.

Although the Sugar Act of 1764 directly affected only the mercantile groups in the colonies, the Stamp Act reached all classes, touching almost every family in one way or another, affecting some persons more than others. Contrary to the impression most Americans have gathered from history textbooks, the Act did not involve gummed stamps, or any other kind of stamps, to be glued by the vendor on pieces of paper or other taxable articles. Actually, the first gummed postage stamps were not used in Great Britain until the 1840s, and at the time of the passage of the Stamp Act, gummed revenue stamps had not yet been developed. What was meant by "stamps" referred to in the Act, was impressions, either imprinted or embossed on sheets of paper, vellum, or parchment by means of a die used in a screw-type printing press. The paper or parchment was first cut to various standard sizes, and each sheet was then imprinted with a tax stamp ranging from one-half pence to £10. The stamped imprint stood out in relief and looked very much like a modern notary seal.

The die, which left clear, colorless impressions on paper, would not register clearly on parchment. To overcome this a small square piece of paper, usually colored blue or beige and slightly larger than the die (which was from one to one-and-one-half inches high), was impressed and glued to the parchment. To prevent its separation in the event the glue dried and lost its adhesion, a reinforcing device like a metal staple was used to hold the impressed paper to the parchment. On the reverse side of the parchment the metal ends were covered by a small "ticket" or "cypher" about the size

*Illustrated below are photographs of three of the thirty differ-
ent stamp dies used in 1765 to imprint the paper shipped to
the American Stamp Distributors. Engraved by Thomas
Major, these die proofs were preserved in record books in
the London Stamp Office and were later deposited at Somerset
House. They were located in 1958 by Marcus Samuel and
used to illustrate his article "The Embossed Die Proofs at
Somerset House," which appeared on pp. 4–16 of* The 1765
Tax Stamps for America, *edited by Adolph Koeppel, published by the American Revenue Association, Boyertown,
Penna., 1962. Permission to reprint these three illustrations
granted by Mr. Koeppel on behalf of the Revenue Association,
is gratefully acknowledged.*

This three-pence stamp, marked with the die letter C, *is engraved with the Tudor rose on which rests a crown. It does
not contain a motto, although the word* America *appears at
the top.*

Valued at one shilling sixpence, this stamp engraved with the die letter B and the word America contains the Cross of St. George imposed on the Cross of St. Andrew on a shield encircled by a garter ribbon on top of which rests a crown. It also bears the motto "Honi Soit Qui Mal Y Pense."

A one-shilling stamp, engraved with the die letter B, *is embellished with the Tudor rose encircled by a garter ribbon on top of which rests a crown. It also contains the motto* "Honi Soit Qui Mal Y Pense," *and the word* America.

of a modern postage stamp, bearing the monogram of George III. The "cypher" was not needed on the reverse side of the stamped paper.

The stamped impressions were usually, but not always, made in the left margin of the paper or parchment, alongside or slightly above a black inked imprint containing a crown and a number in pence, which designated the cost of the paper exclusive of the tax stamp. More than thirty embossing dies were created bearing such designs as the Tudor Rose, the Cross of St. George imposed upon the Cross of St. Andrew, the royal arms of George III on a shield, and a number of others.

The Act required the user to purchase the stamped paper or parchment from a Stamp Distributor, who was both the vendor of the paper and the tax collector. It was a direct tax plainly visible to every taxpayer. Certain tradesmen were required to purchase their licenses on stamped paper. A vendor of spirituous liquors had to purchase a license inscribed on paper that bore a twenty-shilling stamp. But to sell wines in addition to the spirituous liquors, the retailer had to purchase a second license made out on paper bearing a £3 stamp. A college graduate was compelled to have his diploma engrossed on parchment or paper bearing a £2 stamp. If the graduate decided to read law, a license admitting him to practice at the bar was engrossed on parchment or paper bearing a £10 stamp.

There were stamp taxes on pamphlets, playing cards, and dice, but this was not the area that aroused the greatest resentment. The tax fell most heavily on those who dealt with newspapers, almanacs, and legal documents in their daily affairs, namely, editors and publishers, lawyers, judges, and clergymen, and merchants and ships' masters. In the Vice-Admiralty and Common-law Courts stamped paper was required for executing almost every kind of legal document, such as wills, deeds, land warrants, judgments, subpoenas, leases, bills of sale, depositions, and affidavits. It was utterly impossible for a court to function or a lawyer to represent his clients without the use of stamped paper. This not only required an additional fee that would have to be charged the client, but it also caused inconvenience to the attorney because the provisions in the statute were very complicated.

For instance, graduated taxes were called for to execute similar documents within a certain class. Deeds of sale transferring less than one hundred acres of land were required to be drawn up on paper bearing a tax stamp of one shilling sixpence. Deeds covering one hundred to two hundred acres had to be executed on paper bearing a two-shilling stamp; deeds covering land from two hundred to three hundred and twenty acres were taxed two shillings sixpence. Acreage larger than three hundred and twenty acres required additional taxes and the use of correctly stamped paper. Other examples could be cited to show that the statute itself was difficult for even a lawyer to understand and comply with, to say nothing of the inconvenience of purchasing stamped paper for each transaction.

Merchants engaged in overseas trade found most objectionable the provision in the Act that all vessels leaving ports in the North American colonies had to have their clearance papers and bills of lading executed on stamped paper before they could depart. If a vessel sailed from American waters and docked in an English port without having a stamped document authorizing the voyage and covering the cargo, the captain was subject to severe punishment. And, as if to add insult to injury, all stamped paper or parchment had to be paid for in hard cash with the sterling money of Great Britain, which was scarce in the colonies.[20]

Printers and publishers were also severely handicapped by the requirements of the Act. Stamped paper was required for printing all newspapers, almanacs, brochures, and pamphlets, as well as for advertisements appearing in these media. The tax applied to every single copy of an advertisement that appeared in every copy of a newspaper. This was in addition to the tax paid for each sheet of paper on which the newspaper was printed. The stamp on the newsprint was not embossed from a die, but was printed in red ink from engraved copper plates. The imprint usually appeared on the bottom right corner of the paper, and the design consisted of a Royal Crown with the sword and scepter crossed at the back, surrounded by the garter with the inscription *Honi soit qui mal y pense.* The word *America* appeared prominently on the design, as it did on the stamps used on legal documents.

On February 14, 1765, Benjamin Franklin, then living in London, wrote his partner, David Hall, who was publishing the *Pennsylvania Gazette* in Philadelphia during Franklin's absence, advising him that he had obtained information from some of his friends in Parliament that it was certain the Stamp Act would be passed. Franklin had been tipped off that colonial newspapers printed on what were known as full sheets (folded down to page size during the printing process) would be taxed one penny per sheet, whereas those printed on half-sheets would be taxed one-half penny. The *Gazette* was then printed on full sheets, and Franklin, for whom a penny saved was a penny earned, realized there would be a 50% tax saving if Hall converted to half sheets. Accordingly, he purchased 48,000 half sheets in London and shipped the paper to his partner in Philadelphia to be used as soon as the act became effective.

Franklin had been given to understand that, under the provisions of the impending statute, Hall could take the imported paper to the office of the Pennsylvania Stamp Distributor and pay for it to be stamped in the proper denomination to comply fully with the law. When the paper arrived in Philadelphia, Hall learned that it could not be used, because printers and publishers were obliged to buy and use only paper pre-stamped in England. Furthermore, as Hall wrote, the paper was "nothing like so good or fair as ours and comes very high."[21] The cost of shipping the paper across the Atlantic was one of the factors contributing to its higher price.

Most of the paper used in the colonies was imported from the mother country, but there were approximately fifty colonial papermakers who operated their own mills. The Stamp Act had the effect of diverting business from this infant industry to the English government, and by the terms of the Act, the Stamp Commissioners had the power to fix the price of the paper that was stamped for sale in the colonies. A real hardship imposed on the colonial publisher was that he could no longer buy paper on credit. The Act required him to pay cash for his paper, at a higher price, to which he had to add the cost of the tax. The September 23, 1765, edition of the *Boston Evening Post* stated that printers throughout the colonies were demanding that their advertisers pay all outstanding bills immediately, because of the critical need for specie in order to conform to the provisions of the Stamp Act.

The editors had no alternative except to pass the higher costs along to their subscribers and advertisers in the form of price increases. They faced the risk that this would result in a loss of advertising and a decrease in subscriptions. James Adams, a Wilmington, Delaware, printer, advised prospective customers for the 1766 edition of the *Wilmington Almanac* that it would be to their advantage to purchase copies prior to November 1, 1765, the date the Stamp Act was to become effective. Adams stated that thereafter the tax "will raise its value to more than double the usual or old price."[22]

The price of *Ames Almanac* for 1766 (published in Dedham, Massachusetts, by Nathaniel Ames), which normally cost "six coppers single," was also expected to double after the Act became effective. Ames advertised in *The Boston Post Boy And Advertiser* (hereafter referred to as *Boston Post*

Boy) on September 9, 1765, that he was printing his 1766 *Almanac* earlier than usual so that subscribers could take advantage of the lower price.

The stamp tax amounted to four pence per almanac, and the substantial price increases predicted by the two publishers reflected not only the tax but the increased cost of the English paper. Legal action against those who failed to comply with the Act could be initiated in any one of three judicial bodies: the provincial Common-law Courts, the Vice-Admiralty Courts, or the Vice-Admiralty supercourt in Halifax. As the members of Parliament viewed the Act, it, like the Act of 1764, was merely an extension of the Trade and Navigation laws, and no distinction was made between legislation passed to regulate trade and that designed to raise revenue. To Parliament there seemed to be no innovation in giving the Vice-Admiralty Courts jurisdiction over enforcement of the Stamp Act. They failed to understand that Americans would consider this subversive of their rights. Since the colonists did not enjoy trial by jury in the Vice-Admiralty Courts, they saw this provision in the Act as an unwarranted extension of the jurisdiction of civil law.

Obviously the commercial and legal world was affected to a greater degree by the Stamp Act than the average consumer. The ordinary colonist might have accepted the tax with only mild protest if he had not been aroused by the propaganda devised by editors, lawyers, and merchants. Militant editors used the columns in their newspapers to turn public opinion against the tax. Lawyers complained to their clients of the costly inconvenience the Stamp Act imposed on the legal system. Merchants used seamen, clerks, apprentices, and other workmen in their employ to register their protests in the streets and help mobilize dissenters.

The execution of the Stamp Act was a major undertaking, the magnitude of which has not been fully appreciated by most historians of colonial America. First, it was necessary for the British Stamp Commissioners to obtain estimates of the quantities of stamped paper required in all the New World colonies for legal and commercial transactions, as well as of the amount of paper needed by colonial publishers of newspapers and almanacs. These figures were arrived at through special correspondence with royal governors and other officials in each colony, who were requested to submit complete lists of the various kinds of documents used in their respective colonies. The production by English paper mills of the required quantities of paper and parchment in many different sizes, the sheets all bearing tax impressions of differing amounts, was in itself a complicated operation. Production was slow because the sources of mechanical power used in modern papermaking and graphic arts industries were not yet available.

Statistics covering the quantities of stamped paper allocated to each colony have not been found, but there are some fragmentary records of the size of some of the initial shipments. The first shipment, which arrived in the middle of September 1765 for use in Massachusetts, New Hampshire, and Rhode Island, weighed twelve tons![23] The monetary value of the first consigment of paper shipped to New York amounted to £12,934, to Boston £12,413, and to Philadelphia £11,852.[24] Although it is not possible to translate these figures in terms of pounds of paper by making a comparison with the small cost of the individual sheets (see below), it is apparent that a huge volume of paper was transported from England to America.

Scheduling the initial shipments to the mainland colonies with drop-offs in the West Indies was another task that had to be undertaken by the Stamp Commissioners. This involved the use of forty-four different sailing vessels, which departed from ports in England between June and November 1765. (See the list of names of these ships and the names of their captains given in the Appendix.)

After the first shipments were enroute, the Commissioners were obliged to schedule additional consignments on a continuing basis for an indefinite period. Vessels with their holds loaded with bales of stamped paper and parchment weighing as much as one and a half tons delivered their cargoes to New York, Boston, Philadelphia, Charleston, Halifax, and other Atlantic coastal ports, as well as to the British Island possessions. Some of the consignments were intended for more than one colony, and were transferred from the English vessels in the major ports to coastwise vessels, which completed the deliveries. The consignee was the Stamp Distributor, and his shipment contained full instructions for the sale of the stamped paper.

The data reprinted below are taken from a contemporary price sheet published by the Stamp Office, which was located at Lincolns-Inn, London. The sizes and quality of all of the stamped paper to be sold in the colonies, as well as the prices, are enumerated. The prices apply only to the cost of the paper and parchment and do not include the cost of the stamps, which varied according to the end use of the document.[25] For example, if the buyer of a plot of land not exceeding one hundred acres wanted to have the deed executed on a piece of parchment 28 x 23 inches, it would be necessary to pay ten pence for the parchment and one shilling six pence tax, which was the amount of the stamp called for in this particular transaction.

Parchment

Skins 18 inch by 13, at Four-pence
     22 inch by 16, at Six-pence
     26 inch by 20, at Eight-pence   each
     28 inch by 23, at Ten-pence
     31 inch by 26, at Thirteen-pence

Paper

Horn at Seven-pence Fools Cap at Nine-pence Do [Ditto] with printed at 1s. notices for Indentures Folio Post at one Shilling Demi Post at Two Shillings Medium Post at Three Shillings Royal Post at Four Shillings Super Royal at Six Shillings	each Quire [24 or 25 sheets]

Paper for Printing[26]

News Double Crown at 14 s. each Ream Double Demy at 19 s.	[Approx. 480 sheets; a Crown measured 15″ x 19″ and a Demy 15½″ x 20″ to 18″ x 23″]

Almanacks

Book—Fools Cap at 6s. 6 d.
Pocket—Folio Post at 20 s.   each Ream
Sheet—Demy at 13 s.

The majority of the members of Parliament believed that the stamp tax was a fair and equitable method of allowing the colonies to pay part of their own defense. The tax was in no way intended to harass the colonial subjects, but was deemed a small tax spread over a large number of transactions so that no hardship would be imposed on any single class of taxpayers. It was a self-executing tax, requiring a minimal cost to enforce, since the taxpayer himself was required to buy the stamped paper. If the prescribed documents used in commercial or legal transactions did not bear stamps, they were void. There was no easy way to evade the tax, and the only possible danger was that of counterfeiting.

This seemed unlikely, not only because of limited paper production in the colonies, but also because English law made counterfeiting of stamped paper a felony subject to the death penalty.

Although the stamp tax seemed reasonable to Lord Grenville and his associates, none of them had tried to ascertain in advance what the reaction in the colonies would be. They received their information indirectly through the Secretary of State or the Board of Trade, and it is now apparent that British officials miscalculated the colonial response. Perhaps the greatest failure in England was to understand that each of the mainland colonies had acquired a measure of home rule, especially in the Lower Houses of the Assemblies. The Assemblies were regarded as a sort of colonial House of Commons, having the right to levy and collect taxes within each colony. The Lower Houses, elected by the people, included among their members many lawyers, merchants, and editors, who insisted that the tax laws they passed meant that the people were, in effect, taxing themselves. Thus, the colonists possessed the traditional right of all English subjects to be represented in the governing body that taxed them.

The Lower Houses, in fact, wielded considerable power, such as fixing the salaries of certain officials; raising troops, if needed, for protection; regulating the Indian trade; and appointing agents to represent the colony in its dealings in London with the House of Commons, the Board of Trade, and the Committee on Plantation Affairs, and in other matters where Parliament was involved.[27]

Other autonomous functions were performed in the Assemblies, although questions involving international trade, foreign affairs, and matters of peace and war were left to King and Parliament. But the right of taxing their constituents was jealously guarded by the Assemblies, because control of the purse strings gave them political power and prestige.

Apart from political issues, there were practical economic considerations resulting from the actions of Parliament that had repercussions in the Assemblies. Northern merchants suffered restraints on commerce caused by the Sugar Act of 1764; Southern planters, deeply in debt to English merchants, were adversely affected by the tightening of general business and the restrictions on the circulation of paper notes. Small farmers, who made up the largest economic group in both the North and the South, suffered a decline in prices for their crops as a result of pressures on the market. Trade with the West Indies, a favorable market for surplus farm products, was crippled because of the enforcement of the duties on molasses. The passage of the Stamp Act left the impression that the mother country was discriminating against the colonial subjects and setting up a monstrous tax system that infringed their rights as Englishmen.

Merchants in the North American colonies believed that they had benefited the mother country by furnishing her with sugar, tobacco, rice, cotton, indigo, naval stores, lumber, and furs, which she would otherwise have been forced to buy from rival nations. They felt that they were contributing to the prosperity of Great Britain by providing a substantial and ever-increasing market for her manufactured goods. It seemed unfitting that Parliament would respond by levying stamp taxes on them for the upkeep of a large, unrequested, and probably ineffective force of English troops. Parliament had poured money into the North American colonies to finance the French and Indian War, but it seemed to be doing its utmost in the postwar period to bleed the colonies of their money without their consent.

Following the passage of the Act of 1764, James Otis, a prominent Boston lawyer and member of the Massachusetts Assembly, wrote a "Rights" treatise, in which he took the position that every subject born in the English colonies was

Engraving of an original painting by Joseph Blackburn of James Otis (1725–1783), brilliant delegate from Massachusetts described as "the soul" of the Congress. He was a member of the committee that wrote the petition to the House of Commons, and he probably was the author of the first draft.
COURTESY NEW YORK PUBLIC LIBRARY, EMMET COLLECTION NO. 174, MANUSCRIPTS AND ARCHIVES DIVISION, ASTOR, LENOX AND TILDEN FOUNDATIONS.

"entitled to all the natural, inherent, and inseparable rights of our fellow subjects in England."[28] He went on to say that the imposition of taxes on the colonists without their consent—external or internal, direct or indirect—was irreconcilable with their *rights* as British subjects. If Parliament had the authority to tax the colonial trade to raise revenue, Otis argued, it then had the power to tax land or anything else it chose. If it were necessary to station troops in America, he said that Parliament should apportion the cost among the colonies and allow them to raise the money in their own way. Otis's arguments had a pronounced influence on his fellow members of the House of Representatives of the Massachusetts Assembly, where there was strong opposition to Grenville's fiscal policies.

From March 9, 1764, when Lord Grenville introduced his resolution in Parliament regarding a stamp tax, the Colonial Assemblies had almost a year's notice before the Stamp Act was passed. During that interim, eight of the colonies, Massachusetts, Rhode Island, Connecticut, New York, Pennsylvania, Virginia, North Carolina, and South Carolina, sent formal protests to Parliament through their London agents.[29] While the Stamp Act was being debated, none of the petitions was given a hearing! It was not the practice of the House of Commons to hear petitions on money bills and, perhaps more important, the members resented the colonies' questioning their authority. It is true that there was minority opposition to the stamp tax by some of the members, but this opposition was on the grounds of expediency, not of constitutionality. There was no question in the minds of any of the members that Parliament had the legal right to tax the colonies if it decided to do so.[30]

Despite colonial protests, the Stamp Act was enacted into law, after which the first and most effective outcry came from Virginia, the oldest and most populous colony. Members of the House of Burgesses were irritated because Parliament ignored their petition, and when the news reached Williamsburg that the Stamp Act had passed, it caused a heated argument between radical members and the younger conservatives. Patrick Henry, a 29-year-old lawyer and new member of the House, introduced a series of resolutions, four of which were printed in the official journal. The resolutions stated that the two royal charters granted by James I to the first Virginia settlers gave them and their descendants all the liberties and privileges of Englishmen, including the right to be taxed only by themselves or by "Persons chosen to represent them."[31] One of the resolutions, which was not printed in the journal, boldly stated that the Virginia General Assembly had the sole and exclusive right to tax the inhabitants of the colony. These so-called Virginia Resolves were widely reprinted in colonial newspapers, whose editors took every opportunity to condemn the Stamp Act. This stirred up action in the other Assemblies, and eight of them, starting with Rhode Island (the others were Pennsylvania, Maryland, Connecticut, Massachusetts, South Carolina, New Jersey, and New York) passed resolutions denying Parliament's right to tax the colonists. The language of these resolutions was much stronger than in the protests made prior to the passage of the Stamp Act.[32]

Starting April 3, 1765, Grenville began to appoint Stamp Distributors to handle the sale of the stamped paper. He purposely named Americans in the thirteen mainland colonies, no doubt feeling that this would make collecting the tax less objectionable than sending unknown tax collectors from England. Since large sums of money would pass through the Distributor's hands, the position was one of considerable responsibility. The remuneration was so attractive that a number of Americans willingly offered their services, some using their political connections to try to get the appointment. Twelve Distributors were appointed to serve the thirteen colonies (John Hughes, the Pennsylvania Distributor, also handled the Three Lower Counties). It was intended to expand the organization once the system got underway by appointing subdistributors at convenient locations in each colony.

Separate Stamp Distributors were appointed for Montreal, Trois Rivières, Quebec, East Florida, West Florida, Granada (in the West Indies), Nova Scotia, Jamaica, St. Kitts, Bermudas, Barbados, and the Leeward Islands.[33] The list of vessels in the Appendix gives the names of all of the Stamp Distributors designated to receive shipments of stamped paper.

Initially, the Colonial Assemblies blamed Grenville and Parliament for passing the Stamp Act, but as the opposition was organized and riots broke out, there were local personalities against whom the mobs could vent their anger— the Stamp Distributors. In the late summer of 1765, the first riots occurred in Boston, and in the weeks and months that followed, violence spread to the other colonies. These riots were not spontaneous outbursts, but were incited by merchants, editors, and other leaders working behind the scenes, who organized dissenters known as the Sons of Liberty. Although riffraff dominated many of the mobs, it is ironical that the rioters were aroused by respectable, well-to-do men whose professions or businesses were directly affected by Parliament's tax policies.[34]

Rioters hung the Stamp Distributors in effigy, damaged some of their homes and property, and threatened their lives and the lives of their families. Facing threat and intimidation, the terrorized Stamp Distributors were forced to resign, one by one, until there was no one left in the mainland colonies to distribute the stamped paper.[35] It was in this tense atmosphere that the Stamp Act Congress was held.

NOTES TO CHAPTER 1

1. *Knollenberg* (p. 17) states that, among the hundreds of letters written between 1745–1763 that he has read, he found

only two that left an intimation of a desire for independence. Ironically, fears that the colonies might seek their independence were prevalent among many politicans in England. For differing views on the question of independence, see Bernard Bailyn, *The Ideological Origins of the American Revolution* (Cambridge, Mass., 1967), and David S. Lovejoy, *The Glorious Revolution in America* (New York, 1972).

2. *Knollenberg* (p. 11) lists a number of causes of colonial discontent prior to 1763 due to Parliament's actions, but in my opinion none of these had the repercussions of the statutes and proclamations passed after 1763.

3. In *Crisis* (p. 21), the Morgans point out that the figure of £140,000,000 once cited by Grenville as the size of the national debt. and quoted by many historians, was an exaggeration.

4. Public Record Office, London, Out-Letters, Taxes (T. 22), piece 6, p. 65.

5. The Trade and Navigation Acts had their origin in 1650–51, and among their other objectives they were designed to exclude rival Dutch ships from trading with the New World colonies. As modified through a series of additional statutes passed in succeeding years, they bolstered the concept of mercantilism.

6 *Acts of the Privy Council of England, Colonial Series,* ed. J. Munro (Hereford, 1911–12), 4: 569–72.

7. *Knollenberg*, p. 135.

8. *Lovejoy, 1958,* p. 19.

9. *Knollenberg*, p. 137. See also Gilman M. Ostrander, "The Colonial Molasses Trade," *Agricultural History* 30 (1956): 77–84

10. *The Statutes at Large from Magna Charta to the End of the Eleventh Parliament of Great Britain,* ed. Danby Pickering (Cambridge, 1762–1869), 26: 33–52.

11. For a definitive account of these courts see Carl Ubbelohde, *The Vice Admiralty Courts and the American Revolution* (Chapel Hill, N.C., 1960). Cf. David S. Lovejoy, "Rights Imply Equality: The Case Against Admiralty Jurisdiction In America, 1764–1776," *William and Mary Quarterly,* 3d s. 16 (1959): 459–84.

12. *Statutes at Large,* 26: 103–5. For a comprehensive analysis of the financial problems and how the Currency Act of 1751 was a prelude to the Act of 1764, see Joseph Albert Ernest, *Money and Politics in America* (Chapel Hill, N.C., 1973).

13. John Shy, *Towards Lexington* (Princeton, N.J., 1965), pp. 62–67, presents evidence that the majority of British troops were to be stationed in the interior and not in the seaboard towns. He believes that the troops were intended primarily to keep the colonists in subjection to the mother country, and to enforce the imperial management of Indian affairs.
14. There were sporadic efforts on the part of certain of the colonies to act cooperatively, e.g., the United Colonies of New England was formed in 1643. Various regional meetings were held to treat with the Indians, but military affairs were the principal consideration, and the meetings originated with British military leaders or other representatives of the British government.
15. *Gipson, 1961*, vol. 10, chap. 2.
16. Charles R. Ritcheson, "The Preparation of the Stamp Act," *William and Mary Quarterly*, 3d s. 10, (1939) : 543–59; also *Crisis*, p. 54n.
17. Edward Hughes, "The English Stamp Duties, 1664–1764," *English Historical Review* 56 (1941) : 234–59. Cf. Sttphen Dowell, *A History and Explanation of Stamp Duties* (London, 1873) ; idem, *A History of Taxation and Taxes in England* (London, 1888).
18. *Journal of the Legislative Council of New York, 1743–1775* (Albany, N.Y., 1861), pp. 1271, 1276, 1286, 1289; *NYCD*, 7: 163; *Gipson, 1961*, 10: 79; *Crisis*, p. 56.
19. It has been said that the postage paid by the colonists in the English-controlled postal system was a form of direct tax levied on the colonies, but this interpretation seems to be stretching the definition of a tax.
20. *Statutes at Large*, 26: 179–204. In the Stowe Manuscript Room, British Museum, 142: 125, there is a specimen of coarse gray paper embossed with a stamp valued at two shillings six pence, intended for use in the colonies. This stamp is approximately 1½ inches long and 1⅜ inches wide. I was unable to photograph it, but it is almost identical in appearance with a drawing of one of the stamps in Frank M. Etting, *An Historical Account of the Old State House of Pennsylvania* (Boston, 1876), p. 50. There are also two specimens similarly embossed on gray paper, of the same denomination in the Etting Papers, Provincial Council, Historical Society of Delaware. There are also examples in the collections of other historical societies, and the most famous in the collections

of the Massachusetts Historical Society is a sheet of paper to which someone affixed a number of the stamps cut out of the original stamped paper.

21. *The Papers of Benjamin Franklin,* ed. Leonard W. Labaree, (New Haven, Conn., 1968), 12: 64–67, 170–71, 190–91. According to the Stamp Act in force in England, a taxpayer could present his own paper and pay for stamping, making it unnecessary to buy stamped paper supplied by the government unless he so desired; see Stephen Dowell, *A History and Explanation of Tax Duties* (London, 1873). Evidently Franklin assumed that the statute applying to the colonies would include this provision, which it did not. I can find no basis to support the statement made by Charles M. Andrews in *The Colonial Background of the American Revolution* (New Haven, Conn., 1924), p. 133, that the colonial taxpayer could have his paper imprinted with a rubber stamp at the tax office. Section 17 of the act provided that a deed or legal document could be drawn up on unstamped paper only if it was executed by an accompanying certificate impressed with a wax seal by the Stamp Distributor in the presence of a magistrate. This special handling would cost £10 per document, or more, which was far more expensive than the regular tax applying to stamped paper used in the same transaction.

22. *Pennsylvania Gazette,* August 29, 1765. Harold B. Hancock refers to this advertisement in "County Committees and the Growth of Independence in The Lower Counties of Delaware, 1765–1776," *Delaware History* 15 (1973): 271.

23. *Lovejoy, 1958,* p. 113.

24. Marcus Samuel, "The 1765 American Stamp Accounts," in *New Discovery from British Archives on the 1765 Tax Stamps for America,* ed. Adolph Koeppel, American Revenue Association (Boyertown, Pa., 1962), pp. 22–23.

25. The table is reproduced in *The Memorial History of Boston, 1630–1880,* ed. Justin Winsor (Boston, 1881), 3: 12; also in Samuel A. Green, *Ten Facsimile Reproductions* (Boston, 1902), chap. 6, along with an illustration of one of the stamps owned by the author.

26. "Double Demy" was the grade of paper that Franklin shipped to Hall.

27. Jack P. Green, "The Role of the Lower Houses of Assembly in Eighteenth-Century Politics," *The Reinterpretation of the American Revolution, 1763–1789* (New York, 1968), pp. 86–109.

28. James Otis, *The Rights of the British Colonies Asserted and Proved* (Boston, 1764). Another pamphlet that denied Parliament's right to tax the colonies and influenced colonial thought was Stephen Hopkins, *The Rights of the Colonies Examined* (Providence, R.I., 1764).

29. *Prologue*, p. 3; see pp. 8–14 for the New York and Virginia petitions as examples of the colonial position. Grenville made an important concession by stating that the colonies could avoid a stamp tax if they would take action themselves to make the tax unnecessary (*Crisis*, pp. 55–56); also Edmund S. Morgan, "Postponement of the Stamp Act," *William and Mary Quarterly*, 3d s. 7 (1950) : 353–92.

30. Fred J. Ericson, "The Contemporary British Opposition to the Stamp Act, 1764–1765," *Papers of the Michigan Academy of Science* 29 (1943) : 489–503.

31. For a transcript of the Virginia Resolves see *Prologue*, pp. 47–50. When the resolves appeared in colonial newspapers there were seven of them, although the three most inflammatory never passed the House of Burgesses. New York's Assembly a year before had denied Parliament's right to tax the colonists. *Prologue*, pp. 8–14.

32. These resolutions are all quoted in *Prologue*, pp. 50–62.

33. In the Fisher Transcripts, Manuscript 360, Maryland Historical Society, there is a document dated July 1765, entitled "List of Officers of the Stamp Duties in the Gift of the Treasury." It includes five commissioners who received £500 per annum salary, and a long list of employees including forty-one stampers, rolling press printers, clerks, etc. This organization handled the production and distribution of stamped paper both in England and the colonies. *Gipson, 1961*, 10: 277, states that there were nine inspectors who worked under the commissioners, each of whom had direct responsibility for a colonial district.

34. John C. Miller, *Origins of the American Revolution*, rev. ed. (Stanford, Calif., 1959); see also Philip G. Davidson, "Sons of Liberty and Stamp Men," *North Carolina Historical Review* 9 (1932) : 38–56; *Crisis*, pp. 180–204.

35. The Act was enforced in Nova Scotia, Bermuda, Granada, and Quebec against varying protests; in Jamaica and Barbados there was some opposition; in the Leeward Islands there was considerable opposition, and the Stamp Distributor was forced to resign. Stamped paper was burned at St. Kitts

(see *Gipson, 1961,* 10: 326, passim). Sir Alan Burns, *History of the British West Indies,* rev. ed. (London, 1965), p. 517, says stamped paper worth £2,000 was destroyed by rioters at St. Kitts, and that there were riots in Nevis, but there was no opposition in the Bahamas. See also W. B. Kerr, "The Stamp Act in Quebec," *English Historical Review* 47 (1932): 648–51, also his "The Stamp Act in Nova Scotia, *"New England Quarterly* 6 (1933): 552–66.

2

Delegates
to the Stamp Act Congress

Although the petitions passed by the Colonial Assemblies before the Stamp Act was enacted echoed a common note of protest, each colony continued to express itself individually. Grenville's solution for England's financial problems ironically was the catalyst that caused the colonies to seek united action. After passage of the Sugar Act of 1764, the Massachusetts House of Representatives took a step in the direction of colonial unity by urging the other Assemblies to protest and urge its repeal, and also to petition Parliament not to pass the Stamp Act. As a means of communicating with her sister colonies, Massachusetts appointed a Committee of Correspondence of five members, who circulated letters to other colonies in June of 1764.[1]

On October 8, 1764, a similar committee appointed by the Rhode Island General Assembly informed the Secretary of the Connecticut Assembly that its members were authorized to correspond with the other colonies on the question of taking unified action to protest the duties that had been levied, and "the Act in Embrio for establishing Stamp Duties." The following significant paragraph in this letter indicates that the Rhode Island Assembly recognized that if the colonies acted in concert to oppose the Stamp, Act, they might accomplish what they could not achieve individually:

If all the Colonies were disposed to enter with Spirit into the Defence of their Liberties; if some Method could be hit upon for collecting the Sentiments of each Colony, and for uniting and forming the Substance of them into one common Defence of the whole, and this sent to England, and the Several Agents directed to join together in pushing and pursuing it there in the properest and most effectual Manner, it might be the most probable Method to produce the End aimed at.[2]

One writer claims, without citing convincing evidence, that New York's Committee of Correspondence, under the influence of two of its members, John Cruger and Robert R. Livingston, was the first to urge that a convention of delegates from all of the colonies be held to protest Parliament's violation of their rights and liberties.[3]

Another source states that James Otis and his father, James Otis, Sr., during a visit to the home of James Warren in Plymouth, Massachusetts (Warren was married to James Otis's sister Mercy), conceived of a congress of representatives from the thirteen colonies.[4] Otis has been given credit by a number of writers for introducing the idea to members of the Massachusetts Assembly, although acceptable documentation has not been offered. In retrospect, it seems so obvious that the colonies would accomplish more by acting in concert instead of individually, that it would appear to have been the natural course to follow. But in the context of the period it was an innovative approach to the problem, and the originator of the idea of an intercolonial congress made a significant contribution to American political history.

Whether or not Otis first suggested the Congress to the Massachusetts Assembly is a moot question, but the fact remains that the Lower House of the Assembly, of which Otis was a member, took the initial action. This, among other things gave Massachusetts a reputation of being foremost among the colonies in political influence and leadership.

On June 6, 1765, the members of the Lower House discussed the Stamp Act, and other objectionable legislation enacted by Parliament, and reached a meeting of minds with regard to the action that should be taken. Because of the importance of their decision, the details of their deliberations are worthy of careful examination. The following passage is quoted verbatim from the Journal of the Lower House:

> The House taking into Consideration the many difficulties to which the Colonies are and must be reduced by the Operation of some late Acts of Parliament; after some Time spent.
> On a Motion made and seconded, Ordered, That Mr. Speaker [Samuel White], Brigadier *Ruggles*, Col. *Partridge*, Col. *Worthington*, General *Winslow*, Mr. *Otis*, Mr. *Cushing*, Col. *Saltonstall* and Capt. *Sheaffe*, be a Committee to consider what Measures had best be taken, and make Report.
> The Committee appointed for that Purpose, reported as follows:
> The Committee appointed to consider what dutiful, loyal and humble Address may be proper to make to our gracious Sovereign and his Parliament, in relation to the Several Acts lately passed, for levying Duties and Taxes on the Colonies, have attended that Service, and are humbly of opinion:
> That it is highly expedient there should be a Meeting as soon as may be, of Committees from the Houses of Representatives or Burgesses in the several Colonies on this Continent to consult together on the present Circumstances of the Colonies, and the Difficulties to which they are and must be reduced by the operation of the late Acts of Parliament for levying Duties and Taxes on the Colonies, and to consider of a general and humble Address to his Majesty and the Parliament to implore Relief.
> And the Committee are further of opinion that a Meeting of such Committees should be held at *New-York* on the first Tuesday of *October* next, and that a Committee of three Persons be chosen by this House on the Part of this Province to attend the same.
> And that Letters be forthwith prepared and transmitted

to the respective Speakers of the several Houses of Representatives or Burgesses in the Colonies aforesaid, advising them of the Resolution of this House thereon, and inviting such Houses of Representatives or Burgesses to join this with their Committees, in the Meeting, and for the Purposes aforesaid.

And that a proper Letter be prepared and forwarded to the Agent of the Province on these Matters in the mean time.

Read and accepted, and *Ordered,* That Mr. Speaker, Mr. *Otis,* and Mr. *Lee,* be a Committee to prepare a draft of Letters to be sent to the respective Speakers of the several Houses of Representatives in the Colonies and make Report.[5]

Several items in these minutes should be particularly noted. The reference to "levying *Duties* and *Taxes*" appears twice. This phraseology makes it clear that the committee had in mind the customs duties called for in the Act of 1764, as well as the direct, internal stamp taxes. The use of the adjectives *dutiful, loyal* and *humble,* in connection with "our gracious Sovereign," indicates that the committee had no desire to antagonize the King nor to abrogate their relationship as his faithful subjects. The phrase *the several Colonies on this Continent* excludes the island possessions from the invitation, since *Continent* was used to mean the thirteen mainland colonies. Although Nova Scotia, Quebec, and East and West Florida were on the mainland, they were not invited. The latter colonies did not yet have any Assemblies, but Nova Scotia, with a population of about 10,000, had a Governor, Council, and Assembly. Nevertheless, she, too, was excluded.[6] The insular possessions like Jamaica, which also had a Governor, Council, and Assembly, were not invited, although their participation might have strengthened the resistance to the Stamp Act.

The committee specified the place and date of the proposed meeting, namely, New York City on the first Tuesday of October 1765, that is, October 1. It would seem that the committee was of the opinion that the delegates could accomplish their mission in a few days and immediately forward petitions to England, which would result in prompt repeal of the Stamp Act. The committee might have selected Boston or another New England town as the site of the meeting, but the members were fully aware that the three most southerly colonies, Georgia and North and South Carolina, were far distant from New England. New York City, accessible either by land or water, was a more convenient location for them than Boston. New York was also a central point for the Middle Atlantic colonies, and as a commercial city whose life depended upon trade with England, it seemed to be an ideal site. Perhaps there had been some prearrangement with New York's Committee of Correspondence (see below).

The House, after hearing the committee's report, decided to elect three delegates to represent the colony at the proposed meeting, or "Convention," as it was termed in the journal. The members cast their votes in favor of James Otis, Colonel John Worthington, and Colonel Oliver Partridge. The minutes then went on to say:

> Col. Worthington having excused himself from that Service, the House came to the choice of a person in his room, and the Committee reported that Brigadier [Timothy] Ruggles was chosen.

In view of the unusual role he played at the New York meeting, it is of interest that Ruggles was not the first choice of the House.

On June 20, the House resolved that the sum of £450 be appropriated to the three "commissioners" for their expenses in order to "enable them to discharge the important Truth to which they are appointed; they upon their return to be accountable for the same."[7]

The original committee (White, Otis, and Lee), as instructed, prepared an invitation to be sent to the other twelve colonies. This carefully phrased communication, probably drafted by Otis, did not suggest that a momentous precedent was being set, but proposed in matter-of-fact language that each Colonial Assembly send a committee to attend a meeting beginning on the first Tuesday in October in New York City (see Journal below, chap. 4). This meeting, later referred to as the Stamp Act Congress, was scheduled to convene a month *before* the Stamp Act was to become effective on November 1. Perhaps a more descriptive name for it would be "A Congress to Protest the Act of 1764, the Stamp Act, and both Internal and External Taxes Levied by Parliament for Revenue Purposes."

The circular letter was addressed to the Speakers of the respective Assemblies and Burgesses. The Speaker held a position of prestige and importance, and in most colonies was dignified by a long black robe and a wig of state, and he carried an ornate mace as a token of his office. Massachusetts stated in her letter of invitation that her delegation would consist of three members of the Assembly. This may have been a subtle suggestion for the other colonies to appoint three deputies, although the letter did not restrict the number. The authors of the letter were fully aware that a third member of a three-man committee could cast a deciding vote in the event the other two members were deadlocked.

The circular letter gave two reasons for the proposed meeting: first, to consult about the difficulties imposed by "the Operation of the acts of Parliament for levying Duties and Taxes on the colonies." This left no doubt that the discussion would not be confined to internal taxes, which Otis in his "Rights" pamphlet had refused to separate from external taxes.

The second reason was to consider a *"united,* dutiful, loyal and humble Representation [emphasis added]" to be addressed to King and Parliament "to implore relief." The invitation contained no inflammatory words or phrases, and nothing was said from which it could be inferred that the Massachusetts Assembly was questioning Parliament's legislative authority. The first draft of the circular letter was dated June 8, 1765, three weeks before publication of the Virginia Resolves, which prompted Massachusetts and some other colonies, to compose similar resolutions, had reached Boston. None of the riots associated with the opposition to the Stamp Act had yet occurred, and no stamped paper had yet arrived in America. As yet there was no Stamp Act crisis.

The authors of the Massachusetts circular letter knew that if the royal governors were given the impression that the colonies were being importuned to take part in a treasonous meeting, they would be expected to do their utmost to prevent their respective Assemblies from being represented. The governors could exercise their legal right of prorogue, which meant discontinuing a session of the Assembly, thus preventing the members from meeting officially to consider the invitation. Furthermore, the governors could continue to keep their Assemblies prorogued until it suited them to call them back into session again.

The authors of the letter also realized that many members of the Colonial Assemblies would question the propriety of holding any kind of intercolonial meeting without first requesting Parliament or the Crown's permission to do so. It may have been proper for individual colonies to petition Parliament for relief, but inappropriate for thirteen colonies to join in what might appear to be a conspiracy to register a united protest. The majority of the assemblymen throughout the colonies believed in the supremacy of Parliament, and even though Parliament may have overstepped itself in passing the Stamp Act, many felt that the colonies did not have the right to disobey. If that august body erred by illegally taxing the colonists, the solution was not defiance, but submission, and a prudent request for reconsideration of the legislation. Thus, when one examines the action taken by the Colonial Assemblies after receipt of the invitation, the words *dutiful, loyal,* and *humble,* are conspicuous in the minutes of their discussions.

The Massachusetts letter gave the Assemblies three months' notice to consider the invitation and to select their committees. A prompt reply was requested so that the project might be canceled in the unlikely event of receiving a majority of unfavorable responses. At the time the letter was released the Massachusetts House sent a communication to Richard Jackson, a member of Parliament and the London agent for Massachusetts, advising him of the coming meeting, fully aware that he was free to notify his colleagues in England. Once the invitation was sent, no attempt was made to keep the meeting a secret and it was widely publicized in the colonial press.

The three men the Lower House named as their deputies represented the best legal brains to be found in Massachusetts. James Otis, aged 40, a brilliant Harvard graduate then in his prime, was believed by many to have no superior in his knowledge of English common and statute law. He was also well versed in Greek and Roman history, as well as philosophy and poetry. He had an impulsive and somewhat moody personality, and some accused him of being a rabble rouser. Later in life he suffered mental deterioration, which was worsened by a blow on the head in a coffee-house brawl, but there was nothing about his participation in the Stamp Act Congress to indicate any mental derangement.[8] Before he left Boston for New York, the September 23, 1765, edition of the *Boston Post Boy* published an article in which the editor held out the "warmest Expectations" from the New York meeting, and enjoined Otis personally "to contribute the utmost of his Ability in having the Rights of the Colonies stated in the clearest view, and laid before the Parliament."

Oliver Partridge, aged 53, was a Yale graduate of the class of 1730 and a respected citizen of Hatfield, where he held a number of political offices. In 1754 he represented Massachusetts Bay at the Albany convention, where he favored the plan for a colonial union. In 1769 he became Judge of the Common Pleas Court for Hampshire County. As the break developed with England, he initially was slow to favor independence. At the beginning of the Revolution he took a neutral position but was never accused of being a Loyalist. As the events unfolded he embraced the American cause.[9]

Timothy Ruggles, a Harvard graduate aged 54, was an outstanding lawyer, Judge of the Worcester County Court, and a former Speaker of the House of Representatives. He had accumulated a substantial fortune from his law practice. He had served as a Colonel under Sir William Johnson and later as a Brigadier-General under Lord Jeffery Amherst. He was strongly pro-English, and as a conservative, held opposite views from Otis on many political and legal issues.[10]

After the Massachusetts letter was dispatched a series of events took place that could not have been anticipated by the authors of the letter. As the following chronology indicates, the letter could not have been timed better:

June 8 Letter approved and circulated

June 24 Virginia Resolves appear in Newport, R.I., *Mercury*

July 2 *Boston Gazette* publishes Virginia Resolves

July 4 *Maryland Gazette* publishes Virginia Resolves
 Lord Grenville dismissed by King, succeeded by Charles Watson-Wentworth, the Marquis of Rockingham

August-September Stamp riots occur in Boston and in Connecticut. Stamp Distributors in Massachusetts, New York, Rhode Island, New Jersey, New Hampshire, and Connecticut forced one by one to resign

September Rhode Island Assembly issues a resolve challenging Parliament's right to tax the colonies
 Pennsylvania and Maryland issue similar resolves

October 1 Stamp Act Congress scheduled to convene

November 1 Stamp Act to become effective

Since the Massachusetts letter was the instrument that led to the first significant effort toward colonial unification, it is of interest to examine briefly the action taken by each of the Assemblies when the unexpected invitation arrived. The responses of the colonies are discussed below in alphabetical order.

Connecticut

Connecticut was regarded as a liberal and progressive colony and, like Rhode Island, it was self-governing in the sense of electing its own governor (in contrast to royal colonies like Massachusetts, where the King appointed the governor). Nevertheless, there were pro-English conservatives in the Connecticut Assembly who looked with disfavor on anyone who questioned Parliament's authority. Although the Assembly formally protested the enactment of the Stamp Act, the committee who prepared the remonstrance transmitted to the London agent conceded that Parliament had the right to levy external taxes on the colonies both to regulate the trade and to raise revenue. The liberals did not agree, and some assemblymen and editors were outspoken against all forms of English taxation. The *Providence Gazette* urged that the Act of 1764 be repealed, and the *Connecticut Courant* published an article on October 29, 1764, suggesting that the colonies must "unite in such measures as will be effectual to obtain redress."[11]

Business had declined in Connecticut, as it had in Rhode Island and Massachusetts, because of the impact on the economy caused by the Sugar Act of 1764. Merchants and farmers were both experiencing economic reverses. It was inevitable that the imposition of the new stamp tax, requiring payment in scarce sterling, would make the situation worse.

The Connecticut Assembly normally met in May and October, or in special sessions when called by the governor. When the Speaker received the Massachusetts letter in June the Assembly was in recess. Governor Thomas Fitch was under pressure by liberals to call a special session to act on the invitation. If he failed to do so, Connecticut would not be represented at the New York meeting, because it would be too late to take action in the regular October session of the Assembly.

Fitch felt that the imposition of a stamp tax on colonists already burdened with debts would be grievous, but at the same time he wanted to uphold the statutes passed by Parliament. He was dubious about whether or not to call a special session, and this caused more pressure to be put on him by the liberals.

Colonel Jonathan Trimble, a judge and member of the Upper House and later governor of the colony, was among those favoring the special session. He wrote Governor Fitch to the effect that the people in his area of the colony (Windham County) considered stamp taxes and other duties levied by Parliament "to be utterly subversive of their Rights & Priviledges both by Charter, and as English Men; and That a Special Assembly be Called as soon as possible to Appoint Commissioners to Meet with such as are or shall be Appointed from other American Colonies at New York On The first of October next, to prepare and Unitedly Agree on an Address to King & Petition to the Parliament for the Repeal of that Act, and for Redress of the Burdens laid On Trade &c."[12]

Fitch acceded to the demands of the liberals, and issued orders for a special session of the Assembly to be held at Hartford on September 19, 1765. The Assembly met as scheduled, and after consideration of the Massachusetts letter and lengthy debate, the following entry was made in the journal:

> *Resolved by this Assembly,* That Eliphalet Dyer, William Samuel Johnson and David Rowland, Esqrs, or any two of them, be and are hereby appointed Commissioners on behalf of this Colony, to repair to New York to attend the proposed Congress in the matters above referred

to. And his Honour [Gov. Fitch] is hereby desired to commissionate them accordingly."[13]

Instructions were then prepared for the delegation and placed on record in the journal. These were substantially the same as those appearing in the Journal (chap. 4 below), except that the latter omits reference to the resolution that £100 be appropriated to cover the expenses of the delegation.[14] One of the sentences in the instructions indicates that the conservatives in the Assembly succeeded in imposing an important restriction on the delegation:

> In your proceedings you are to take care that you form no such junction with the other Commissioners as will subject you to the major vote of the Commissioners present.

This meant that the three delegates did not have the authority to sign any petitions or remonstrances. That decision could be made only by the members of the Assembly after the delegates returned from New York.

Like the Massachusetts delegates, the three commissioners from Connecticut were all well informed in the law. Eliphalet Dyer, aged 44, a graduate of Yale law school who held M.A. degrees from both Yale and Harvard, served as a Lieutenant-Colonel in the French and Indian War. Between 1747 and 1762, he was elected a deputy from Windham in eleven sessions of the Assembly. He became a member of the Governor's Council in 1762, and in 1763 the Susquehanna Company, of which he was one of the principals, sent him to England as its agent. He was in London when Lord Grenville's tax program was being formulated, and prior to the passage of the Stamp Act he wrote cynically that he thought it was intended "to fix upon us a large Number of regular Troops under pretence for our Defence; but rather designed as a rod and Check over us, etc."[15] In later years he became Chief Justice of the Connecticut Superior Court, and he was a delegate from the colony to the First Continental Congress.[16] John Adams said of him that "Dyer is long-winded and roundabout—obscure and cloudy, very talkative and very tedious, yet an honest worthy man and judges well."[17] When named as a deputy to the Stamp Act Congress he was not a member of the Lower House but was a governor's assistant, a member of the Council, and Comptroller of His Majesty's customs at the port of New London.

William Samuel Johnson, a distinguished conservative aged 38, widely read in law, history, and literature, was the son of a well-known Anglican clergyman. After receiving an education for the ministry at Yale, where he earned a master's degree, Johnson turned to law and became a recognized leader at the bar. He received an honorary master's degree from Harvard, and Oxford University awarded him an honorary doctor's degree in Civil Law in 1766. He served as a Lieutenant-Colonel in the Connecticut militia (resigning his commission when rumors of war were heard), and was selected a delegate to the First Continental Congress but refused to attend. He believed in a firm union between Britain and the colonies, but he was not a true Tory because he did not overtly support England. He summed up his position as follows: "I would not serve the people against the Crown nor can I [serve] the Crown against the people." During the Revolution he retired to his home in Stratford, where he maintained his neutrality, although he later took the oath of allegiance to the independence of Connecticut. He became one of the most respected members of the convention that framed the U.S. Constitution, and he was elected by the Assembly as one of Connecticut's first U.S. Senators. He also distinguished himself by being appointed in 1787 as president of Columbia College. A contemporary wrote that he had "a voice of finest and richest tones, a copious and flowing elocution, a mind stored with elegant literature."[18]

Judge David Rowland, aged 51, was also a graduate of Yale, where he had studied theology, but he spent his life as a civilian in Fairfield. He represented the town in the General Assembly from 1747 to 1765. He also served as Judge of the Fairfield County Court and the Fairfield Probate Court. He died in 1768, less than three years after the adjournment of the Stamp Act Congress, and did not participate in the Revolution.[19]

Georgia

Alexander Wylly, Speaker of the Commons House, as the lower branch of the Georgia General Assembly was known, received the Massachusetts letter at Savannah after the Assembly had adjourned and was then in recess. Governor Wright had prorogued the Assembly until October 22, 1765, which would be too late to attend the New York meeting. Recognizing the importance of the proposed meeting, Wylly sent personal messages to the twenty-five representatives of the Commons House, and sixteen of them met with him at Savannah to discuss the Massachusetts proposal. They agreed to request the royal governor, James Wright, to call a special session of the Assembly where the members could take action on the invitation. Governor Wright refused to call a special session.

Wylly then sent a letter to Speaker Samuel White of Massachusetts, explaining the situation and requesting that copies of any of the representations agreed on by the delegates be sent to him to present to the Assembly when it reconvened in October. This letter was received by the Massachusetts delegation in New York City while the Stamp Act Congress was in session (see Journal below, chap. 4).[20]

Although Governor Wright, one of Georgia's wealthiest men, shared the general opinion of the colonists that the stamp tax was ill-advised he was neverthless determined to uphold the authority of Parliament.[21] His refusal to call a special session prevented Georgia from acting on the invitation and sending delegates to New York. The members of the Commons House might have acted on their own initiative without the governor's consent, as did the New Jersey Assemblymen (see section on New Jersey below), but they were unwilling to do so without Wright's calling them into session. They considered it illegal for them to meet without his approbation, and consequently Georgia was not represented at the Congress.

Maryland

The Massachusetts letter was delivered to Speaker Robert Lloyd of the Maryland Assembly while that body was still in recess. The minutes of the Assembly state that delivery was made by the Deputy Postmaster of the city of Annapolis. This is an interesting detail because it indicates that the invitation was carried by post riders in the colonial postal system.

Because an epidemic of small pox had broken out in Annapolis in February of 1765, the proprietary Governor Horatio Sharpe prorogued the Assembly until October. The members were fully in accord with his action because it was believed that assemblages would spread the disease. After two months had passed following receipt of the invitation, the disease abated, but Sharpe continued to keep the Assembly in recess, and no action could be taken on the invitation. It appeared that Maryland would not be represented at the Congress.

A petition was drawn up and signed by all of the practicing lawyers in the Provincial Court, and by a number of other gentlemen, urging Governor Sharpe to convene the Assembly in order to permit action on the invitation. As a result, he called the members into session on September 23, and the members of the Lower House heard the invitation read the following day. After a discussion they passed a resolution unanimously approving the appointment of three of their members to attend the New York meeting.[22]

Up to this time, the letter from the Massachusetts Speaker, dated almost four months earlier, had gone unanswered. It was apparent to the Speaker that there was not sufficient time for a reply to be delivered in Boston before the scheduled date of the meeting, either by the regular post riders or a special courier. It was therefore, decided to dispatch a messenger to New York with a reply addressed to the Massachusetts committee. Incidentally, the courier's fee for running this errand was £15 (see expense account of the Maryland delegation, Journal, chap. 4 below).

The Lower House then passed the following resolution on Wednesday, September 25:

> On Motion Resolved that Col. Tilghman [,] William Murdock Esqr. and Thomas Ringgold Esqr. be a Committee to meet the Committees from the Houses of Representatives or Burgesses of the several British Colonies on this Continent at the City of New York on the first Tuesday of October next for the purpose mentioned in the said Letter of the 8th of June.[23]

A committee was then appointed to draw up instructions for the three delegates (see Journal below, chap. 4).[24] It was also agreed that £500 be appropriated as a lump sum to cover the expenses of the delegates, and that permission be given them to exceed this amount if necessary.

The Upper House concurred in the measures taken by the Lower House to send delegates to the meeting, but disagreed that the delegates should be given what they termed "Unlimited credit." They insisted that the three deputies should keep an account of any disbursements in excess of £500 and submit a detailed record on their return to Annapolis before being reimbursed.[25]

Governor Sharpe subsequently signed the "Ordinance" presented to him for his assent, which signified that he consented to having Maryland represented at the New York meeting. However, he insisted upon signing it in confidence.[26]

After completing this business, the Lower House discussed the grievances the Province would suffer if the Stamp Act were allowed to become effective November 1. After lengthy debate the members agreed to prepare and publicize a set of resolutions as a sort of "position paper." These resolutions were drawn up by a committee of fourteen members, including Murdock, Tilghman, and Ringgold, the three delegates.[27] Among other things the resolutions stated that trial by jury "is the Grand Bulwark of Liberty the undoubted Birthright of every Englishman," and that only the Maryland Assembly had the sole right to tax the inhabitants of the Province. These resolutions left no doubt what position the Maryland delegates would take on any petitions drawn up at the Congress in New York.

The members of the Maryland delegation were all gentlemen farmers, landowners, and leaders in the anti-proprietary party in the Assembly. Edward Tilghman, 52-year-old member of a prominent Maryland family, owned extensive property in Wye, Queen Anne's County, where he was born. He had been active in political life in the county for a number of years, having held the position of High Sheriff. He was one of the leading members of the Assembly, and in 1770–71 served as Speaker of the Lower House. He was also an officer in the Maryland militia.[28]

Thomas Ringgold of Chestertown on the Eastern Shore, aged 50, was a merchant and a landowner, who served in the House for five different sessions. Inasmuch as he died in 1772, he did not play any part in the events immediately preceding the break with England and the war for independence.[29]

William Murdock, who owned 2,662 acres in Prince George's County, was 55 years of age. He was High Sheriff of the county in 1740, and in 1749 was elected to the Assembly, where he served until his death in 1769. Like his friend Ringgold, his early death prevented his participating in the critical events immediately prior to the Revolution.[30]

The October 10, 1765, edition of the *Pennsylvania Gazette* stated that the three delegates from Maryland belatedly passed through Philadelphia on Thursday, October 3, enroute to New York to attend the meeting scheduled to begin on October 1. They learned in Philadelphia that the Pennsylvania delegation had left for the Congress a week before (see section on *Pennsylvania* below)

New Hampshire

Henry Sherburne, Speaker of the New Hampshire Assembly, received the Massachusetts letter, and presented it to members on June 29. After some discussion a committee was appointed to consider the invitation, and when the committee reported, the members passed the following resolution:

> Resolved, That notwithstanding we are sensible such a Representation ought to be made & approve of the proposed method for obtaining thereof, yet the present situation of our government affairs will not permit us to appoint a Committee to attend such meeting but shall be ready to joyn in any Address to his Majesty & the Parliament we may be honored with the knowledge of [,] probable to answer the proposed End.
>
> A copy of this give[n] the Speaker in order to forward to the Speaker of the Honble House of Representatives of the Massachusetts Bay.[31]

Thus, because of unsettled conditions in the colony occasioned by boundary and currency problems, and strained relations between the Assembly and Governor Benning Wentworth, the majority of the members believed that it would be ill-advised to send deputies to the Congress.

After reflection, some of the members apparently felt that the decision had been too hasty, for less than a week later, at the final session held July 4, 1765, it was moved and passed that the Speaker withhold the resolution until the next session of the Assembly, scheduled for August 28. Evidently there was a minority opinion that delegates should be sent to New York despite the unsettled state of the colony. Unfortunately, Governor Wentworth recessed the Assembly until November 19, and there was no opportunity to reverse the earlier decision. Later, as the reader will see, the New Hampshire Assembly fully approved the proceedings of the Stamp Act Congress but did not participate because the invitation arrived at an inopportune time.

New Jersey

The New Jersey Assembly was meeting the last day of the session when Speaker Robert Ogden received the Massachusetts letter of invitation. Ogden promptly read the letter to the members, and his reply to the Massachusetts Speaker, dated Burlington, New Jersey, June 20, 1765, indicates what action was taken:

> Yours of the 8th Instant came opportunely to my Hands on the last Day of the Sitting of our Assembly. Having communicated it to them, they took it into deliberate Consideration, and desired me to inform, through you, the General Court of the Massachusetts [another name for the Assembly], That though they are not without a just Sensibility respecting the late Acts of Parliament affecting the Northern Colonies, yet apprehending, whatever Reasons may be thought proper to be urged against them may be better received after some Time elapse; our Assembly, on that Account & because the Trade of this Province is insignificant in Comparison of others, are unanimously against uniting on the present Occasion. They, however, cannot but wish such other Colonies, as think proper to be active, every Success they can loyally reasonably desire.[32]

Having politely declined the invitation, which proved to be an unwise decision, the Assembly adjourned. Following the adjournment strong sentiment grew in the colony against the impending stamp tax when the details of the Act were better understood. Extremely active opposition developed among New Jersey lawyers, who had agreed to cease doing business in court after November 1 rather than pay the required tax to execute legal documents on stamped paper.

News that the other colonies would be represented at the New York meeting also reached New Jersey. For instance, *The New York Gazette and Weekly Post Boy* (hereafter referred to as the *New York Post Boy*), reported in its September 26 edition that Rhode Island and Connecticut had appointed commissioners to attend. The action taken in Pennsylvania's Assembly on September 10 (see below) to send representatives to New York was reported in the *Pennsylvania Gazette,* which had many readers in northern New Jersey. These and other factors caused residents of New Jersey to feel that their Assembly had acted prematurely and unwisely in declining the Massachusetts invitation.

Speaker Ogden was under strong pressure from his constituents to reconsider the invitation. Consequently, on his own authority he reconvened the members of the Lower House in a meeting at the home of Robert Sproul in Perth Amboy, Middlesex County, on October 3, which was attended by twelve of the members.[33]

This was not a legal act on Ogden's part, since only the royal governor, William Franklin, had the authority to summon members of the Assembly into special session. Although Governor Franklin did not take issue with Ogden and the assemblymen, he considered Ogden's act improper and illegal. After the Assembly had previously adjourned its regular session in September, he had written on September 23 to the Secretary of State of the Southern Department, General Henry S. Conway, assuring him that the members "were determined to conduct themselves on the Occasion as became sober, dutiful, and loyal subjects . . . notwithstanding the Phrensy [over the stamp tax] which prevailed in other Colonies."[34] Having given Conway this assurance, he did not relish having the Assembly take action that would reverse the original decision.

At their extra-legal session the assembly selected three delegates to represent New Jersey at the Stamp Act Congress: Speaker Ogden, Joseph Borden, and Hendrick Fisher.

With the Congress scheduled to convene two days before, New Jersey's acceptance came at a very late date. Speaker Ogden hastily sent a courier to New York to advise Massachusetts that New Jersey would attend.[35] There was no time to prepare lengthy instructions for the deputies, who were briefly instructed to attend the Congress and then make a report of the discussions at the next meeting of the General Assembly (see Journal below, chap. 4).

Governor Franklin was irritated when he learned what had happened. It was within his authority to dissolve the Assembly as punishment for the rash, illegal act of some of the members. But, in a letter written on December 18, two months later, to the Lords of Trade, he excused himself by stating "but there was Reason to apprehend I should thereby have thrown the Province into the utmost Confusion. However, at the late Meeting of the General Assembly, I took an Opportunity of declaring my Disapprobation of their Conduct in pretty strong terms, lest there [word missing] should hereafter make it a Precedent for such kind of Meetings."[36]

Franklin appears to have tried to straddle the issue in order to pacify the authorities in England and also keep the New Jersey colonists from finding fault with him. In a letter dated October 1, 1765, quoted in its entirety in the October 3 edition of the *Pennsylvania Gazette,* replying to an accusation made by James Biddle that he blocked the appointment of delegates to the Congress, he maintained that he had had nothing to do with declining the Massachusetts letter of invitation. He said that he had never seen the letter, and that he had never been requested by any of the members of the Assembly to call them into special session to consider whether or not to attend. His letter allowed colonial readers to draw the inference that he did not oppose the Congress, but at the same time the records indicate that in his letters to England he was voicing his disapproval.

In view of the lateness of the acceptance, New Jersey was

fortunate that three members of the Assembly were willing to undertake the assignment on such short notice. Ogden doubtless felt an obligation to attend, since he was the Speaker and his name had appeared as the signatory to the refusal letter. Born in Elizabethtown, Essex County, New Jersey, on October 7, 1716, he celebrated his 49th birthday in New York while the Congress was in session. He had inherited extensive property in Essex County that had belonged to his father and grandfather, as well as half ownership of a tanyard and bark mill. He was first elected to the General Assembly in 1751, and was reelected the following year and became the Speaker, the position he was still holding in 1765. He also served as Clerk of the Essex County Court and a Surrogate in the Orphans' Court of East New Jersey. During the French and Indian War he was appointed Commissary and Barrack Master for the King's troops, a position he also held at the time of the Stamp Act Congress.[37]

Joseph Borden, aged 46, was a merchant and storekeeper who, along with his father, Joseph Borden, Sr., operated a stage and boat line for the transportation of mail, merchandise, and passengers between Philadelphia and New York.[38] A month before the Stamp Act Congress convened, the elder Borden died at the age of 79. His obituary in the October 10, 1765, edition of the *Pennsylvania Gazette* said that in 1735 he had founded the settlement in Burlington County, New Jersey, known as Bordentown. Joseph Borden, the delegate, took over the control of the business after his father's death, and later laid out the streets and residential sites in Bordentown. He was said to have been one of the wealthiest men in the Jersies. He also became a Colonel in the Burlington County militia and a Judge of the Court of Common Pleas. His daughter Mary was married to Thomas McKean, a delegate to the Congress from the Lower Counties. His son, another Joseph Borden, was a Captain during the Revolution, who died at Bordentown in 1788 at the age of

33. It was said that the younger Borden never fully recovered from the effects of a musket wound received in the Battle of Germantown. The male line of the family became extinct with his death.[39]

Hendrick Fisher was born in the Lower Palatinate in Germany, and although the date of his birth has not been corroborated, he was in his late sixties, perhaps seventy, when he attended the Congress. As a small boy he had come to America with his parents, who bought a farm on the south bank of the Raritan River near Bound Brook in Somerset County. He inherited the property after his father's death, and he became a successful farmer and mechanic. A man of unusual intelligence, he was elected to the General Assembly from Somerset County in 1740, and continued to be reelected for thirty consecutive years. He also served as a Deacon and Elder in the Dutch Reformed Church at New Brunswick, and assisted the pastor as a lay preacher. Some of his sermons were published and widely circulated. He served on numerous committees in the Assembly, and also held office in New Jersey's Provincial Congress.[40]

New York

The New York General Assembly was also in recess when the Massachusetts letter was received. It was a foregone conclusion that Lieutenant-Governor Cadwallader Colden would not call a special session to permit the members to act on the invitation. He had already prorogued the Assembly on March 13 until May 14, and he continued to keep it in recess, finally permitting it to convene almost a month after the Stamp Act Congress had adjourned.[41]

A Committee of Correspondence was originally authorized by the Assembly on April 4, 1761, to conduct correspondence with the London agent when the Assembly was in recess. The Assembly subsequently decided that its representatives from New York City, or the major part of them, would act *ex officio* as the Committee of Correspondence. Accordingly,

this Committee corresponded with Committees of Correspondence in the other colonies, and at its October 1764 session,
the Lower House authorized the Committee to correspond
on the subject of the Stamp Act or other acts of Parliament
(see Journal below, chap. 4).

When the Massachusetts letter was received, the Committee consisting of Robert R. Livingston, Philip Livingston,
John Cruger, William Bayard, and Leonard Lispenard considered itself empowered to represent the colony in the Congress. With the Assembly in recess, and the certainty that
Colden would not summon the members into a special session,
the Committee reasoned that this was the only legal way the
colony could be represented. These five New Yorkers, constituting the host delegation, probably assumed some of the
responsibility of making arrangements to accommodate the
visiting deputies. They also entertained the delegates at
dinners and suppers.

John Cruger, an amiable bachelor aged 55, was the incum-
bent Mayor of New York, having been elected in 1756 and
having served consecutive terms ever since. His late father
had previously served in the same office. Cruger had been
an alderman prior to his election as Mayor, and in 1759 he
was elected to his first term in the New York Assembly.
Both Cruger and Leonard Lispenard, a Huguenot descendant
aged 49, were successful merchants who represented society,
wealth, and power.⁴² Lispenard's wife inherited property in
New York City from her father, and as an importer,
Lispenard conducted a very prosperous business. He too
had served as an alderman and, like his friend Cruger, was
elected to the Assembly in 1758. He became one of the
principals in the New York Sons of Liberty, and was more
radical in his thinking than Cruger. When the Revolution
broke out Cruger, then aged 65, seems to have been unde-
cided whether or not to support the colonial cause, but he
was not a Tory.

William Bayard, aged 36, was also a prominent and prosperous merchant, who owned most of the land where present Hoboken is situated. When the break with England finally came, his conscience would not allow him to take an active role in the movement for American independence. He was a close friend of Major General Thomas Gage, Commander-in-chief of the British forces in America, and he had a son-in-law in the British army and a son in the employ of the British East India Company.[43] When war became inevitable he raised a Loyalist regiment in New York, and when hostilities ended he left New York and sailed to England, where he died in 1804. His property in New York, along with that of other Loyalists, was confiscated by the colonial authorities.[44]

Robert R. Livingston, aged 47, a lawyer, a large landowner, and a justice of the New York Supreme Court, was generally referred to as "Justice" or "Judge." His wife came from a wealthy family and inherited both money and property. At birth he was named Robert Robert Livingston to distinguish him from a number of male relatives also named Robert. His prominent son, also named Robert Robert Livingston, became Chancellor of New York and was usually indentified by his colleagues as "Chancellor," to avoid confusing him with his father. Judge Livingston died in 1775 as the opposition in the colonies to England's policies neared the breaking point.[45]

Philip Livingston, his cousin, aged 49 (erroneously referred to in many sources as a brother), graduated from Yale in 1737 and went into business in New York City. During the French and Indian War he was joint owner of several vessels engaged in privateering against the French, which proved to be a very profitable undertaking. He opened a store on the dock at the foot of Wall Street, where he sold hardware, general merchandise, and rum made in his own distillery in Brooklyn, where his country home was located. In 1754 he was elected an alderman in New York, and in 1759 became a member of the General Assembly. He was a delegate to both the First and Second Continental Congresses and a signer of the Declaration of Independence.[46] When John Adams met him in Philadelphia in 1774 at the First Continental Congress, Adams noted in his journal, probably with some exaggeration, that Philip Livingston was "a great rough, rappid [abrupt] Mortal. There is no holding any Conversation with him. He blusters away. Says if England should turn us adrift we should instantly go into Civil Warrs among ourselves to determine which colony should govern the rest."[47] Despite Adams's characterization, Philip Livingston gave generously of his own fortune to help the Continental Congress.

North Carolina

While the Massachusetts House of Representatives was debating the question of inviting the colonies to a meeting, North Carolina was still mourning the royal governor, Arthur Dobbs, who died March 28, 1765. At this critical period he was succeeded by William Tryon, the Lieutenant-Governor, an army officer 36 years of age. (Later that year Tryon received his commission as full governor of the colony.) Less than two months after Dobbs's death, the General Assembly convened at a regular session on May 3, 1765, at New Bern. There was outspoken opposition among the assemblymen to British tax policies, and the story goes that at the first session he attended, Lieutenant-Governor Tryon asked John Ashe, the Speaker of the House, what the people of North Carolina intended to do about the taxes levied by Parliament, especially the stamp tax. "Resist unto blood and death," is the reply that has been attributed to Ashe.[48]

Tyron, who was in ill health, must have become nervous about the radical trend developing in the Lower House, which seemed to foreshadow trouble at the very outset of his administration. He was not in favor of the Stamp Act and felt that it would fail, but as a soldier he had been trained to obey the orders of his superiors. The House recessed on Saturday, May 18, expecting to resume its unfinished business when it reconvened at 10:00 A.M. on Monday. Without advance notice, Tryon issued a proclamation dissolving the General Assembly until November 27.[49] Since the Massachusetts letter was not written until June 8, Tryon's action had nothing to do with blocking the invitation to attend the meeting in New York City, as some historians have inferred. When the Massachusetts letter was being written, a month had elapsed since Tryon issued his proclamation and the North Carolina Assembly was still in recess. The records do not clearly state that Speaker Ashe ever received the invitation, but if he did no action was taken. The members were unable to meet legally until Tryon called them into session, which he failed to do.

Thus North Carolina was not represented at the Congress, but by no means did the colonists quietly accept the stamp tax. There were public demonstrations at Cross Creek, Edenton, New Bern, Wilmington, and other cities, and violent opposition on Lower Cape Fear where Tryon lived. There were located the chief ports where the vessels landed bringing paper from England.[50]

Pennsylvania

Speaker Joseph Fox of the Pennsylvania Assembly received the Massachusetts letter about three weeks after the Assembly adjourned on May 18, 1765. He felt it necessary to reply to the letter before the new Assembly convened on September 9, and he invited a number of members who lived in or near Philadelphia to consult with him. They approved the proposal in principle, and Fox accordingly, on June 27, acknowledged the Massachusetts letter, stating that Pennsylvania's initial reactions were favorable. He added that the proposal would be brought before the Assembly in September for official action.[51]

This information was enthusiastically received in Boston, because Pennsylvania with its 300,000 people was an important colony, second in population to Virginia, and its main center, Philadelphia, was then the largest city in the colonies.

On June 24, three days before Fox acknowledged the Massachusetts letter, Thomas Wharton of Philadelphia wrote to Benjamin Franklin, who was then in London, telling him he had seen the letter inviting Pennsylvania to attend the Congress in New York. He also told Franklin that Speaker Fox had met informally with some of the local members of the Assembly to sound them out. Franklin received the news in England of the coming Stamp Act Congress before most of the members of the Pennsylvania Assembly knew about it.[52]

The Assembly met in Philadelphia on September 9, as scheduled, and on September 10 there was heated debate on the question whether or not to accept the Massachusetts invitation. At this time the existing proprietary government was opposed by an articulate faction that favored a royal government. The divergent political views held by the members strongly influenced their vote, and it was finally decided by a close vote of 15 to 14 that a committee of three or more deputies should be appointed "to attend the general Congress of Committees from the several assemblies on this continent. . . . ."

The committee selected for the important mission consisted of Speaker Joseph Fox, John Dickinson, John Morton, and George Bryan.[53] Another committee was appointed to prepare instructions for the delegation, and these were completed and approved on September 11 (see Journal below, chap. 4). The views of the conservatives are reflected in the caution given the delegates to make certain that any addresses originating in the Congress should be drawn up in decent and respectful terms to avoid offending King or Parliament.[54] The House also authorized the sum of £99, 8 shillings to cover the expenses of the delegates during their sojourn in New York City.

When this business was completed the Assembly prepared a series of resolves, approved September 21, which had been drafted by John Dickinson. They dealt with the Stamp Act, and other tax measures, and stated that taxing the inhabitants of Pennsylvania by persons other than their own representatives in the Assembly was unconstitutional and "subversive of their most valuable rights." Reference was also made to the Vice-Admiralty Courts, which were destructive of the precious right of trial by jury guaranteed all Englishmen.[55] It was ordered that the resolutions be published in both German and English newspapers in Philadelphia.[56]

Exactly a year before, September 22, 1764, Benjamin Franklin, then Speaker of the House, had written the Pennsylvania agent in London on behalf of the Assembly, stating that under the Pennsylvania royal charter the colonists could be taxed only by their duly elected representatives. Franklin suggested modification of the Act of 1764 and requested that Parliament lay aside any plans to impose a stamp tax on the colonies.[57] Parliament ignored his request, and the members of the Assembly had no reason to think that their latest resolutions would fare any better. It seems inconsistent that the Assembly would pass resolutions critical of England's tax policies in such provocative language and yet be sharply divided on the question of attending the Congress in New York.

Joseph Fox did not attend the meeting in New York, probably because he believed that his duties as Speaker were more important and that he should remain in Philadelphia. He knew that the Province would be well represented in the Congress by the other three delegates. John Dickinson, a patriot 33 years of age, was destined to become a distinguished statesman. He was practicing law in Philadelphia when he was elected to the Assembly in 1764, and in later years, as a resident of both Delaware and Pennsylvania, he was active in the political life of both colonies. He became known as the

"Penman of the Revolution," primarily because of his famous *Letters from a Farmer in Pennsylvania.* He was a delegate to both the First and Second Continental Congresses, and although he opposed English tax policies, he was a conservative who held out for reconciliation until the last moment. He was also a leading member of the Constitutional Convention in 1787. When John Adams met him for the first time in 1774, Adams wrote "He is a Shadow-tall, but slender as a Reed—pale as a [quill] pen. One would think at first Sight he could not live a Month. Yet upon a more attentive Inspection he looks as if the Springs of Life were strong enough to last many Years."[58]

John Morton, a self-made man aged 41, was a farmer descended from early Swedish settlers, who supplemented his income by surveying. He had also developed some knowledge of the law as a county Sheriff. He was elected to the Assembly in 1756 and served a number of terms. Shortly after his return from the Stamp Act Congress he became a Justice of the Pennsylvania Supreme Court. He served as Speaker of the Assembly and was a member of the two Continental Congresses and a signer of the Declaration of Independence.[59]

George Bryan, aged about 34, born in Dublin, Ireland, was engaged in business in Philadelphia at the time he was elected to the Assembly. Like his two associates, he remained active in politics, and in 1780 was elected a Justice of the Pennsylvania Supreme Court.[60]

The Pennsylvania delegates, according to the September 26 edition of the *Pennsylvania Gazette,* set out that day for New York City. They arrived on September 30, one day ahead of the scheduled meeting date. Upon their arrival they learned that the other delegates, including those from South Carolina, who had arrived two weeks before (see South Carolina below), were patiently awaiting word from Maryland and New Jersey advising whether they would be represented.

Rhode Island

With a population of less than 50,000 (in contrast to approximately 250,000 in neighboring Massachusetts), Rhode Island contained a smaller land area than any of the other mainland colonies. Despite this smallness, dissenters in Rhode Island protested just as loudly against the British tax program as those in the larger colonies. The importance of molasses to the thirty rum distillers in the colony caused the Assembly to register strong objections to the Lords Commissioners of Trade and Plantations on January 24, 1764, prior to the passage of the Sugar Act of 1764.[61] Later, on November 29, 1764, the Assembly formally protested to the King about the tax on molasses and the impending stamp tax.[62]

In July of 1764, the Assembly appointed three of its members as a Committee of Correspondence to confer and communicate with Committees from the other colonies in an attempt to obtain repeal of the Sugar Act of 1764 and prevent passage of the Stamp Act.[63] With this background, there was little doubt that Rhode Island's reaction to the Massachusetts invitation would be favorable. When the General Assembly convened at East Greenwich on September 9, 1765, the second Monday of the month, the Speaker of the Lower House read the Massachusetts letter and the members promptly voted in favor of attending. It was decided to appoint commissioners to represent the colony, but before they were named, another committee was appointed to prepare instructions for the committee "*to be* appointed."[64]

The committee prepared a letter of instructions authorizing the commissioners to join the committees from the other colonies to prepare representations to King and Parliament, as proposed in the Massachusetts letter. The letter gave the commissioners authority "to sign the same in behalf of this colony; and also to join with the other commissioners in taking the proper measures for laying the said representation and address before his Majesty and the Par-

liament, at the first opening of the session."[65] The latter
phrase had reference to the session of Parliament scheduled
to open in December of 1765.

The instructions phrased by the committee were somewhat
different from those incorporated in a letter signed by
Governor Samuel Ward which the Rhode Island delegates
carried with them to the Congress (see Journal below, chap.
4). The former instructions were much stronger, and although expressing affection and loyalty to the King and
"the highest sense of their subordination to that august assembly, the British Parliament," the members asserted certain
rights and privileges that belonged to the colonies. The levying of stamp duties (and extending the jurisdiction of the
Vice-Admiralty Courts), the instructions stated, is "oppressive and injurious and deprives us of some of our most
essential rights and liberties."

It may have been these instructions, which were reported
to Thomas Whately in the Treasury Office in London, that
he referred to as treasonable in a letter to Lord Grenville on
October 17, 1765:

> . . . the Assembly of Deputies from the several provinces,
> in order to apply jointly for the Repeal of the Act, is soon
> to be held at New York. The instructions given by one
> of the Colonies to their Deputies on this occasion are come
> over, and as I hear from one who has seen them, are
> directly treasonable. I suppose no representation from
> such a convention of States will be received by Parliament,
> at least it is worth considering whether it should or not.[66]

After approving the letter of instructions, the members of
both Houses of the Rhode Island Assembly resolved themselves into a grand committee, and chose Metcalf Bowler
and Henry Ward to represent the colony at the Congress.
An appropriation of £100 was voted to cover their expenses.

With this business concluded, the Assembly then set about
preparing a set of resolutions denying Parliament's right

to levy stamp duties and other internal taxes on the residents of Rhode Island. The resolutions stated that only the General Assembly had the right to levy taxes on the inhabitants of the colony, and that the colonists *are not bound to yield Obedience to any Law or Ordinance* imposing internal taxes on them other than tax laws passed by the General Assembly.[57] This meant, in effect, that the Assembly was encouraging the colonists to disobey the Stamp Act; no other colony, not even Virginia, had gone that far in its protests or petitions.

Both delegates to the Congress were prominent in Rhode Island politics and were held in high regard in the colony. Metcalf Bowler, aged 39, was born in London, and as a young man he accompanied his father to America, ultimately settling at Newport. He was a successful farmer and merchant, and owner of several vessels used in foreign trade. He became an Associate Justice of the Superior Court of Rhode Island, and Speaker of the Lower House of the Assembly. In 1776 he held the position of Chief Justice of the Rhode Island Supreme Court, but with the approach of the Revolution he sympathized with his homeland. Although he gave every evidence of supporting the American cause, it is now known that he was a traitor and rendered aid to the English by surreptitiously supplying General Sir Henry Clinton with useful military intelligence.[58]

Henry Ward, aged 33, came from one of Rhode Island's most active political families. His father, Richard Ward, was Secretary of the colony for eleven years, and served three terms as Governor. Henry's brother Thomas was also Secretary of the colony, and his older brother, Samuel, was Governor at the time of the Stamp Act Congress. Henry was elected Secretary in 1760–61, a position he held for thirty-seven years. He was a member of several important committees of the Assembly, and helped to revise the laws of Rhode Island for publication in a single volume He and his brother Governor Samuel Ward were both strong supporters of colonial rights, and later worked untiringly for independence.[69]

South Carolina

The Commons House of the General Assembly of South Carolina, a colony of 150,000 people, then larger than the Province of New York, took the Massachusetts circular letter under consideration at its session on Friday, July 19. Speaker Rawlins Lowndes did not approve of resisting the laws of the mother country, and lengthy debate ensued on the propriety and legality of joining the other colonies in a protest meeting. It was during a lively discussion of the pros and cons that a member of the Assembly is reported to have addressed the members humorously as follows:

> If you agree to the proposition of composing a Congress of deputies from different British colonies, what sort of a dish will you make? New-England will throw in fish and onions, the middle colonies flax-seed and flour, Maryland and Virginia will add tobacco. North-Carolina pitch, tar and turpentine. South-Carolina rice and indigo, and Georgia will sprinkle the whole composition with sawdust. Such an absurd jumble will you make if you attempt to form an union among such discordant materials as the thirteen British provinces.[70]

One of the witty country members of the Assembly is supposed to have replied, "He would not choose the gentlemen who made the objection for his cook, but nevertheless he would venture to assert that if the colonies proceeded judiciously in the appointment of deputies to a continental Congress, they would prepare a dish fit to be presented to any crowned head in Europe."[71]

Speaker Lowndes did not agree and, in consequence of his unwillingness to resist the Stamp Act, he was unseated at the next issue of the Assembly. (Later he redeemed himself by becoming a patriot, and he was elected Speaker of the House in 1772, and President [Governor] of the colony in 1778.)

When the debate was over, the Massachusetts letter was referred to a special committee of ten members appointed by the Speaker. The following Friday, July 26, the committee reported that after full consideration the proposal seemed to them to be both prudent and necessary. The committee recommended that commissioners be appointed to attend the New York meeting. The committee report was read a second time, and the House voted affirmatively to approve the report.

On Friday, August 2, a resolution was passed that a sum not to exceed £600 be authorized to cover the expenses of the delegation, and the following three members were named to represent the colony: Christopher Gadsden, Thomas Lynch, and John Rutledge.[72] These same three delegates were later to represent South Carolina in both the First and Second Continental Congresses (although Lynch's health failed during the Second Congress, and he was succeeded by his son, Thomas, Jr., who was a signer of the Declaration of Independence).

Christopher Gadsden, aged 41, was an aristocrat, a wealthy Charleston merchant who owned a large plantation, stores, and a wharf. Despite his wealth, he was a leader of the South Carolina radicals, was a dominant figure in the Sons of Liberty, and was elected a Brigadier-General in the Continental Army during the Revolution.[73]

John Rutledge, then aged 26, the youngest member of the Stamp Act Congress, had studied law in England and was a persuasive orator. The previous year he was appointed Attorney General of South Carolina, the youngest man ever to hold the position. "He fronts a fact more quickly than anyone I ever knew," a client once said of him. During the Revolution he was Commander-in-chief of the colony's military forces, and later became Governor.[74] George Washington later appointed him to the Supreme Court of the U.S.

Thomas Lynch, Sr., aged about 38 and one of South Carolina's landed gentry, had inherited large estates on the North and South Santee Rivers. Like his friend Gadsden, he fearlessly advocated colonial resistance to the encroachment of Parliament on the rights of the colonists.[75]

These three South Carolina delegates who traveled the greatest distance to attend the Congress were the first to arrive in New York City, which may be a reflection of their eagerness to join in a concerted colonial protest. An article in the September 26 edition of the *Georgia Gazette* reported that the three South Carolina delegates left Charleston September 4 on the brigantine *Carolina Packet*. The October 10 issue of the same publication reported that they arrived in New York on September 16, twelve days later.[76] This was two weeks ahead of the scheduled date of the meeting. One wonders how these southerners occupied their time while awaiting the arrival of the other delegates. Unfortunately, the contemporary documents do not provide any enlightenment.

The Three Lower Counties (Delaware)

At the time of the meeting of the Stamp Act Congress the present state of Delaware was known as "the Three Lower Counties," having been an appendage to Pennsylvania, which William Penn acquired from the Duke of York. In 1704, with Penn's permission the Lower Counties formed their own House of Assembly, although continuing to share Pennsylvania's governor. The Assembly was a unicameral body of 18 delegates, six elected annually from each county every October. (Not until "the Delaware State" was created in 1776 was there a bicameral legislative body.)

When the Massachusetts letter was received the Assembly had adjourned. No business could officially be transacted until the forthcoming session in October 1765, which would be held following the election of new assemblymen on October 1. The new session was scheduled to convene too late for the body to act on the Massachusetts letter and to decide whether or not to send representatives to the Congress.

Recognizing that they lacked authority to act officially, but aware of the significance of the meeting and its importance to the colonies, the members of the previous Assembly decided to take action on the letter. The legal procedure required their requesting Governor John Penn to call them into a special session, but they decided to proceed without this formality. It was later recorded in the minutes of the May 1766 session of the House that the members held a meeting in September to consider the Massachusetts invitation, and they decided to participate by sending the three delegates named below to New York. There is no other record of this extralegal meeting, but the phraseology of the three letters signed by the assemblymen indicates that they knew they were following an unorthodox procedure (see Journal below chap. 4, for transcripts of the three letters).

The first letter, dated September 13, 1765, and signed by five members of the former Assembly from Kent County, appointed "Jacob Kollock Esqr, Caesar Rodney Esqr and Thomas McKean Esqr members of said Assembly to be a Committee, to meet with the other Committees . . . at the City of New York, on the first Tuesday in October next. . . ." The letter had stated at the beginning that the signers were "sensible of the impropriety of assuming the Functions of Assembly Men, during the Recess of Our House." but felt that under the circumstances their action was justifiable.

On September 17 five members of the former Assembly from Sussex County appointed the same three men to represent the Three Lower Counties at the New York meeting. They too stated that they realized the impropriety of the action they were taking, but they were "Zealous to Concur in any measures which may be productive of Advantage to this Government, and the other British Colonies on the Continent of America in general. . . ."

On September 21 five members of the former Assembly from New Castle County appointed the same three delegates to represent the Lower Counties at the New York meeting. Their letter stated that taking into consideration the misfortune "we at present labour Under in not haveing it in our Power to Convene as a House, and in a Regular manner to appoint a Committee. Yet, zealous for the happiness of Our Constituents, think it Our duty in this Way to serve them as much as in Us lies (Assured of the Hearty Approbation of any future House of Assembly of this Government), etc." This letter was more forceful than the other two in its assertion that the colonies should be excluded from Parliamentary taxation, and should not be denied trial by juries of their peers.

(When the new Assembly met at New Castle the following October, the newly elected members approved the action taken by their predecessors during the recess and retroactively allowed the delegates £140 for their expenses during their trip to New York.)[77] The reader has already seen that the Pennsylvania Assembly in its session on September 10 had approved attending the Congress, and perhaps the Lower Counties felt justified by Pennsylvania's action in doing what they did. There is no record that Governor John Penn ever offered any objections to the procedure that was followed.

The delegate from New Castle County, Thomas McKean, aged 31, was an able and highly successful lawyer, having practiced in Pennsylvania and the Lower Counties for a number of years. In 1758 he was admitted to practice before the Supreme Court of Pennsylvania, a very distinct honor in the colonies. In 1762 he had been elected a member of the Assembly of the Lower Counties, and he was reelected for seventeen consecutive terms. Three months prior to the convening of the Stamp Act Congress McKean became Justice of the Peace and Justice of the Court of Common Pleas and Quarter Session, and of the Orphan's Court for

New Castle County. No delegate to the Stamp Act Congress had a longer or more distinguished career in colonial government than McKean. He represented the Lower Counties in the First and Second Continental Congresses, was a signer of the Declaration of Independence, and also served as President of the Congress. In July of 1777, at which time he was the Speaker of the Delaware Assembly, he was commissioned Chief Justice of Pennsylvania. Six weeks later he became Acting President (Governor) of Delaware, holding both positions at the same time. In 1799 he was elected Governor of Pennsylvania and served in office for nine years.[78]

Caesar Rodney, a planter, had been in local politics for about ten years at the time of the Stamp Act Congress, serving as High Sheriff in Kent County, followed by other county political positions including that of trustee of the Loan Office. Like Robert Ogden of New Jersey, he too had a birthday in New York, celebrating his 37th year on October 7. In the years that lay ahead, despite poor health due to a cancer that infected his face and nose, he had an illustrious career as jurist, Speaker of the Assembly, delegate to the two Continental Congresses, signer of the Declaration of Independence, Revolutionary officer, and President of Delaware.[79]

The third delegate, Jacob Kollock, a landowner 73 years of age, was senior in years to any of the other delegates selected to attend the Congress. He was a prominent citizen of Lewes, holding office as a co-trustee of the Loan Office, Justice of the Peace, and Judge of the Common Pleas Court of Sussex County. Following Braddock's defeat, when there was fear of a French invasion, Kollock helped raise a regiment of eight companies of militiamen in the county, and was commissioned a colonel as their commanding officer. He was an assemblyman for forty consecutive years, and at the time of the Stamp Act Congress he had served as Speaker since 1759.[80]

Kollock's name is not found in the Journal of the Stamp

Caesar Rodney (1728–1805) celebrated his 37th birthday on October 7, the day the Congress convened in New York. He later became President (Governor) of Delaware, was a member of the First and Second Continental Congresses, and was a signer of the Declaration of Independence. H. B. Hall etched this likeness in 1871 from an unidentified portrait, executed in profile perhaps to hide the cancer on his face and nose. COURTESY NEW YORK PUBLIC LIBRARY, EMMET COLLECTION NO. 213, MANUSCRIPT AND ARCHIVES DIVISION, ASTOR, LENOX AND TILDEN FOUNDATIONS.

Act Congress as a delegate when the Congress officially convened, which has led historians to conclude that he did not go to New York. However, an article in the October 3, 1765, edition of the *Pennsylvania Gazette* reads as follows:

> The Assembly of Maryland, we hear, have appointed Messieurs Tilghman, Ringold and Murdoch to assist at the General Congress in New York. Messieurs Kollock, Rodney and M'Keane are gone on the same Business from the Government of New-Castle, Kent and Sussex upon Delaware.

Also the October 10, 1765, edition of the *New York Post Boy* lists the following among the gentlemen who had arrived in New York to attend "the most important [Congress] that ever came under Consideration in America":

> Government of the Counties of New-Castle, Kent and Sussex on Delaware—Jacob Kollock, Caesar Rodney, and Thomas M'Kean, Esqrs.[81]

If Kollock accompanied his two associates to New York who arrived on September 30, he must have returned home before the opening of the Congress. He had every reason to believe that the meeting would convene on October 1, as announced in the Massachusetts invitation, but after arriving in New York he found it to be delayed a full week. Having served as Speaker in the Assembly of the Lower Counties for six consecutive sessions, he doubtless went to New York in the expectation of returning in time to be reelected Speaker of the new session.[82] Not only was the opening of the Congress delayed, but informal discussions with the delegates who had arrived on time may have indicated that the sessions were going to cover a longer period of time than he had expected. If this hypothesis is correct, he would have felt that his return to New Castle before the formal opening of the Congress was fully justified. In any event, on October 21 he was present at the new session of the Assembly of the

Lower Counties, where he was reelected Speaker for the seventh time.[63]

Virginia

Governor Francis Fauquier dissolved the Virginia House of Burgesses on June 1, 1765, because he was displeased over the resolutions introduced by Patrick Henry and passed by the House. The House was in recess when the Massachusetts letter was received by John Robinson, Speaker, and no action could be taken on the invitation until the members reconvened. Robinson was also treasurer of the colony, and was very favorable to the Crown. Through a series of prorogations Governor Fauquier deliberately prevented the House from meeting, and the recess was extended until November 6, 1766, long after the Stamp Act Congress had met and adjourned.[64] As a result of the governor's refusal to call the members into session, it was ironical that Virginia, the oldest and most populous colony, which had lighted the fuse of resistance with its Resolves, was not represented at the Stamp Act Congress. Of course, there could be no misunderstanding of where the colony stood on the question of the Stamp Act even though it was unable to send delegates to New York.

NOTES TO CHAPTER 2

1. This letter may be found in *Connecticut Historical Collections,* 18: 284–85.
2. *Ibid.,* pp. 290–92.
3. *Journal of the First Congress of the American Colonies . . . .* ed. Lewis Cruger (New York, 1845), pp. iii, vi. On August 24, 1764, Ogden of New Jersey wrote a letter in which he indicated that the colonies should unite in opposing English taxes. *NJCD,* 9: 449–51.
4. William Gordon, *The History of the Rise, Progress and Establishment of the Independence of the United States* (London, 1788), 2: 172. Mercy Warren is supposed to have

said that the proposal for the Congress originated in her home (George Bancroft, *History Of The United States*, 12th ed. [Boston, 1858], 5: 279n.) Ezra Stiles, writing in 1767, also states that James Otis first proposed the Congress. *Crisis*, p. 186; cf. John Gorham Palfrey, *A Compendious History Of New England* (Boston, 1873), p. 388.

5. *Mass. Journals*, 42: 108–9.

6. I am grateful to C. B. Fergusson, Provincial Archivist of Nova Scotia, who examined the Journal of the House for 1765–66, and could find no reference to the receipt of an invitation from Massachusetts.

7. *Mass. Journals*, 42: 108–9. When the delegates returned from New York and made an accounting, Partridge had spent £115 and Ruggles £102, 6s, 8p, and each remitted to the Treasurer the difference between these amounts and £150. Otis was allowed the full £150 for "services ordinary and extraordinary," and for losses sustained in his business during his absence. *Ibid.*, p. 277.

8. *Appletons' Cyc.*, 4: 605–6. See also William Tudor, *The Life of James Otis of Massachusetts* (Boston, 1823); cf. Ellen Elizabeth Brennan, "James Otis: Recreant and Patriot," *New England Quarterly* 12 (1939): 691–725; John J. Waters, Jr., *The Otis Family in Provincial and Revolutionary Massachusetts* (Chapel Hill, N.C., 1968).

9. *Appletons' Cyc.*, 4: 667.

10. *Ibid.*, 5: 344–45; Henry Stoddard Ruggles, *General Timothy Ruggles* (privately printed, n.p., 1897). Governor Francis Bernard of Massachusetts claimed that he influenced the selection of Partridge and Ruggles, whom he termed "prudent and discreet men" because they were not likely to be swayed by Otis, nor to consent to any action in the Congress inimical to England's best interests (*Crisis*, p. 104). Ruggles learned after accepting the appointment that the House had instructed the delegates to insist that the colonies had the right of self-taxation. "He determined to excuse himself, but being urged by friends he changed his mind" (Thomas Hutchinson, *The History of the Colony and Province of Massachusetts-Bay*, ed. Lawrence Shaw Mayo [Cambridge, Mass., 1936], p. 85).

11. *Knollenberg*, pp. 178–79.

12. *Conn. Hist. Colls.*, 18: 355–56.

13. *Conn. Recs.*, 12: 410.

14. *Ibid.*, pp. 410–11.

15. "Ingersoll Papers," New Haven Colony Historical Society, *Papers*, 9: 289.
16. *Appletons' Cyc.*, 2: 285; *Knollenberg*, p. 172. Cf. George C. Groce, Jr., "Eliphalet Dyer: Connecticut Revolutionist," pp. 290–304 of *The Era of the American Revolution*, ed. Richard B. Morris (Gloucester, Mass., 1971).
17. *Adams Diary*, 2: 173.
18. *Dict. Amer. Biog.*, 5: 131–34; George C. Groce, Jr., *William Samuel Johnson, a Maker of the Constitution* (New York, 1937), pp. 25, 94–95.
19. Franklin Bowditch Dexter, *Biographical Sketches of the Graduates of Yale College* (New York, 1885), p. 463; *History and Genealogy of the Families of Old Fairfield*, ed. Donald Lines Jacobus (Fairfield, Conn., 1932).
20. The letter also appears in *The Colonial Records of the State of Georgia*, compiled by Allen D. Candler (Atlanta Ga., 1907), 14: 273–74. The *Georgia Gazette*, October 31, 1765, reported on the "rump session" of the Assembly that Wylly held in Savannah.
21. W. W. Abbot, *The Royal Governors Of Georgia, 1754–1775*, (Chapel Hill, N.C., 1959), pp. 107–8.
22. *Proceedings and Acts of the General Assembly of Maryland, 1764–1765*, ed. J. Hall Pleasants (Baltimore, Md., 1942); *Maryland Archives*, 59: 19–20; also *ibid.*, 14: 201, 230.
23. *Maryland Archives*, 59: 21. (Daniel Dulany was not a delegate to the Congress from Maryland as stated in error by Samuel Eliot Morison, *The Oxford History of the American People* [New York, 1965], p. 187, nor was Charles Thomson the Secretary, as stated by William Thompson Read, *Life and Correspondence of George Read* (Philadelphia, 1870), p. 497.
24. *Maryland Archives*, 59: 22–23 for the same instructions.
25. *Maryland Archives*, 59: 10.
26. *Maryland Archives*, 59: 34. See also Paul H. Giddens, "Maryland and the Stamp Act Controversy, *"Maryland Historical Magazine* 27 (1932): 79–98.
27. *Maryland Archives*, 59: 31–32; see also *Prologue*, pp. 52–53, for a transcript. It is amazing how quickly news from one colony spread to the others. The Maryland resolutions were published in the October 21, 1765, issues of the *Boston Post Boy* and the *Boston Evening Post*.
28. *Dict. Amer. Biog.*, 9: 542; *Nat'l. Cyc.*, 13: 421 gives his birth as ca. 1720, but the exact date, July 3, 1713, is given by

Christopher Johnston, "Tilghman Family, "*Maryland Historical Magazine* 1 (1906) : 283–84.

29. George A. Hanson, *Old Kent* (Baltimore, Md., 1878), p. 66.
30. *Nat'l Cyc.*, 13: 45; cf. William B. Marye, "The Murdock Family of Maryland and Virginia," *Maryland Historical Magazine* 25 (1930) : 269.
31. *N.H. Recs.*, 7: 81. Jere R. Daniell, *Experiment in Republicanism* (Cambridge, Mass., 1970), p. 71, states that members of the New Hampshire Assembly desired a reversal of the decision that gave to the New York colony lands they owned west of the Connecticut. Thus, they did not want to antagonize the ministry by participating in the Congress. I was not fully satisfied with this explanation and wrote Professor Daniell asking if he still held the opinion. He kindly replied on June 21, 1974, expanding on his published observations. "Government affairs were indeed in an unsettled state that summer," he wrote. "The boundary decision had been announced, rumors circulated that Benning Wentworth was on the way out as governor, the newly arrived Peter Livius seemed bent on stirring up trouble, and commercial depression threatened the personal fortunes of many Assembly members; the impending Stamp Act only added to a general sense of malaise. Since political leaders in New Hampshire were generally satisfied with the government, they had no desire to disrupt things further. On the other hand, condemning the proposed congress—especially given economic circumstances—would have seemed like condemning motherhood. The Assembly therefore took the obvious middle road: they gave verbal support but refused to participate." Quoted by permission.
32. *NJCD*, 9 : 496.
33. *Ibid.*, 24: 682. Evidence that Ogden was under pressure is shown in a letter written him Sept. 13, 1765, by Richard Stockton, urging him to request Governor Franklin to call a special session to "reconsider the propriety of sending deputies to New York." *Proceedings*, N.J. Historical Society, 1st s. 2 (1846–47) : 149–50.
34. *NJCD*, 9 : 492–94, 524–25. Governor Franklin sent a copy of Ogden's letter declining the invitation to Secretary Conway, indicating that he knew more about what was going on than his letter published in the *Pennsylvania Gazette* would suggest.
35. This was reported in the *Boston Post Boy* on October 14, 1765, another example of good communications.

36. *NJCD*, 9: 525.
37. Edmund Drake Halsey, *Descendants of Robert Ogden 2nd, 1716–1787*, (Amenia, N.Y.: Walsh & Griffen, 1896); *Appletons' Cyc.*, 4: 561.
38. *Nat'l Cyc.*, 13: 428.
39. *South Jersey, a History, 1664–1923*, ed. Alfred M. Heston, (New York, 1924), 2: 655. I am grateful to Herbert Bernstein for this reference.
40. I am indebted to Henry H. Bisbee for supplying me with biographical notes on Fisher appearing in Theodore Frelinghuysen Chambers, *Early Germans of New Jersey* (Baltimore, Md., 1969), pp. 360–62; see also Rev. T. E. Davis. "Hendrick Fisher," *Proceedings*, N. J. Historical Society 3d s. 4 (1907): 129–46.
41. *Journal of the Legislative Council of New York* (Albany, N.Y., 1861), 2: 1562–64.
42. *Appletons' Cyc.*, 2: 22–23; 3: 735; *New York Genealogical and Biographical Review* (New York, 1875), 6: 74–80; 24 (1893): 109. See also Virginia Draper Harrington, *The New York Merchant on the Eve of the Revolution* (New York, 1935).
43. *Adams Diary*, 2: 106.
44. *Appletons' Cyc.*, 1: 199; *Nat'l. Cyc.*, 1: 498, says that he had two sons who served in the British army.
45. *Dict. Amer. Biog.*, 6: 319–20. Cf. George Dangerfield, *Chancellor Robert R. Livingston of New York, 1746–1813* (New York, 1960). "The Chancellor," who had a more illustrious career than his father, administered the presidential oath to George Washington, and served as Minister to France from 1801–1804.
46. *Appletons' Cyc.*, 3: 742. *Gipson, 1961*, 10: 329, says incorrectly that Robert R. and Philip Livingston were brothers. For additional data about Philip Livingston, see B. J. Lossing, *Biographical Sketches of the Signers of the Declaration . . .* (Glendale, N.Y., 1970), pp. 67–68; also Robert Warren Anthony, *Philip Livingston, a Tribute* (Albany, N.Y., 1924).
47. *Adams Diary*, 2: 107.
48. Samuel A'Courte Ashe, *History of North Carolina* (Greensboro, N.C., 1925), p. 314.
49. *The Colonial Records of North Carolina*, ed. William Saunders (Raleigh, N.C., 1890), 7: 88.
50. C. Robert Haywood, "The Mind of the North Carolina Opponents of the Stamp Act," *The North Carolina Historical*

Review 29 (1952) : 317–43. Cf. Hugh Tallmadge Lefler and Albert Ray Newcome, *North Carolina* (Chapel Hill, N.C., 1954).

51. *Pennsylvania Archives*, 8th s., ed. Charles F. Hoban (Harrisburg, Pa., 1935), 7: 5765.
52. *Letters and Papers of Benjamin Franklin and Richard Jackson, 1753–1785*, ed. Carl Van Doren, American Philosophical Society (Philadelphia, 1947), pp. 191–92.
53. *Pennsylvania Archives*, pp. 5768–69. Information that the vote was 15 to 14 is mentioned by John Hughes in a letter to Benjamin Franklin, September 10, 1765, *The Register of Penna.*, ed. Samuel Hazard, 2, no. 16 (Philadelphia, Nov. 1, 1828) : 249.
54. The same instructions to the delegates are found in *Pennsylvania Archives*, p. 5769.
55. *Ibid.*, pp. 5779–80. A transcript of these resolutions appears in *Prologue*, pp. 51–52.
56. The first public printing of the resolutions was in the *Pennsylvania Gazette*, September 26, 1765. The news spread quickly, and both the *Boston Post Boy* and the *Boston Evening Post* published the same resolves in their October 7 editions.
57. *Papers of Benjamin Franklin*, 12: 183–87.
58. *Adams Diary*, 2: 117. For biographical data see *Historical and Biographical Encyclopedia of Delaware*, ed. J. M. McCarter and B. F. Jackson (Wilmington, Del., 1882), p. 243; Charles J. Stillé, *The Life and Times of John Dickinson, 1732–1808*, Historical Society Of Penna. (Philadelphia, 1891) ; David Louis Jacobson, *John Dickinson and the Revolution in Pennsylvania, 1764–1776*, University of California Publications in History, 78 (1965).
59. *Nat'l. Cyc.*, 10: 127. See also John Morton Scrapbook in Harley Collection, B-82, Historical Society of Penna.
60. *Pennsylvania Magazine of History and Biography* 26 (1902) : 339–40. The George Bryan Papers, Historical Society of Penna., include only some receipts and a few business letters—nothing pertaining to Bryan's biography.
61. *R.I. Recs.*, 6: 378–83.
62. *Ibid.*, pp. 414–16.
63. *Ibid.*, p. 403.
64. *Ibid.*, p. 449. As early as August 27, residents of Little-Compton at a town meeting urged their representatives in the Assembly to vote to attend the Congress. *New York Post Boy*, Sept. 19, 1765.

65. *Ibid.*, pp. 450–51.
66. *Grenville Papers*, ed. William James Smith (London, 1953), 3: p. 100. Whately wrote the text of the Stamp Act.
67. *Ibid.*, pp. 451–52. See *Prologue*, pp. 50–51 for a transcript. These resolves were published in the *Boston Evening Post* on September 23, and by October 17 they had got as far south as the *Georgia Gazette*.
68. *Dict. Amer. Biog.*, 1: 512; *Lovejoy, 1958*, pp. 118, 121; Jane Clark, "Metcalf Bowler as a British Spy." *R.I. Hist. Colls.*, 23 (1930): 101–17.
69. *Lovejoy, 1958*, pp. 9, 113, 191.
70. David Ramsay, *The History of the Revolution of South Carolina* (Trenton, N.J., 1785), 1: 13–14. This excerpt is inaccurately quoted by *Pitkin*, 1: 178–79.
71. Ramsay indicates that it was Gadsden who influence! the Assembly to participate in the Congress. *The History . . . .*, 2: 457–59.
72. *Journal of the Commons House of the Assembly of South Carolina, Jan. 8, 1765 – August 9, 1765* (Columbia, S.C., 1949), pp. 141, 150, 158.
73. *Appletons' Cyc.*, 2: 567; Richard Frothingham, *The Rise of the Republic of the United States* (Boston, 1886), p. 182.
74. *Appletons' Cyc.*, 5: 357-58; Richard Barry, *Mr. Rutledge of South Carolina* (New York, 1942).
75. *Appletons' Cyc.*, 4: pp. 64–65. Cf. "Death Notices from the South Carolina and American General Gazette, etc." *S.C. Historical and Genealogical Magazine* 17 (1916): 123.
76. On September 30 the delegates from Pennsylvania and Rhode Island arrived and the representatives from Massachusetts and Connecticut were expected momentarily. *New York Mercury*, September 30, 1765. Gov. Colden wrote on September 23 that the South Carolina delegates had already been there a week. *NYCD*, 7: 760.
77. *Minutes Lower Counties*, pp. 40, 51.
78. *Historical and Biographical Encylopedia of Delaware*, p. 235. Roberdeau Buchanan, *Life of The Hon. Thomas McKean, L.L.D.* (Lancaster, Penna., 1890). See also G. S. Rowe, "The Legal Career of Thomas McKean, 1750–1775," *Delaware History* (April 1974), pp. 22–46, and note footnote references to other papers, and a doctoral dissertation written by the same author on McKean. I am indebted to Professor John M. Coleman for his kindness in permitting me to read in advance of publication the chapter in his biography of Thomas McKean

dealing with the Stamp Act Congress. While the present manuscript was being edited Professor Coleman's book was published, *Thomas McKean, Forgotten Leader of the Revolution* (Rockaway, N.J., 1975). Chapter 6 in the volume is entirely devoted to McKean's role at the time of the Stamp Act Congress.

79. *Historical and Biographical Encylopedia of Delaware*, p. 528. See also biographical sketch of Rodney in *Letters to and from Caesar Rodney, 1756–1784*, ed. George H. Ryden, Historical Society of Delaware (Wilmington, 1953).

80. Daniel F. Wolcott, "Ryves Holt, of Lewes, Delaware, 1696–1763," *Delaware History* 8 (1958): 16; 26–27; also Edwin Jaquette Sellers, *Genealogy of the Kollock Family of Sussex County, Del., 1657–1897* (Philadelphia, 1897). Professor Harold Hancock has brought to my attention Kollock's obituary in the *Pennsylvania Gazette*, March 26, 1772. He died February 7, 1772, aged 80, having served forty years in the Assembly.

81. The same article appears in the October 14 edition of the *New York Mercury* with Kollock's name included, also in the October 17 issue of the *Pennsylvania Gazette*. These notices appear to have been overlooked; Gipson, for example, in *The Coming of the Revolution*, p. 96 n31, says Kollock did not appear at the Congress. J. Thomas Scharf, *History of Delaware* (Philadelphia, 1888), 1: 84 says Kollock did not attend, and Henry C. Conrad, *History of the State of Delaware* (Wilmington, Del., 1908), 1: 90 makes the same assumption.

82. On Oct. 6 or 7 Caesar Rodney received a personal message in New York from his brother Thomas indicating that he, McKean, and Kollock had all been reelected to the Assembly at the election held Oct. 1. This adds further weight to the hypothesis that Kollock decided to return home to stand for reelection as Speaker. Letters sent by Thomas Rodney, Brown Manuscript Collection, Historical Society of Delaware, Box 6, Folder 2.

83. *Minutes Lower Counties*, October 21, 1765 session.

84. *Journals of the House of Burgesses*, ed. John Pendleton Kennedy (Richmond, Va., 1906–7), 1761–1765, p. 364; 1766–1769, pp. 5–9.

3

Discussions
in the Stamp Act Congress

According to Stokes, who carefully chronicled the events in
the history of New York City, the Stamp Act Congress was
held in the old City Hall. As of 1765, the city had a population of less than 20,000, living in some 3,200 houses, and
the City Hall was the seat not only of the municipal government, but it also contained offices, courts, jail, a library, and
a fire department.[1] The New York Assembly, which was in
recess, usually met in a chamber in the east wing on the
second floor. Since this room was vacant, it would have
been a logical place for the delegates to meet.

The following twenty-seven delegates assembled for the
first official session on Monday, October 7, a week later than
the scheduled date suggested in the Massachusetts letter. The
delay was due to the late arrival of the delegates from Maryland and New Jersey:

Connecticut	Eliphalet Dyer, David Rowland, William Samuel Johnson
Massachusetts	James Otis, Oliver Partridge, Timothy Ruggles
Maryland	William Murdock, Thomas Ringgold, Edward Tilghman

New Jersey	Joseph Borden, Hendrick Fisher, Robert Ogden
New York	William Bayard, John Cruger, Leonard Lispenard, Philip Livingston, Robert R. Livingston
Pennsylvania	George Bryan, John Dickinson, John Morton
Rhode Island	Metcalf Bowler, Henry Ward
South Carolina	Christopher Gadsden, Thomas Lynch, John Rutledge
Lower Counties	Thomas McKean, Caesar Rodney

To sum up the brief biographical data given in the previous chapter, the delegates were all propertied men ranging in age from the youngest, aged 26 (Rutledge), to one who was over 65 (Fisher), although his exact age is not known. Seventeen were older than 40, and the average age was about 41. Ten were practicing lawyers, and ten were merchants. The other seven were planters or farming land-owners, although one was also a mechanic and lay preacher, and another practiced surveying as a sideline to farming. All were politicians in the sense that they had all served in elective positions in the Assemblies of their respective colonies. All but three (Fisher, Bryan, and Bowler) were born in America. All had been brought up with a deep sense of loyalty to their King, whom they then cherished.

James Otis stated in his "Rights" pamphlet, "If I have one ambitious wish, 'tis to see Great-Britain at the head of the world, and to see my King, under God, the father of mankind." John Dickinson, who fought the Stamp Act as fiercely as any man in the colonies, spoke of George III as "the best of Kings," and "our excellent Sovereign" to whom he held inviolable loyalty.[2] The other delegates were no less ardent in their attachment to their beloved monarch, and nothing said or done at the Congress weakened this affection. When these loyal British-American subjects socialized together following their formal sessions, one may be sure that glasses were raised to toast the health of George III and wish him good health and long life.

The modern view of this period in history is colored by knowledge of the events that occurred later and completely changed the attitude toward the mother country of men like Dickinson, Otis, McKean, Rodney, Gadsden, Rutledge, Dyer, and others. Even the motives of the delegates attending the Stamp Act Congress have been misunderstood. A popular notion that they assembled in this first Congress to throw off the British yoke, which was dramatized in their opposition to the stamp tax, is untrue. Instead of considering their protests against the Stamp Act as a step toward independence, they believed that their efforts would *strengthen the ties* between England and the colonies.

Here is how Robert R. Livingston expressed this viewpoint in an unpublished letter written to John Sergeant, New York's special agent in London:

> but here we seem to think it as clear as any proposition of Euclid that if America submits to be taxed at the pleasure of the house of Commons the power will be too great & uncontrolable to remain long abused, & that the abuse of it will naturally render the colonies independent, therefore you must not look on the opposition made to the Stamp Act as proceeding from factions spirit, but from a real patriotic desire of promoting the general interest of the Empire. . . . *if I really wished to see America in a state of independence I should desire as one of the most effectual means to that end that the stamp act should be inforced*. This would unite the whole colony in disaffection, etc.[3] (Emphasis added)

When the Stamp Act was finally repealed, the grateful, unsolicited letters sent to the King by a number of the Assemblies were sincere expressions of relief that the crisis was over. These letters reinforce Livingston's view that repeal would bring the colonies back willingly to the bosom of the mother country.

Although some of the delegates to the New York Congress knew each other, particularly those from the bordering New England colonies, it was the first time that many of the others had met. Otis, Johnson, and Mayor Cruger were probably known to some of the others by reputation. Bayard, as a member of the New York Committee of Correspondence, had visited the Massachusetts Assembly the previous year, and Cruger had been in Boston on a number of occasions to conduct personal business matters. Johnson often came from his home in nearby Stratford, Connecticut, to visit New York City, where he had a number of important clients. His mother came from a good Long Island family, and she and Johnson's father had many friends in the city. Johnson and Dickinson were introduced at the Congress, and Johnson developed a high regard for the brilliant Pennsylvania delegate, and in their later correspondence he did not hesitate to express his esteem and admiration.[4]

Dickinson and Otis met for the first time, and their meeting was the beginning of a warm friendship and a correspondence that continued until Otis's sudden death eighteen years later. This remarkable scholar was struck dead by a bolt of lightning on May 23, 1783, in a farmhouse at Andover, Massachusetts, where he was living with close friends. Although he was only 58, it was a merciful death, because the mental derangement that he suffered had robbed him of his reasoning powers.

Tilghman from Maryland was introduced to Gadsden from South Carolina at the Congress, and Tilghman gave Gadsden a pamphlet published in Virginia having to do with colonial rights, which Gadsden enjoyed reading.[5] Gadsden also met Johnson for the first time, and they corresponded with each other long after the Congress adjourned. Gadsden also wrote letters to Dickinson after the meeting was over.[6]

The delegates from the Lower Counties, as well as those from South Carolina and Maryland, were strangers to most of the northerners, although Dickinson had previously met

Rodney and he and McKean were good friends. Caesar Rodney, coming from a farming section of Kent County in the heart of the present state of Delaware, was much impressed by the delegates. He may even have stood in awe of some of them, especially the wealthy, well-dressed New York merchants, and the brainy New England lawyers. He characterized the members as "an Assembly of the greatest Ability I ever yet saw."[7]

Never again would the same twenty-seven men assemble in one place. In the trying years that followed, four would die before the American colonies declared their independence (Murdock, Robert R. Livingston, Rowland, and Ringgold). Among the more aggressive delegates, whose reputations were enhanced through their participation in the Stamp Act Congress, nine would meet again in Philadelphia in 1774 as delegates to the First Continental Congress (Dyer, Dickinson, Gadsden, Philip Livingston, Lynch, Morton, McKean, Rodney, and Rutledge). The same nine would attend the Second Continental Congress the following year. Four of the boldest were present to sign the Declaration of Independence, risking their necks if the British had been victorious during the Revolution (Philip Livingston, Morton, McKean, and Rodney). One pretending to be a patriot (Bowler) was paid by the British as a spy during the Revolution, although his contemporaries were unaware of his duplicity. Three would bear the stigma of Loyalists (Johnson, Bayard, and Ruggles), and the latter two would be forced to leave the colonies, paying the full penalty of exile and expropriation. Johnson did not overtly support the British cause, but neither did he actively participate in the movement for independence. Although he retired during the Revolution to his home in Stratford where he maintained his neutrality, he managed to retain the respect of his constituents. When the Constitutional Convention was held in Philadelphia in 1787, Connecticut sent him as a delegate, and he renewed his friendship with Rutledge and Dickinson, who also attended. The signatures of all three appear on the U.S. Constitution.

When the twenty-seven delegates converged on New York during the rainy fall of 1765, some traveling on horseback with bulging saddlebags, others coming by stagecoach, and still others by sailing vessel, they represented unaffiliated colonies that were then principally concerned with their own local matters. None of the delegates could have anticipated the grave years that lay ahead, and the break that would occur with the mother country over issues that transcended their parochial problems. They were not together very long in New York before they realized that they were all in the same boat in opposition to the Stamp Act, and that they shared other common economic problems.

John Watts, a prominent New York merchant, saw the delegates arriving, and he met and dined with some of them. He wrote a letter while the Congress was still in session in which he gave the colonial Assemblies a compliment for their choice of delegates. "To do 'em justice," he wrote, "I believe they have deputed some of their best people, and I imagine the fruits of their deliberations will be sensible and moderate enough."[8]

General Gage, Commander-in-chief of the British armed forces in America, in a letter written from New York October 12, 1765, to General Henry S. Conway, Secretary of State for the Southern Department, said of the delegates:

> They are of various Characters and opinions, but it's to be feared in general that the Spirit of Democracy is strong amongst them. . . . There are some moderate Men among the Commissioners from whence will Meaning People hope that the meeting will end in drawing up a Modest, decent and proper Address; tho' there wants not those who would Spirit them up to the most violent, insolent and haughty Remonstrance.[9]

Each delegate arranged for his own lodgings, staying with friends or relatives, in boarding houses, or in one of the

Photograph of a copy of a portrait by Charles W. Peale of John Dickinson (1732–1808), one of Pennsylvania's delegates at the Congress and author of the original draft of the Declaration of Rights. His mansion south of Dover, Delaware, has been restored and furnished by Delaware's Division of Historical and Cultural Affairs. COURTESY DIVISION OF HISTORICAL AND CULTURAL AFFAIRS, STATE OF DELAWARE.

numerous taverns and inns. Among the most popular were the King's Arms, Queen's Head, Sign of the Bunch of Grapes, and the City Arms.[10] The last, on the west side of Broadway overlooking the bowling green and owned by George Burns, was a favorite meeting place for New York's merchants and lawyers, and the delegates frequently dined there. In the City Arms and the other hostelries, one could rent a comfortable bed and enjoy meals of beef and cabbage, leg of pork and turnips, mutton and pickles, puddings and pies, strong coffee and tea, with plenty of claret, beer, or Madeira.

In a letter John Dickinson wrote to his mother on October 7, he said he was lodging with a cousin on "Waln Street." He indicated that the business of the first morning session was interrupted by an invitation to dinner with "the gentlemen of the town & long sittings afterwards which I am afraid will consume the greatest part of our afternoons."[11] Some of the business of the Congress was conducted at these informal sessions where the delegates gathered together to socialize at dinner about 4:00 P.M., and continued their discussions around the dinner table. They also had a number of supper meetings later in the evening, although most of these were attended by small groups, or the individual delegations, in order to reexamine what had been discussed in the larger meetings. Most of the formal sessions were probably held in the City Hall, and the dinner and supper sessions were conducted in private homes or inns. On a number of occasions some of the New York businessmen who were not participants at the Congress invited groups of delegates to dine with them.

Dickinson told his mother in his letter that his lodgings were close to one of the coffee houses, of which there were several near the City Hall. From time to time the delegates also gathered in small groups in these establishments to exchange views, although they took pains to make sure that they were not overheard when they discussed what had taken place in their formal meetings and after-dinner sessions.

The delegates permitted no audience at any of their sessions, and no information about their discussions was released to the public either during, or at the close of the meeting. Evidently they had little time for backgammon, chess, or cards, or to enjoy the bowling green. After tense and heated discussions, some of the delegates relaxed, as did William Samuel Johnson (see his *Diary* in the Appendix), by taking long walks before retiring.

Despite the social aspects of the Congress, the meetings were long and tiresome, and usually argumentative. All of the delegates felt the heavy responsibility of the assignment they had undertaken. Judge Livingston wrote a note to his father while the Congress was in session telling him that he was so busy attending the meetings and trying to handle his active cases in court that he had little time for personal business. In the same letter he wrote that on the previous day "I had the whole Congress to dine with me & in one place or another we dine together every day so that beside business this engrosses much time." He went on to say that the Congress faced a number of problems, but the "three great points" the delegates had to contend with were "trials by Juries; a right to tax ourselves; the reducing admiralty courts within their proper limits."[12]

The other New York delegates, including Mayor Cruger, took turns at playing host to the visiting delegates at dinner, either at their homes or, usually, at Burns's tavern. Like the other dinner meetings, these too were followed by long and often acrimonious discussions.

Lieutenant-Governor Cadwallader Colden, a man with scientific and philosophical leanings who had formerly practiced medicine in Philadelphia, opposed this Congress's being held in New York without his prior consent. Perhaps he felt that he could be criticized in Whitehall for tolerating an extraordinary meeting of colonial leaders, which had not been approved by Crown or Parliament. Unswerving in his loyalty to the King, he feared that as the ranking English official, he would be held responsible for what happened in New York. Actually, he was serving only as the temporary head of the colony, a substitute for the royal governor, General Robert Monckton, who returned to England in ill health in June of 1763.

On September 23, a week after the South Carolina delegation arrived in New York, Colden wrote Secretary Conway in London, telling him, "This Meeting was kept secret from me till lately, I have in discourse discountenanced it, as an illegal convention, and inconsistent with the Constitution of the Colonies, by which their several Governments are made distinct and independent of each other. Whatever possible pretences may be used for this meeting their real intentions may be dangerous."[13] Colden's comments leave no doubt that he was suspicious that something politically unhealthy was afoot.

Colden was frustrated in his disapproval of the Congress, because there was nothing he could do to prevent it. Governor Bernard of Massachusetts, the political head of the colony whose Assembly was responsible for initiating the Congress, was in a like position. He too had misgivings, but was helpless to interfere. What the Congress intended to do as a group was legal if performed by the individual colonies.

Despite Colden's disavowal that he was aware that a Congress was going to be held, the colonial newspapers widely publicized the event, and he should have known about it long before the South Carolina delegation arrived in New York. On August 15, 1765, the *Georgia Gazette* published the Massachusetts letter of invitation verbatim, and on August 22, the names of the South Carolina delegates who would attend. The September 5 edition carried a story giving the names of the Massachusetts delegates, and an editorial stating in part, "It is hoped that neither the governor of Virginia nor any other governor on the continent, will think this is so improper a set as to dissolve their assemblies to prevent it. . . ." The article went on to say that it was the right of English subjects to petition King and Parliament for a redress of their grievances. Georgia's governor James Wright paid no attention to the editorial; he kept the Georgia Assembly adjourned (as did Governor Fauquier of Virginia), which prevented their participation.

On September 23, the *Boston Evening Post* announced the names of the Pennsylvania and Rhode Island delegates to the Congress, and the September 23 edition of the *Boston Post Boy* stated that it afforded the editor satisfaction to learn that the Congress proposed by the Massachusetts Assembly had been consented to by "the Representatives of most of the other colonies on the continent."

The *Massachusetts Gazette* also kept its readers fully informed going so far in the October 10 edition as to report the names of the three delegates appointed by the Assembly of the Three Lower Counties in far-away New Castle on the Delaware. The *Boston Post Boy* on October 21 published a list of all the delegates attending the Congress, and the *Evening Post* on the same day reported the elections of Ruggles as chairman and Cotton as clerk at the first session in New York. Despite the secrecy at the Congress, there were apparently some leaks to the press.

Both the *New York Post Boy* and *New York Mercury* kept their subscribers informed as they received messages reporting the arrival of the various delegations in New York. After the Congress convened, both papers published a complete list of the names of all the delegates.[14] Many other examples could be cited to show that the gathering of the delegates was widely reported in the colonial press, especially in the New York and Boston papers, which were quoted by newspapers in Philadelphia and elsewhere. Reference is often made by historians to the undeveloped methods of communication and transportation during the colonial period; nevertheless, it is amazing how quickly the news of the assembling of the Stamp Act Congress was disseminated.

When the delegates from Massachusetts arrived in New

York, they called on Lieutenant-Governor Colden to pay their respects, and to assure him that they upheld the authority of King and Parliament. Colden received them coldly and rebuffed them by saying that their Congress was unlawful and unconstitutional.[15]

It is not difficult to understand Colden's apprehensions. Serving in office until General Monckton returned from England, or until a new governor was appointed, he knew that he was sitting on a powder keg in New York, the British military headquarters in the colonies. It was a logical place for a clash to take place between the troops and New York mobs, and events leading to such a confrontation were taking place all too fast. For a man in his twilight years (he was aged 77), Colden no longer had the stamina of youth as an ally, and the Stamp Act, which he had taken an oath to enforce, was already causing him too many annoyances. The Congress meeting on his front doorstep added more anxiety to his troubles. In no colonial community was the populace more aroused by the Stamp Act than in New York City.

On August 26, 1765, James McEvers, a leading New York merchant and William Bayard's father-in-law, suddenly resigned the commission he had accepted as Stamp Distributor. After learning that a mob had harassed Andrew Oliver, the Stamp Distributor in Boston, destroying his office, stoning the windows of his residence, and forcing his resignation by threatening his life, McEvers decided that he had accepted the job in haste. News that he had relinquished the office tended to add weight to the growing opposition to the stamp tax in New York's business and legal circles. No one wanted the job McEvers had resigned. Colden knew that if New York did not have a Stamp Distributor, it would be impossible to purchase the stamped paper, and he would not be able to enforce the Stamp Act. To make matters worse, the Sons of Liberty, encouraged by some of the leading merchants, were recruiting members in New York City, and they threatened violence against anyone who sold or used the pre-stamped English paper.

With no one to sell the stamped paper, Colden fully expected the commercial and legal activities of the city to come to a halt on November 1. He knew that under the provisions of the statute the courts could not sit and act without the use of stamped paper or parchment, newspapers could not legally be published, and ships could not be permitted to sail from New York harbor. Colden did not then realize that the Sons of Liberty had decided that the Stamp Act should be ignored as though it did not exist, and they encouraged merchants, editors, and lawyers to carry on their business affairs as usual without the use of stamped paper.

On October 22, during these tense days and while the Stamp Act Congress was in session, the *Edward* entered New York harbor after a nine-week voyage from England, bringing the first consignment of stamped paper intended for use in New York and Connecticut. This was not the first shipment made from England to the colonies, as the list of vessels in the Appendix will indicate, but it was the initial shipment to New York. Captain William Davis, skipper of the *Edward,* anchored off the Battery, where several thousand angry, noisy citizens incited by the Sons of Liberty gathered to protest the delivery of the stamped paper. Captain Davis discreetly waited until after nightfall, and then, escorted by two frigates, the *Coventry* and *Garland,* secretly landed the cargo at Fort George for safekeeping.[16]

A few days later, placards inspired by the Sons of Liberty appeared on the doors of public offices and stores, threatening bodily injury to anyone who distributed or used the stamped paper. The delegates to the Congress could not help seeing this literature on their way to the City Hall.

To protect the stamped paper from being burned by the mobs, Colden was forced to turn it over to Mayor Cruger and the Corporation at the City Hall, where it was put in storage. It was humiliating to His Majesty's government to be forced to rely on the city authorities to guard the stamped paper, especially since the Mayor was opposed to the Stamp Act and was attending a Congress that Colden considered illegal. The delegates to the Congress were all fully aware of the situation and must have realized its gravity.

Colden had another problem to deal with when Zachariah Hood, an Annapolis merchant and the Maryland Stamp Distributor, arrived in New York, dusty, unshaven, and distraught. Hood was forced to flee from Annapolis when crowds whipped, pilloried, hanged, and burned him in effigy, and damaged the building where he intended to stock and sell the stamped paper. Unwilling to give in to the rioters by resigning, as other Stamp Distributors had done, he fled to New York to seek protection. Initially he was given quarters in the King's Arms, but the New York rabble found him there and harassed him. Colden was forced to find refuge for him in Fort George, where he was protected by Gage's troops.[17]

In England, when news that the colonies were going to hold a Congress reached the Lords Commissioners for Trade and Plantations, the honorable members addressed a communication to the King on October 1, 1765, from which I have extracted the following significant paragraph:

> The Object of the Foregoing Resolutions and proceedings of the House of Representatives of Massachusets Bay is to recommend to, and induce the Rest of your Majestys Colonies in America to join in a General Congress of Commee's from the several Assemblies independant of the other Branches of the Legislature and without any previous Application to your Majesty to consider and deliberate upon the Acts of Parliament of this Kingdom. *And as this appears to us to be the first Instance of any General Congress appointed by the Assemblies of the Colonies without the Authority of the Crown a Measure which we Conceive of dangerous Tendency in itself,* and more Especially so when taken for the purpose Expressed

in the above mentioned Resolution and Connected with the Spirit that has appeared throughout the whole Conduct of this particular Assembly; We therefore think it our Indispensible Duty to Submit this Matter to your Majesty's Consideration for such Direction as your Majesty with the Advice of your Council may think proper and expedient to give thereupon.[18] (Emphasis added)

This letter was referred to the Lords of the Committee of Council for Plantation Affairs, whose members reported as follows on October 3:

That this is a Matter of the Utmost Importance to the Kingdom and Legislature of Great Britain, and is of too high a Nature for the Determination of your Majesty in Your Privy Council, and is Proper only for the Consideration of Parliament.[19]

By the time Parliament was fully informed, the die was cast. The Stamp Act Congress was in session, and it was too late to halt it.

With the excitement and outbursts in New York reaching a crescendo, the delegates to the Congress were brought face to face every day with the vehement opposition to the Stamp Act. Public pressure in New York had mounted, making the delegates keenly aware of their responsibility to take action to relieve the crisis. They were anxious to convene their meeting, and even though all the delegates had not yet arrived, they decided to hold a preliminary session on September 30, after the Massachusetts delegation arrived in New York. The Rhode Island members arrived Saturday, September 28, and the South Carolina delegation was already in New York, which meant that three visiting delegations and the New York representatives were on hand.

The brief account of this meeting, since apparently no minutes were kept, is found in the following letter dated Thursday, October 3, published in the *Boston Evening Post* on October 14:

On Monday afternoon [September 30] the Commissioners had a meeting at which were present those from Boston, Rhode Island, South Carolina, and a standing committee from the lower House of this province [New York] appointed to hold a correspondence with the neighboring Governments upon the Stamp Act &c. On Tuesday [October 1] arrived an express from the Speaker of the Maryland Assembly informing that at the request of some of the members Governor Sharpe immediately and chearfully called the Assembly who appointed Messers. Tilgham [*sic*], Ringold and Murdock, three of the House to Attend the Congress, who are expected this Evening, as are also those from Pennsylvania and Connecticut [the Lower Counties also arrived on the 30th]. Yesterday [October 2] a letter from the Lower House of the Jersies came to hand informing that on this day the members would convene and appoint a Committee to join the Congress.[20]

On Monday, October 7, representatives from all nine of the colonies assembled in the first official meeting of the Congress. The first item of business was to elect a chairman. Since Massachusetts was responsible for the Congress, it seemed only fitting that one of her representatives should occupy the chair, and Timothy Ruggles and James Otis were nominated. It might be said that Ruggles was the spokesman for the conservatives, and Otis the radicals, although the latter had moderated many of his earlier views. Referring to the contest for the chairmanship, to which Otis aspired, John Watts wrote that

"Otis aimed at it and would have succeeded but they thought as he had figured much in the popular way, it might give their meeting an ill grace, but it is observed Otis is now quite a different man, and so he seemed to me, to be, not riotous at all."[21]

Watts obtained his information about the voting at secondhand, probably from his good friend Mayor Cruger, but Thomas McKean, who participated in the election, explained in a letter he later wrote to John Adams how Ruggles defeated Otis by a close margin:

"Mr. James Otis appeared to me to be the boldest and best speaker. I voted for him as our President, but Brigadier Ruggles succeeded by one vote, owing to the number of the committee from New York as we voted individually."[22] John Adams, who received information about what went on at the Stamp Act Congress from Caesar Rodney, Thomas McKean, and others, wrote Thomas Jefferson on December 25, 1813, that although Ruggles was the president, Otis was "the soul" of the Congress.[23]

Caesar Rodney later wrote that Otis "displayed that light and knowledge of the interest of America, which shining like a sun, lit up those stars which shone on this subject afterwards."[24]

In an unpublished letter that John Adams wrote to Caesar A. Rodney (nephew of Caesar Rodney) on April 4, 1819, he had this to say about some of the delegates:

> Caesar Rodney your Uncle was in my opinion a Judicious and Sagacious Judge of Men and things. I knew only three of the Delegates to the Congress of 65, General Timothy Ruggles was a Man of a Strong Mind, but devoted to Great Britain, James Otis possessed as great talents as any Man that ever arose in North America, and was wholly devoted to his Native Country. Oliver Partridge was a Gentleman of Education, but not greatly distinguished, more inclined however to Great Britain than to his own Country, Governour McKean and his talents you know. These are all I ever knew except your Uncle. I have heard that Mr. [Robert] Ogden was distinguished, but he was on the side of Ruggles and Great Britain.[25]

Following the election of Ruggles as their chairman, the delegates resolved that John Cotton, aged 37, a Harvard graduate, should be the Clerk, or Secretary, of the Congress, and would keep whatever records were necessary. Cotton was the Deputy-Secretary of the Massachusetts House of Representatives, and the Massachusetts delegates, anticipating the need for a professional penman at the Congress, engaged him to accompany them to New York.[26] At the session the following day, Robert R. Livingston, McKean, and Rutledge were elected as a committee to inspect the minutes and proceedings to make certain that they were correctly recorded. This committee excercised strict censorship, as indicated by the brevity of the Journal; the delegates obviously wanted their statements "off the record."

The Congress then turned to an examination of the credentials of the representatives from New York, New Jersey, and the Lower Counties, inasmuch as these delegations had not been appointed by their respective Assemblies in official sessions. This was putting the cart before the horse, because the three delegations had already participated in electing the chairman who was then presiding over a meeting to determine their eligibility to participate and vote! After reading the letters submitted by each delegation, the decision was made, with no dissenting votes, to admit all of them.

Next came the question of what method of balloting should be adopted for the deliberations to follow in the plenary sessions. One of the problems was that New York was represented by five deputies, Rhode Island and the Lower Counties had only two, whereas the other six colonies were each represented by three. The election of Ruggles by the slim margin of one vote indicated plainly to McKean and Rodney that it would not be fair to allow New York more than twice as many votes as the Lower Counties. No doubt Bowler and Ward, the two delegates from Rhode Island, also had something to say on this subject, since their colony had only two votes. Representatives from the more populous colonies felt that their weight should be stronger than the small provinces like the Lower Counties, which had a population of less than 25,000. After further discussion it was resolved that each colony would have one vote on all questions that arose in the Congress thereafter. McKean must have argued this point passionately, for some years later he wrote that "a vote by states was by me made a *sine qua non* in the first

Congress held in New York in 1765."[27] Had this system been followed in selecting the chairman, Otis might have won the election and achieved his ambition to preside over the Congress. Incidentally, Cotton used the word *congress* in his minutes on the first day of the assembly, and continued to use the term throughout the Journal.

An article in the *Boston Post Boy* published April 21, 1766, stated that, to avoid disputes in the Congress and to promote harmony, "it was agreed in Voting, and in the Proceedings, to begin at one End of the Continent and go through, only as Massachusetts first proposed the Measure, the Compliment was paid by the Gentlemen of the other colonies of placing them first; but it was merely a Compliment, and it is to be hoped that on all future Occasions as on this, the Colonies will consider themselves as on the same Footing without the least Claim of Pre-eminence one over the other." This meant that when a vote was called, each colony held a caucus to determine how its single vote would be cast, and then the colonies voted in geographical sequence, going from North to South.

After resolving the questions of voting, the Congress adjourned until the following morning, Tuesday, October 8, at which time the delegates assembled to begin discussing the serious questions that had brought them together. There is no reference in the Journal to the presence of a minister or opening the Congress with prayer. That practice would be introduced in 1774, when the Reverend Duché, an Anglican priest, opened the First Continental Congress in Philadelphia with an eloquent invocation.

As of the first morning of the Stamp Act Congress, none of the delegates could have realized how many days they would be away from their homes.[28] The discussions required more time than any of them had anticipated when they accepted the assignment. The last session took place on Friday, October 25, two weeks and five days after the delegates formally convened. Altogether, seventeen official sessions were recorded in the Journal, but no record was kept of the numerous dinner and supper meetings.

Details about the debates, and the positions taken by the individual delegates on the issues under discussion and how they voted, would be more significant than information about the number of sessions and where they were held. Unfortunately, this information was not recorded and its omission was obviously intended. Fragmentary accounts have been gleaned here and there from contemporary newspapers, or from letters written by some of the delegates, or by residents of New York while the Congress was in session. These data are tantalizing in their incompleteness, and it is frustrating to try to weave them into a continuous narrative.

Unfortunately, none of the deputies attending the Congress kept private minutes of the discussions, as James Madison did during the Constitutional Convention of 1787. It would appear that the members of the Stamp Act Congress deliberately chose to keep the subtance of their debates from being recorded. If the speakers were certain that their remarks would never be published, they would be less inhibited in their comments, and knowledge that the speeches were "off the record" probably contributed to frank discussions.

Apparently the first subject brought up for discussion was the hardships the colonies suffered as a result of the late acts of Parliament—not only the Stamp Act, but the Sugar Act and the Currency Act. Of course the Stamp Act took precedence in the discussions, and doubtless there was a recounting of what had taken place in each of the nine participating colonies—the Stamp Act riots, the forced resignations of Stamp Distributors, and the widespread opposition to the impending stamp tax. The merchant delegates, whose business had been affected by the Sugar Act of 1764, probably related their experiences. Discussions of the problems, and the best method of approaching them, continued from October 8 to October 19. In his second letter to his brother Thomas,

Caesar Rodney explained why the business of the Congress was not yet finished and what was keeping him in New York:

> You, and many others, perhaps are Surprised to think We Should set So Long When the business of our Meeting Seemed only to be Petitioning the King, and Remonstrating to both houses of Parliament—But When you Consider That We are Petitioning & addressing That august Body the great Legislative of the Empire for Redress of Grievances: That in order to point out Those Grievances it Was likewise Necessary to Set forth the Liberty We have, and ought to Enjoy (as freeborn Englishmen) according to the British Constitution.[29]

Rodney also went on to explain that the members decided first to phrase a Declaration of Rights, forerunner of what in American politics two centuries later would be termed a "party platform." This Declaration would be written as a self-contained document enunciating in a series of resolutions the principles that would become the foundation for the petitions to be addressed to the King and Parliament. The delegates planned, at some later, unnamed date after the petitions had been received in England, to release the Declaration in America as the official expression of the Congress. "It was also recommended by the Congress," Rodney and McKean later reported to their Assembly, "that the greatest Precaution be used to prevent any of the Addresses [petitions] being printed before they were presented, lest they might be considered as an Appeal to the People rather than an Application to our Sovereign and the British Parliament."[30]

In his letter to his brother, Rodney explained that phrasing the Declaration turned out to be a much more difficult task than the members had imagined it would be, because they did not want to infringe on either the prerogative of the Crown or the power of Parliament. They wanted to assert what they believed to be the rights and privileges of the colonies, and at the same time to show their respect for

British authority. As Dickinson phrased it, "Let us behave like dutiful children who have received unmerited blows from a beloved parent. Let us complain to our parent, but let complaints speak at the same time the language of affection and veneration."[31]

In view of the Declaration of Independence eleven years later, and the bloody battles that followed, the attitude of the delegates in retrospect may seem weak and conciliatory. But it must be remembered that in 1765 they considered themselves British subjects owing allegiance to their King. They were engaged in a struggle to preserve their rights as Englishmen, nothing else. They did not then conceive of rebelling, nor of withdrawing from the Empire. They were not questioning the authority of their sovereign, nor the right of Parliament to legislate in their behalf. Their aim was to formulate a prudent Declaration in which they would respectfully challenge Parliament's right to tax the colonies without their consent for the purpose of raising revenue. The majority of the members agreed with Dickinson, who was then firm in his belief that the colonies should remain united to Great Britain and that Parliament should continue to have certain jurisdiction over all the English colonies in North America. The delegates knew that they would be fully supported by their constituents as long as their goal was to preserve their rights, as well as their obligations, as Englishmen. They also knew that such radical proposals as outright disobedience to the laws, secession from the Empire, or talk of independence, would be strongly opposed in the colonies. How to express their devotion and loyalty to the mother country without yielding any of the taxing power of the Colonial Assemblies was the delicate point at issue.

Dickinson was able to get the support of the New Englanders and the delegates from the Middle Colonies regarding English supervision of the trade. "The Parliament unquestionably possesses a legal authority to *regulate* the trade of Great Britain and her colonies," he wrote. "Such an authority is essential to the relations between a mother country and her colonies; and necessary for the common good of all."[32] On the other hand, Dickinson strongly opposed Parliament's levying either internal or external taxes for the purpose of raising revenue. Some of the Southern members disagreed that Parliament should levy taxes either for revenue, or for the purpose of regulating the trade, or for any other purpose. Rutledge and Lynch took this position and argued against Dickinson.

There apparently was a lengthy discussion about the difference between external and internal taxes, with some quibbling over the definition of terms. The delegates even differed on the definition of the word *tax*, Dickinson arguing that it meant "an imposition on the subject for the sole purpose of levying money." He later wrote, "I am satisfied that the congress understood the word 'tax' in the sense here [above] contended for."[33]

It was one thing to admit that Parliament had the right to regulate the trade by imposing customs duties, provided such duties were not intended to raise revenue, and another thing to acknowledge that right in a formal document. Robert R. Livingston was one who felt that the Declaration should explicitly state that Parliament had the sovereign power to legislate on behalf of trade, and that the delegates should frankly acknowledge that authority. He reasoned that if Great Britain could not regulate the trade of her colonies, the colonies would be of no use to her. He also argued that if Parliament's right to levy external taxes for the regulation of the trade was conceded in the Declaration, then Parliament would more readily accept the position held by the Congress that internal taxes should not be levied on the colonies.[34] Other delegates felt that this admission would be misconstrued to mean that external taxes, levied to regulate the trade and also as a source of revenue (such as the Sugar Act of 1764), were acceptable to them.

The arguments advanced by Robert R. Livingston, and

supported by his cousin Philip, angered the delegates from South Carolina. In March of 1773, when Josiah Quincy, Jr., visited Thomas Lynch in South Carolina, the latter was reminiscing about the Stamp Act Congress and he described some of the maneuvers made by the delegates. Lynch said that "the conduct of Livingston ought to be remembered with unrelenting indignation and his name loaded with infamy—Caesar Rodney of Pennsylvania, Lynch and Gadsden of South Carolina were heroes and patriots."[35]

On the question of Parliament's authority, Otis probably reiterated the position he had expressed in his "Rights" pamphlet, namely, that Parliament was the supreme legislative body and had the right to legislate for the colonies on all matters that did not infringe on their liberties. Levying taxes without their consent, he argued, was an example of such infringement, because taxes were considered in the context of depriving a person of his property, and thus, *per se*, of his liberty and freedom. However, there was a strong feeling among some of the other delegates that the Congress should not concede too much authority to Parliament. Dickinson felt that the issue could be straddled by loosely defining Parliament's authority in the Declaration in the following words: "That all acts of Parliament not inconsistent with the principles of freedom are obligatory on the colonies."[36]

Some of the delegates, including Rutledge, felt that this was too broad an assertion of Parliament's power.[37] Others must immediately have recognized that Parliament's conception of *the principles of freedom* might substantially differ from what the delegates meant by the term.

Ruggles, the archconservative, had serious reservations about what he considered radical proposals being advanced by his colleagues, although he decided to keep his objections to himself instead of arguing from the chair. He had come to New York with the hope of convincing the delegates that they should recommend submission to the Stamp Act until Parliament, through the established channels of communication with each colony, could be persuaded to repeal it. That was the position Governor Bernard had taken in a speech to the Massachusetts Assembly and that he reiterated in a personal letter he wrote Ruggles on September 28. Bernard went so far in his letter as to tell Ruggles that he thought he should recommend this course of action to the Congress.[38] Although Otis believed that the colonists would be justified in refusing to pay the stamp taxes, he agreed with Ruggles that they "should yield obedience to an act of Parliament, tho' erroneous, 'till repealed."

The Congress was not in session very long before it became plain to both Ruggles and Otis that the majority of the delegates were not in a mood to accept this choice. Even as the Congress met, the Sons of Liberty, growing in strength and numbers, were inciting resistance to the stamp taxes, not only in New York and New England, but in Virginia and the Carolinas. News reached New York that John Hughes, the Pennsylvania Stamp Distributor, had assured dissenters who besieged his home and office in Philadelphia that he would not sell any of the stamped paper unless the other colonies agreed to conform to the act. A curse had already developed on the stamped paper—the Stamp Distributors appealed to the royal governors to take the shipments in custody before crowds of rioters destroyed the paper, and the governors appealed to commanders of the British armed forces to protect the stamped paper from the mobs.

In view of the trend of public opinion, the majority of the members of the Congress had no inclination to urge compliance with the Stamp Act; they were more concerned about justifying the rights of the colonists to tax themselves. This was one of the freedoms that John Locke had emphasized in 1690 in his *Two Treatises of Government*, with which the lawyer delegates were familiar. With their keen legal minds, Otis, Johnson, Robert R. Livingston, McKean, and Dickinson insisted that the right of self-taxation must have a sound legal basis. There was a great deal of argument about

whether this right should be attributed to the charters issued
by the Crown to the individual colonies at the time land was
patented to their founders. The Virginia Resolves, which
brought to a head the opposition to the stamp tax, referred
specifically to the rights granted the colonists by their royal
charters.³⁹ The first colonial charter was issued to the Virginia
Company in 1606 by James I, granting to the settlers at
Jamestown and their progeny all the rights enjoyed by Englishmen at home.⁴⁰ In the Charters later issued to Lord Baltimore as the Proprietor of the Province of Maryland, and to
William Penn as Proprietor of Pennsylvania (and in other
colonial charters), there were similar provisions relative to
individual rights.

In the resolves that the Assemblies of Maryland and
Rhode Island had passed, both colonies followed Virginia's
example by referring to their respective charters as guaran-
tees of their essential rights as British subjects. Benjamin
Franklin had also invoked charter rights, on September 22,
1764, when, as Speaker of the Pennsylvania Assembly, he
wrote a letter protesting Parliament's tax policies.

William Samuel Johnson, who was thoroughly familiar
with the Connecticut charter issued by Charles II in 1662,
knew that the General Assembly of his province derived its
legal authority from this charter, which also granted the
colonists "all the Liberties and Immunities of Free and
Natural Subjects." He advocated adducing the charter rights
of the respective colonies (although some did not have
charters) as an important legal basis for the rights claimed
for the colonists. Johnson saw the charters as medieval
compacts, or grants, between the King and his subjects,
which Parliament could not abrogate. With this interpretation, buttressed by common law and the British constitution,
only the Colonial Assemblies had the right to tax the colonial
subjects.

Otis had leanings in this direction, too, since it was also
one of the ideas he had expressed in his "Rights" pamphlet.

Christopher Gadsden (1724–1805) of South Carolina is pictured as an elderly man, but he was only 41 when he attended the Stamp Act Congress. One of the foremost of Southern patriots, he was a Revolutionary officer, and led the fight for independence as a delegate to the First and Second Continental Congresses. COURTESY NEW YORK PUBLIC LIBRARY, EMMET COLLECTION NO. 221, MANUSCRIPTS AND ARCHIVES DIVISION, ASTOR, LENOX AND TILDEN FOUNDATIONS.

Despite the brilliant part he played in the Congress, Otis had a tendency to shift from one position to another. In fact, in two tracts published the year following the "Rights" pamphlet, he contradicted some of the views that he had previously expressed. Also, in conversation he appeared to retract statements that he had made in print.

Christopher Gadsden never vacillated in his attitude toward the colonial charters, which he strongly opposed as the basis for adducing individual rights. He insisted that basing individual rights on the charters, which differed in content by colony, would necessarily require each colony to act individually in its own interests. That would negate the concept of colonial unity, which he strongly favored, and would make it extremely difficult to formulate a Declaration of Rights that all could approve. He may also have been aware that some English officials like Governor Bernard, well educated in the law, considered the Massachusetts charter of 1691, and other colonial charters, as temporary trusts, which could be revoked at will by Parliament.

Gadsden argued that the colonies should all endeavor to stand upon "the broad common ground of those natural and *inherent* rights we all feel and know, as men, and as descendants of Englishmen, we have a right to. . . ."[41] This meant the rights found in the Magna Charta and the great Bill of Rights of 1689. He maintained that these rights took precedence over the colonial charters, and were the indubitable natural rights of all Englishmen under the British constitution, which Parliament could not annul.

On this point Dickinson agreed with Gadsden. His position was that the liberties given to the colonial subjects in the charters were favors granted by the Crown. He admitted that such rights could be withdrawn, but neither King nor Parliament could give or take away the natural rights essential to happiness that are born in all men. These natural rights, Dickinson maintained, included freedom and security of one's property without confiscatory taxes. As he phrased it, those taxed without their consent were no better than slaves.[42]

In the Pennsylvania Resolves, drafted less than a month before, Dickinson had wrestled with the same problem, and he decided to omit any reference to charter rights. Instead, he took the following position, as it was phrased in the third paragraph of the Resolves, which the Pennsylvania Assembly unanimously approved:

That the inhabitants of this Province are entitled to all the Liberties, Rights and Privileges of his Majesty's Subjects in Great-Britain, or elsewhere, and that the Constitution of Government in this Province is founded on the *natural rights of Mankind, and the noble Principles of English Liberty, and therefore is, or ought to be, perfectly free.* (Emphasis added)

Otis expressed the same thoughts in his "Rights" pamphlet, using the terms *inherent* and *by the law of God and Nature.* Dickinson and Otis were both trying to say, without being able to find the exact words, what Thomas Jefferson a decade later in the Declaration of Independence was to call the "unalienable rights" of "life, liberty, and the pursuit of happiness."

These acrimonious discussions involving legal technicalities must have become tedious to some of the nonlawyers, who were impatient to begin writing the petitions to the King and Parliament, which was the reason that they had made the trip to New York in the first place. Even McKean, who understood the law as well as any of the delegates, felt that there was too much pussyfooting and that the Congress should take a bolder stance. Many years later, reminiscing about the Stamp Act Congress, in contrast to the later Congresses where the belligerent members were outspoken in their criticism of both King and Parliament, McKean wrote, "There was less fortitude in that body than in the succeeding Congress of 1774; indeed some of the members seemed as timid as if engaged in a traitorous conspiracy."[43]

In retrospect, this timidity seems excusable in view of the time, the circumstances, and the personalities of the delegates, who were setting a precedent in American political life. The hour was not yet at hand for rebellion.

There is record of two interruptions to the business of the Congress. Mayor John Cruger (who was also Water Bayliff and Clerk of the New York Market, *ex officio*) was kept busy trying to keep abreast of the city's affairs while he was participating as a delegate in the Congress. On the morning of October 14, he found it necessary to excuse himself from the discussions between 10:00 and 11:00 in order to attend an important meeting with his aldermen in the Common Council Chamber of the City Hall, He and the aldermen were entering a new term of office, and the Council records indicate that the entire group had to leave City Hall and go to the Governor's Palace at Fort George, where Lieutenant-Governor Colden administered their oaths of office."

The second interruption was a more dramatic one. During the final discussion on colonial rights, a courier from the Georgia General Assembly delivered the letter previously referred to (see Georgia, chapter 2 above). The unnamed messenger, who had departed Savannah on horseback on September 6, passed through Philadelphia on October 17, according to a brief note in the October 28 edition of the *Boston Evening Post,* and arrived in New York on October 18 or 19. The letter carried in his saddlebags, signed by Speaker Alexander Wylly, seems to have been the first acknowledgment Georgia made to the Massachusetts letter of invitation. The delegates to the Congress were aware that no reply had been received from Georgia, and were doubtless delighted to greet the messenger. They were gratified to read Wylly's reply asking for copies of whatever petitions they drew up, because he wanted to present them to the Georgia Assembly for authorization to be transmitted to Great Britain (see his letter in Journal below, chap. 4).

The Journal of the Congress provides no clue as to the

identity of the delegate who drew up the first draft of the Declaration of Rights. It has been said that Cruger prepared the first draft, although evidence is completely lacking to support this assumption. Robert R. Livingston, in a letter written to his father while the Congress was in session, complained of the loss of valuable time by "employing a person to draw a state of the rights of the colonies who did not effect it in the manner intended."[45] He neglected to name the person.

Evidently some of the other Eastern delegates felt that, with a certain addition to it, this first draft was acceptable, but the Southern delegates objected. Gadsden later wrote, "But had we consented to the addition that was so strenuously proposed to be made to the first Declaration of the opinion of the Congress, I am sure we should have been far, very far from having the thanks of our House."[46]

The "Papers of William Samuel Johnson, 1745–1790" in the Library of Congress Collections, contain an eleven-page manuscript in Johnson's hand entitled, "Report of Committee at Congress."[47] Although the members of the committee are not named, the opening sentence begins, "The Comm[itt]ee to whom was refered the Consider[ati]on of the Rights of the British Colonies, etc." This seems to mean that a committee not named in the Journal, possibly to guarantee anonymity, undertook the task of framing the Declaration. The October 8 entry in Johnson's *Diary* (see Appendix) supports this assumption. After a wordy introduction the report presents eight numbered arguments protesting British colonial policies. The delegates may have used this report as a basis for discussion and to crystallize their own views, but they rejected it as a model for the Declaration they finally approved and adopted.

The Johnson collection also contains a page of notes entitled "Some General Hints for the Connecticut Commissioners to be used or not as shall be tho't best by them [during the discussions in the Congress]."

Photograph of a portrait of William Samuel Johnson (1727–1819), delegate from Connecticut, painted in 1793 by Gilbert Stuart. Member of the committee that prepared the address to the King and author of the Diary appearing in the Appendix of this volume, Johnson was a member of the Constitutional Convention of 1787, and became the first president of Columbia University.

Another document, of only three pages, entitled "Notes at Congress," reveals the logic of Johnson's mind in organizing his argument to challenge Parliament's right to tax the colonies. He reasoned that the American colonies were formerly under the jurisdiction of Parliament and were absolutely liable to English laws and taxation by Parliament. This system, based on charters in some colonies and on royal instructions in others, would have been continued if King and Parliament had not permitted another to take its place. "But," he wrote. "ye Crown having Establish'd Legislatures with Compleat & full powers of Govern[men]t the most essential of which is the power of taxation—some for more than a century—Parliament has admitted these powers to be executed—it must be considered as having fully ratified and confirmed them, as instituted by the Crown—thereby transfering to Provincial Assemblies full & perfect powers of Legislation & government."

It seems safe to infer from the nature of the notes that Johnson must have expressed these thoughts in the Congress during the discussions on the Declaration of Rights.

In the John Dickinson Papers in the collections of the Historical Society of Pennsylvania, there is evidence that, after the Congress rejected the earlier draft, Dickinson undertook the task of composing the Declaration of Rights. He first prepared a preliminary text in his own hand, which he then corrected. Next he prepared a second draft, incorporating additional thoughts, which bears notations and deletions in the handwriting of others, suggesting that it was read and corrected by one or two fellow delegates. Last, he prepared a third version, which bears a note in his hand reading, "the original Draft of the Resolves of the first Congress held at New York in the year 1765."[48]

When this final draft is compared with the Declaration as approved by the Congress, it is evident that the text of the latter is derived from the former, preserving many of Dickinson's crisply written phrases. Even the arguments in the

Dickinson draft conform to those in the final Declaration, with some changes in the indentifying numbers. Comparison of the two texts provides clues to the drift of the discussions in the closed sessions.[49]

The majority of the delegates felt that it was highly desirable to point out that the colonists were affectionate and dutiful subjects of the King and owed him their allegiance. This would make the record clear that the Congress was not engaged in a conspiracy against their monarch nor could they be accused of insubordination. There was no opposition on this point which became the opening statement in the Declaration.

The question of Parliament's authority came next, and this provoked considerable discussion and argument. Dickinson's draft stated that all acts of Parliament were obligatory on the colonies except those that violated their freedoms. The majority of the delegates could not accept this definition. It was agreed to borrow a phrase that Johnson had used in the first committee report, that is, *due subordination* and to state that the colonies owed all "due subordination" to Parliament, without amplifying or explaining what was meant. The inference that the delegates apparently intended to be drawn was that Parliament had the right to regulate trade, and to exercise legislative authority so long as it did not conflict with taxing or other prerogatives of their colonial Assemblies.[50] The Congress made no effort to clearly define the relationship that should exist between Parliament and the colonies.

On the question of justifying colonial rights and liberties, it was decided to omit all references to the charters, which is what Dickinson had done in his draft. He had merely stated "That his Majesty's liege subjects in these colonies, are as free as his subjects in Great Britain." The delegates felt that this should be strengthened by stressing that the colonists were entitled to all the inherent rights and liberties enjoyed by all other natural-born British subjects. This provided the opportunity to specify the right of trial by jury and to protest the Vice-Admiralty Courts, wherein the absence of a jury tended to subvert individual rights and liberties.

The majority of the delegates also agreed that the most important point at issue was the right guaranteed to all Englishmen to be taxed by a legislative body in which they had chosen the representatives. To do otherwise was to allow their property to be confiscated, which was inconsistent with the principles of the British constitution. Thus, Article 5 of the Declaration stated that no taxes (both internal and external taxes were implicit in the statement) could be imposed upon the colonists "but by their respective Legislature," which meant their own Assemblies.

The delegates also debated the question as to whether or not the colonies should request the privilege of sending elected representatives to Parliament.[51] Such representation would invalidate the argument that they were suffering from taxation without representation. Since there were more than five hundred members in the House of Commons, it was apparent that the colonies could not send a sufficient number of representatives to block the votes of the English majority. It was expensive to reside at court in London, and the cost of sending colonial representatives to England and supporting them there would be prohibitive. Although the members of Commons received no salaries, it was unreasonable to expect Americans to serve abroad without remuneration. Even if the colonies could afford to support representatives in Commons, there were no American peers, and the colonies could not be represented in the House of Lords. Perhaps the most convincing argument against the plan was that if the colonies had representatives both in Parliament and in their own Assemblies, the legislative processes would become hopelessly confusing, and eventually the authority of the Assemblies would become subordinate to Parliament.

In many respects these discussions were academic. The

Assemblies of South Carolina and Virginia had already
gone on record the previous year as opposing representation
in Parliament, and the Massachusetts delegation had been
specifically instructed by their Assembly to resist such proposals if they were made at the Congress.

When the discussion ended, the delegates agreed to point
out in the Declaration that due to "their local circumstances,"
they could not be represented in Parliament, *nor did they
want such representation*. This, of course, strengthened their
argument that their own Assemblies were the only legislative
bodies having legal power to tax them. At the same time they
agreed to refer to the colonial Assemblies as "subordinate"
legislative bodies.

Finally, the Congress discussed the specific language to be
used in protesting the Stamp Act, and other acts of Parliament that they felt should be repealed. The merchant members insisted upon including a passage relating to the scarcity
of specie in the colonies, which made payment of the taxes
levied by Parliament "absolutely impracticable." This was
a point that Dickinson had overlooked in his draft. The
merchants also stressed another point that Dickinson had
not included, namely, that the restrictions imposed by the
acts of Parliament would "render them unable to purchase
the Manufactures of Great Britain." The full text of this
remarkable Declaration appears in the Journal (see chap. 4
below), and the reader will note how the carefully chosen
words reflect the sentiments of the majority of the delegates,
as discussed above.

Having completed and approved the Declaration of Rights
on Saturday October 19, the Congress then opened the discussion on the nature of the petitions to be submitted to the
King and Parliament. Once more the lawyers asserted themselves in the matter of using correct legal terminology. They
believed that an *address* should be prepared for the King;
a *memorial* to the House of Lords; and a *petition* to the House
of Commons. Implicit in the technical meanings of these

terms were diplomatic nuances that are partially lost today; an *address* was a written or formal message of respect to a superior, whereas a *petition* was a formal request seeking redress for injuries. Just how the Congress defined a *memorial* is uncertain, but the term later proved to have an objectionable connotation to members of the House of Lords. In the diplomatic language of the day, a *memorial* was a state paper presented by one government to another, usually through an ambassador, embodying a statement of facts. It also had the meaning of a document containing instructions relating to some matter under negotiation, delivered by a minister of foreign affairs to one of his own diplomatic agents. This subject is discussed further in chapter 5. (In the present text, for simplicity, I sometimes use the word *petition* to refer to any of the three documents.)

Although most of the delegates agreed that three separate instruments should be prepared, Gadsden, Rutledge, and Lynch all took exception, maintaining that an address to the King was all that was necessary. The Southerners reminded the Congress that the King, not Parliament, was their monarch, and that all authority in colonal matters sprang from the Crown. They further argued that the colonies held no political rights either from the House of Commons or the House of Lords, a technicality that caused further debate. Gadsden also insisted that petitioning Parliament was a waste of time, for had not the House of Commons flatly refused to hear the earlier resolves submitted by a number of colonies?

The majority of the other delegates felt that to ignore Parliament would be an unnecessary affront to the body that had enacted the objectionable tax legislation, and the Southerners were voted down. Having expressed their opinions as convincingly as they could, they finally consented to compromise and go along with the majority.[52] Throughout the long discussions in the Congress other compromises had been made, and no doubt many of the delegates were influenced to change opinions they had held when they heard opposing ideas expressed and debated pro and con.

The committee named to prepare the document addressed to the King consisted of Robert R. Livingston, Johnson, and Murdock. This committee, and the other committees, were evidently not appointed by Chairman Ruggles, but according to the Journal were selected "Upon Motion Voted." This seems to mean that the delegates had a voice in the selection of the committees, but unfortunately the Journal does not clarify either how the members were nominated or the nature of the balloting.

The committee assigned to prepare the memorial to the House of Lords consisted of Rutledge, Tilghman, and Philip Livingston.

The committee assigned to prepare the petition to the House of Commons was composed of Lynch, Otis, and McKean.

Members of these three important committees represented six of the colonies, with two committeemen from New York, two from Maryland, two from South Carolina, one from Connecticut, one from Massachusetts, and one from the Lower Counties. Three of the colonies, New Jersey, Rhode Island, and Pennsylvania, were not represented on any of the three committees, although this probably has no significance.

The committees were requested to submit their reports on the following Monday, October 21 at 12:00 o'clock, and there can be little question that they spent Sunday working on their respective assignments. No minutes of these committee meetings were kept, but by Monday morning each committee had finished its assignment.

When the Congress reconvened on Monday, the members first took up the address to the King. Robert R. Livingston has been credited with having prepared the first draft.[53] The Johnson Papers in the Library of Congress contain no less than four corrected drafts of the address in Johnson's hand, which indicates that he took an active part in its composition. In his *Diary* (see Appendix), Johnson indicates that he spent all day Sunday October 20, at the home of Robert R. Livingston, and they may have worked together on the draft. Perhaps Murdock, the third member of the committee, was also present.

Although Dickinson was not a member of this committee (nor of the other two), the aforementioned John Dickinson Papers contain a printed copy of the address to the King as it was published some months later in the *Pennsylvania Gazette*. The clipping bears a note made with pen and ink in an unknown hand stating that Dickinson "drew up the resolves [Declaration of Rights], and the petition to the Crown, which was altered, particularly in the title and middle of it, after he left the Congress." (Dickinson was summoned home on urgent business, and he returned to Philadelphia before the debates were concluded.) The published petition contains longhand corrections made by Dickinson, presumably to make it conform to an original draft and to show wherein the Congress had altered the text.[54] This seem to be very frail evidence, especially since Dickinson himself makes no reference in his political writings to having been the author.

The Journal of the Congress states that the address to the King was read first, and approved after the members made the minor amendments. The memorial to the House of Lords was next read, amended, and approved. Which member of the committee was responsible for preparing the original draft is not known, although Rutledge may have been the author. Finally, the petition to the House of Commons, probably drafted by Otis, was read, several amendments made, and it, too, was approved.[55] The Congress then voted that all three documents should be engrossed, which meant copying them formally in a fine hand.

The next day, Tuesday, October 22, the Congress met at 9:00 A.M. and, following the practice of most Colonial Assemblies before bills were passed, read the engrossed copies for the second time. After some debate the address to the King and the memorial to the House of Lords were formally accepted but, evidently due to the lateness of the hour, time did not permit a rereading of the petition to Commons. The Congress adjourned after deciding to reconvene at 9:00 A.M. the following day, Wednesday, October 23. The members met on Wednesday as scheduled, and the engrossed copy of the petition was read and accepted.

Whereas the Declaration of Rights was written to influence public opinion in the colonies, the three petitions, conciliatory in tone, were intended to provoke sympathetic action in Parliament and to win the support of the King. The flattering address to George III briefly recounted that the colonies were planted by subjects of the British Crown who were animated with the spirit of liberty, and implored the monarch to allow them to continue to receive the liberties they had formerly enjoyed under the British constitution. Among these liberties were those of taxing themselves, and enjoying trial by jury of their peers.

The memorial to the House of Lords reiterated that the colonists were entitled to the inherent rights and liberties of the natives of Great Britain, and the Lords were entreated to restore these rights, which were being denied them. The rights included trial by jury, and taxation by a legislature in which they were represented. The memorial went on to say that the authors had the warmest sentiments of filial affection for the mother country, but they found the restrictions on trade resulting from the recent acts of Parliament detrimental to the colonies and their commerce with Great Britain. The memorial specifically acknowledged "due Subordination to that August Body the British Parliament."

The petition to the House of Commons was lengthier than the other two documents and incorporated strong economic arguments that had been advanced by the merchant delegates. It again emphasized that specie was scarce, which made it difficult for the colonial merchants to pay their debts to British manufacturers. It discussed trade relations between Great Britain and the colonies, and how the mother country had prospered by selling manufactured goods in America. The petition also repeated the several legal premises expressed in the other two petitions: how the colonies derived their civil and religious rights and liberties from the English constitution; why the punitive taxes should be repealed; and how their continuance would be injurious to Great Britain's commercial interests.

The petition stated that the statutes extending the jurisdiction of the Vice-Admiralty Courts should be repealed and that the newly erected Vice-Admiralty Court at Halifax would cause "immense expense" to colonial litigants. In the third paragraph, the authors again emphasized that the colonies owed "due subordination" to Parliament, and the next-to-last paragraph stipulated that "Subordination to Parliament is universally acknowledged."

All three instruments stated that they originated with the "Freeholders and other Inhabitants" of the respective colonies. The meaning is clear that the delegates considered themselves not only as agents for the Assemblies that had sent them to the Congress, but as representatives and spokesmen for the general population of the colonies. The full texts of the three petitions are given in the Journal (chap. 4, below), and are worthy of careful study.

The delegates met again at 10:00 A.M. Thursday, October 24, for the express purpose of deciding on the proper method to bring the petitions to the attention of the King and Parliament. Since the Stamp Act Congress was a sort of *ad hoc* committee, it had no political indentity and thus lacked formal channels of communication with the mother country. It was decided that all the members present should sign the three documents, and then deliver them to their respective

Assemblies with the recommendation that each colony should employ a special agent (or utilize one of the existing agents in London) to deliver the petitions.

The members also unanimously voted that the clerk, John Cotton, should transcribe copies of the Journal, supplying a copy to each of the nine participating delegations, and one to each of the four absentee colonies. It was also ordered that Cotton should affix his signature to all of the copies.[56] The Journal included the text of the Declaration of Rights, as well as the address to the King, and the memorial and petition to Parliament. Although the three signed petitions would be sent separately to England by each Assembly, each would also have a copy of the Journal containing the text of the petitions. Everything seemed to be going smoothly up to this point, when a series of unexpected developments threw the Congress into turmoil and upset the well-laid plans.

The five delegates constituting New York's Committee of Correspondence reminded the chairman that since they had not been appointed by their Assembly to attend the Congress, they were not authorized to sign the documents without the approval of the Assembly.

The Connecticut delegates also said that their instructions from their Assembly prohibited their signing any documents until the matter had been discussed and approved in the Assembly following their return from New York.

The members of the South Carolina delegation also stated that they were similarly obligated by their instructions, which had previously been read to the Congress, to report back to their Assembly, the members of which would make the decision whether or not to sign the petitions.

That left only six colonies whose delegates were authorized to sign, or felt qualified to do so, without further instructions from their Assemblies: Massachusetts, Maryland, New Jersey, Pennsylvania, Rhode Island, and the Three Lower Counties. This was probably disappointing to Massachusetts, because the intent from the beginning was to prepare documents in the Congress that all the delegates were willing to sign and forward to England without delay. Since the approbation of six colonies, although not a majority of the thirteen, was better than none, the Congress decided that the sixteen delegates representing these colonies should sign the documents. This triggered an argument that soon became very heated. Sharp words passed among the Massachusetts and New Jersey delegations, because Ruggles and Ogden suddenly expressed an unwillingness to sign. Ruggles then made a motion that *none* of the delegates should sign the petitions, and that the documents should be taken back to their respective Assemblies for adoption. This was an unusual motion, since the Massachusetts Assembly had empowered Ruggles and his associates to sign any petitions drawn up at the Congress. Otis responded to Ruggles's motion by stating that his motion would defeat the whole purpose of the Congress, which had met to take concerted action.[57]

It would seem that at the last minute Ruggles was doing his utmost to prevent approval of the petitions. On his return to Boston he was called before the Lower House to explain his actions. This is what he said:

First, my Instructions from this Honourable House conceived in the following words, viz., "It is the expectation of the House that a most loyal and dutiful Address to his Majesty and his Parliament will be prepared by the Congress praying as well for the removal of the grievances the Colonies labour under at present, as for the preventing others for the future, which Petitions if drawn up as far as you shall be able to judge, agreeable to the Mind of this House, you are empowered to sign and forward."

The Petition agreed on by the Congress to be presented to His Majesty, not being conceived in Terms clearly enough expressive of that Duty and Loyalty which are due to the best of Sovereigns, and consequently not agreeable to my above Instructions from this House, left as a mere Matter of Judgment and Discretion, if I had signed it, I must have acted in direct opposition to those Instructions, and thereby have exposed myself not only to the Censures of this House, but to the Reproaches of my own Conscience, a Tribunal more awful to me than this (however great) by which I have been condemned.

Continuing to rationalize his behavior, Ruggles said he also felt that it would have been more regular and constitutional for the three petitions to be authenticated by the colonial Assemblies and signed by their respective Speakers. He also said it was not truly a "general Congress" because representatives of three of the colonies present were not empowered to sign for their Assemblies, and four colonies were not represented at all. Last, he admitted that he could not accept the premise that the colonies had the exclusive right of self-taxation as expressed in the documents![58]

These arguments—especially his opposition to self-taxation—have a strange sound coming from the chairman of the Congress, who had presided without protest during the long discussions challenging Parliament's right to tax the colonies. If he had had such substantial differences in political philosophy from the other delegates, why did he not resign his seat and return to Boston when he heard the trend of the discussions?

Robert Ogden of the New Jersey delegation gave a different reason for not signing the petitions. When he appeared before the New Jersey Assembly at Burlington on his return from New York, he said he refused to sign because he believed that separate petitions originating with each colony and submitted to Parliament would have greater probability of achieving the desired results.[59] This too was a peculiar position, since the individual colonial petitions protesting enactment of the Stamp Act had been ignored by Parliament, and in Dickinson's words were "treated with contempt."[60] Ogden also added that since the other two New Jersey delegates were willing to sign, their signatures would, in effect, indicate that New Jersey endorsed the documents. The omission of his signature (since he was the Speaker of the House) would leave open to the Assembly the option of directing a separate petition to the Crown if the members so decided. This too was a tenuous argument, because he knew that the Assemblies of Rhode Island, Pennsylvania, and Maryland had drawn up separate resolves immediately prior to the convening of the Congress. The omission of his signature on the petitions approved by the Congress had nothing to do with New Jersey's preparing its own resolves. In fact, the New Jersey Assembly did prepare them on November 30, 1765.[61]

Ogden may have been concealing the real reasons for not signing, which he was unwilling to admit. Perhaps he and Ruggles sensed the beginning of a rupture with the mother country, and, in good conscience, they were opposed. Their refusal to sign was an unhappy note in the Congress and occasioned "a long and warm debate upon which it was determined by a vote, that the Address to his Majesty, which was at that time in a fair draught, together with those of the Lords and Commons should be laid on the table until the next morning [i.e., Friday, October 25] in the form they had passed before the Congress and entered upon the journal, to be signed by such of the members as thought proper."[62]

Dyer of Connecticut took the floor at this point to share his views with the other delegates. "Union is so necessary, disunion so fatal in these matters," he said, " that, as we cannot agree upon any alteration, they ought to be signed as they are by those who are authorized to do so."[63]

During the debate on the question of signing the petitions, McKean became embroiled in an argument with Ruggles, and he evidently lost his temper, exhibiting an explosiveness that characterized some of his later political encounters. In recounting the incident, McKean said he pressed Ruggles to give his reasons for not signing the petitions. Ruggles, more than twenty years McKean's senior, with much broader legal experience, resented being cross-examined by the younger lawyer, and replied that he did not feel it necessary to explain his refusal. McKean persisted by saying that the dele-

Reproduced from a gouache portrait believed to be by Rembrandt Peale, of Thomas McKean (1734–1817), a delegate from the Lower Counties to the Stamp Act Congress, and to the First and Second Continental Congresses, and a signer of the Declaration of Independence. He was a member of the committee to inspect the minutes at the Stamp Act Congress and also a member of the committee to prepare the petition to the House of Commons. COURTESY HISTORICAL SOCIETY OF DELAWARE.

In his later years Thomas McKean continued his activities in colonial politics serving as Acting President (Governor) of Delaware, Governor of Pennsylvania, and Chief Justice of Pennsylvania. This engraving by T. B. Welch from a painting by Gilbert Stuart shows McKean at age 68 wearing the medal of the Society of the Cincinnati. COURTESY NEW YORK PUBLIC LIBRARY, EMMET COLLECTION, NO. 210, MANUSCRIPTS AND ARCHIVES DIVISION, ASTOR, LENOX AND TILDEN FOUNDATIONS.

gates had all come together in good faith to obtain repeal of the unconstitutional and oppressive acts of Parliament, "and as unanimity & sociability had hitherto prevailed among them, it appeared to him strange to find anyone decline to sign his name to what he had at least apparently approved without any excuse or observation on the occasion; that if there was anything treasonable, offensive or indecent in their proceedings, he thought it an act of comity, nay of duty, to inform his brethren of it; some others spoke briefly to the same purpose."[64]

After a considerable pause to digest these remarks, Ruggles gave McKean a short answer by saying that it was against his conscience to sign the petitions. This arbitrary reply irritated McKean as much as the older man's refusal to sign, and he gave him a tongue-lashing before the entire company. Ruggles, who was taller than six feet, rose to his full height, and challenged McKean to a duel. "Young man," he said, "you shall hear from me tomorrow." To which McKean, as he later told the story, replied that he would not only be available the next morning to give Ruggles pleasure, but would wait in New York for ten days, if necessary, to oblige him.[65] The duel did not take place, nor did Ruggles sign the three petitions. He left New York early the next morning before daylight and headed for Boston.

After his return home, Ruggles was reprimanded by the Speaker of the Massachusetts House of Representatives in the presence of the members for his conduct in not signing the petitions, and for leaving New York before the Congress officially adjourned.[66] He asked permission to prepare a written defense, which he read before the House, but the members refused his request to allow it to be published in their journal. Although he was subject to criticism, Ruggles was not dismissed from the House, and he continuel to retain membership on the committees to which he had been appointed. He remained firm in British interests, and when the Revolution broke out he joined General Howe in New York

Photo of a lost portrait by an unknown artist of Timothy Ruggles (1711–1795), a delegate from Massachusetts who presided at the Stamp Act Congress. Ruggles challenged Thomas McKean to a duel in a dramatic moment while the Congress was in session. Ruggles was a Loyalist and during the Revolution fled to Nova Scotia. COURTESY LIBRARY OF CONGRESS.

and commanded a company of Loyalists. His property, along with that of other Tories, was confiscated, and after the war he went to Nova Scotia, where England gave asylum to many of those who were loyal to the mother country. He died there in 1795 at the age of 84.[67]

McKean never forgot his confrontation with Ruggles, and in 1774, at the First Continental Congress, he told John Adams the whole story while they were sipping claret in Philadelphia's City Tavern, where the representatives socialized. Adams made note of the incident in his diary and referred to Ruggles's conduct at the New York Congress as "dishonourable."[68] Almost forty years later, McKean then aged 78, rehashed the same story in a letter he wrote to Adams on August 20, 1813, evidently forgetting that he had told it to him before. He added an additional point of information in his letter; he said that after the Stamp Act Congress adjourned, Otis told him that he had suspected Ruggles's sincerity throughout the meeting when he was giving the others the impression of being fully and heartily in agreement with the decisions that were made.[69]

Robert Ogden, aware that his refusal to sign the petitions would result in his being censured by his constituents, requested his colleague, Joseph Borden (McKean's father-in-law), not to mention it when they returned home. He also asked McKean not to talk about his refusal to sign the petitions when he rode through New Jersey enroute to New Castle. After McKean and Borden both did their best, without success, to persuade Ogden to sign, McKean said he would remain silent only if no questions were put directly to him. As he passed through New Jersey on his way home, McKean was asked about the Congress and for the names of those who would not sign the petitions, and he had no hesitancy in naming Ogden.[70] As a result, McKean heard rumors that he was going to be threatened with a second duel, although Ogden never openly challenged him.

Ogden left New York before the Congress adjourned, and the *Boston Post Boy* in its April 21, 1766, edition reported that both Ruggles and Ogden "for reasons best known to themselves, if they had any, refused to sign and abruptly left the Congress before the Business was completed." Ogden was burned in effigy in many towns in New Jersey for his actions in the Congress, and on November 28, 1765, was rebuked in an official session of the Assembly. He felt compelled not only to resign as Speaker, but to give up his seat in the House. Some historians have concluded that he was requested to resign, which is incorrect, because it was a voluntary act on his part. In fact, the session in which he attempted to explain his actions and then submitted his resignation, was called by Governor Franklin at Ogden's request.[71]

Ogden seems to have been misunderstood, despite his plea to the Assembly that "I trust that Providence will, in due time, make the rectitude of my inviolable affection to my country appear in a fair light to the world, and that my sole aim was the happiness of New Jersey." Following his resignation he resumed his private business in New Jersey, and in 1776 became Chairman of the Elizabethtown Committee of Safety. Two of his sons were officers in New Jersey regiments during the Revolution, and as a patriot, Ogden supported the colonial cause.[72]

The Stamp Act Congress met for the last time at 9:00 on the morning of October 25, the fifth anniversary of the accession of George III, and "broke up" at 3:00 P.M. It is not known who, if anyone, presided in Ruggles's absence, but thirteen delegates from six colonies affixed their signatures to the petitions and then prepared for their departures from New York. The signatories were Otis and Partridge for Massachusetts; Ward and Bowler for Rhode Island; Fisher and Borden for New Jersey; Morton and Bryan for Pennsylvania; Rodney and McKean for the Lower Counties;

and Tilghman, Murdock, and Ringgold for Maryland. John
Dickinson, who had been summoned back to Philadelphia on
important business, was not present to sign. However, "there
was no doubt in the Minds of any but he was a sincere friend
to his Country."[73]

Those delegates whose Assemblies were still in session
were eager to return home to make their reports before
adjournment. The South Carolina representatives were informed by a messenger that their Assembly would convene
on October 28. After discussion they decided that Gadsden
should take advantage of an opportunity to return to Charleston on a small schooner anchored in New York harbor, where
there was a berth for one additional passenger. He took with
him a copy of the Declaration of Rights, the Journal, and
three signed petitions. As a result of poor navigation the
vessel did not reach the Charleston harbor until November
13. The return trip took a week longer than the voyage from
Charleston to New York. Meanwhile, Rutledge and Lynch,
who went overland from New York to Charleston via Philadelphia, a trip of 850 miles, arrived home forty-eight hours
after Gadsden debarked.[74]

It is uncertain how many copies of the three petitions
were signed on the morning of October 25, but it was a
chore if thirteen copies were engrossed, because each signatory had to sign his name thirty-nine times When Rodney
and McKean made their report to the Assembly of the Lower
Counties they stated that only nine engrossed copies were
signed by deputies from six colonies. They said one set was
forwarded to London, and sets sent to the four absent colonies, New Hampshire, Georgia, Virginia, and North Carolina, and also supplied to the nonsigning delegations, Connecticut, New York, and South Carolina.[75] If only nine copies
were made, the inference to be drawn is that Cotton did not
have sufficient time to have copies made for all the colonies.
But when Bryan and Morton reported to the Pennsylvania

Assembly on their return from New York, they stated that engrossed and signed copies were transmitted to England, and that similar copies were given to each delegation to lay before their respective Assemblies.[76]

The record is clear that after the signatories had affixed their names, Otis and Partridge decided to send copies immediately to Richard Jackson, the Massachusetts agent in London, for presentation to King and Parliament. There were two vessels scheduled to leave New York harbor during the week of October 28, one of which was the *Edward,* which had brought the stamped paper to New York. One set of petitions was carried by each vessel as a safety measure in the event of the loss of one of the ships.[77]

Thirteen copies of the Declaration of Rights were also engrossed, one copy for each of the colonial Assemblies, although these did not require the signatures of the delegates.[78] There is no evidence that a copy of the Declaration, intended for home consumption, was sent to England.

It seems evident that Cotton must have found it necessary to employ penmen in order to prepare thirteen copies of the *complete* Journal, as the Congress ordered him to do on October 24. It was too arduous a task for one man to undertake, working by candlelight at night and attending the Congress by day. Due to the limited time, Cotton and his scribes were able to complete only nine copies of the Journal before the Congress adjourned. Consequently, on the last day of the Congress, the delegates resolved that when the Massachusetts delegation returned home they should have an extra copy transcribed and delivered to the New Hampshire Assembly; the Maryland delegates were commissioned to make a copy for Virginia; and the representatives from South Carolina to have copies made for Georgia and North Carolina.[79] I have taken pains to clarify what may appear to be unimportant details regarding these instruments, because most authors of history textbooks have not been aware that the three petitions, the Declaration of Rights, and the Journal were all separate documents, but the three petitions and the Declaration were also duplicated in the Journal.

John Watts, in a letter written to General Monckton from New York on October 26, the day after the Congress adjourned, said, "The Congress is broke up, their transactions not publickly known, as decency forbids they should. How their addresses will be received [in England] you are the best judge. I take their resolves to be pretty much upon the Philadelphia plan with some elucidations. I mean the resolves of that colony."[80]

Watts meant by his use of the word *decency* that it would have been improper for the delegates to release the texts of the petitions for publication until the documents had first been received in London and considered by King and Parliament. The "Philadelphia plan" meant the Pennsylvania Resolves, to which previous reference has been made, although the Declaration of Rights was by no means an imitation of the Pennsylvania document even though it incorporated some of the same protests. The Declaration was a distinctive document that one author has termed "the first American state paper that can claim the slightest element of nationality."[81]

The Congress adjourned, its discussions still veiled in secrecy. This is shown in a letter that John Rodney, a half cousin of Caesar Rodney, wrote to Caesar, December 3, 1765, two months after the adjournment. He was curious to know more "of that most Important Congress, in whose hands we have as it were Intrusted our Liberties. I do not know that Ever was I so desirous of seeing anything of a publick Nature as I have been to see the Petition and Memorial to the King and both houses of Parliament, but have little hopes of seeing it now 'till the same is made publick. . . ."[82]

Of course, all eighteen members of the Assembly of the Lower Counties had listened to the reading of the petitions when Rodney and McKean returned from New York, and the Assembly was in possession of a copy of the Journal.[83] The Assemblies in the other colonies were also familiar with the contents of the Declaration and the petitions, although every effort seems to have been made not to reveal their contents prematurely. The Rhode Island House of Representatives, for example, turned all the documents over to Secretary Henry Ward for safekeeping, and resolved that no copies should be released until the Assembly was informed that King and Parliament had received their signed copies.[84]

Alert newspaper publishers were fully aware that the Congress had adjourned after writing a Declaration and three petitions, but they exercised restraint, not trying to print the contents of the documents, A number of colonial newspapers reprinted the small paragraph that appeared in the New York papers to the effect that the Congress had adjourned, but they gave no further details. On November 4, 1765, the *Boston Evening Post* reported that the action of the Congress had been approved by the Massachusetts House of Representatives, and that petitions had been sent by the House to the King, the House of Lords, and the House of Commons, "setting forth a final Declaration of the Rights of the Colonists and a Representation of the Grievances they labour under." But no information relative to the contents of the Declaration or the petitions was disclosed.

Not until March 24, 1766—five months after the Stamp Act Congress had adjourned—did the *Boston Post Boy* carry a complete transcript of the Declaration of Rights, which it reprinted as an "extraordinary" item lifted from the most recent edition of the Providence *Gazette*. The Declaration was preceded by a line that said, "The following is said to be a copy of the Resolutions of the Congress Held at New York." Thereafter many other colonial newspapers reprinted the Declaration.

The contents of the three petitions drawn up at the Stamp Act Congress remained undisclosed to the American colonists until the *Boston Post Boy*, at long last, reprinted the petitions in its April 21, 1766, edition. Other colonial newspapers promptly copied the texts of the petitions for their readers. This was almost a month after Parliament had repealed the Stamp Act. Colonial readers naturally associated the repeal with the petitions and concluded that Parliament must have been swayed by the actions taken in the Stamp Act Congress. That was not the case; the petitions drawn up by the delegates at New York after their lengthy discussions had little to do with Parliament's decision to repeal the Stamp Act.

NOTES TO CHAPTER 3

1. I. N. P. Stokes, *The Iconography of Manhattan Island* (New York, 1915), 4: 751. See *ibid.*, vol. 3, plate 4, for a drawing by Du Simitière that shows how the building appeared in 1765; note description, p. 863. The structure was situated on the northeast corner of Broad and Wall Streets, where the Federal Hall National Memorial now stands. I have failed to find in either contemporary newspapers or letters written by the delegates a specific statement that the City Hall was the site of the Congress, but several earlier works indicate that it was the meeting place: William C. Bryant and Sydney H. Gray, *A Popular History of the U.S.* (New York, 1879), 3: 341; Richard Frothingham, *Rise of the Republic* (Boston, 1886), p. 184; James Grant Wilson, *Memorial History of the City of New York . . .* (New York, 1892), 2: 355; and *Scribner's Popular History of the United States* (New York. 1897), 3: 340.
2. *Dickinson*, pp. 22, 27.
3. Livingston Papers, Bancroft Transcripts, New York Public Library, letter dated December 20, 1765. Opposition was organized not to overturn the government, "but to prevent isolated exertions of unlawful power." Pauline Maier, *From Resistance to Revolution* (New York, 1972), p. 38.
4. Letter from Johnson to Dickinson, May 24, 1766, R. R. Logan Manuscript Collection, John Dickinson Papers, 1756-1769, Historical Society of Pennsylvania.
5. Richard Walsh, *The Writings of Christopher Gadsden* (Columbia, S.C., 1966), p. 68.

6. R. R. Logan Collection, letter dated June 22, 1766.
7. *Letter to and From Caesar Rodney*, p. 26. It is curious that Rodney makes no reference to Kollock in his letters. Various sources indicate that 28 delegates attended the Congress, e.g., *Scribner's Popular History*, 3: 340, Malcolm Decker, *Brink of Revolution* (New York, 1964), p. 47. This is erroneous because Kollock was not present at any of the formal sessions.
8. *Mass. Hist. Colls.*, 10: 580. Cf. *Letter Book of John Watts, 1762–1765*, New York Historical Society Collections (1928), 61: 393.
9. *The Correspondence of Major General Thomas Gage*, ed. Clarence Edwin Carter (New Haven, Conn., 1931), 1: 69–70.
10. When he was enroute to Philadelphia to attend the First Continental Congress, John Adams referred to a number of these taverns. *Adams Diary*, 1: 102–6.
11. R. R. Logan Collection. Richard H. Barry, *Mr. Rutledge of South Carolina* (New York, 1942), says that Gadsden went to a boarding house but that Lynch and Rutledge had rooms at the King's Arms, and the latter's room adjoined Ruggles's (pp. 103, 111). Regrettably, the author does not adequately document these details, and it is difficult to separate fact from fiction in his book.
12. Bancroft Transcripts, New York Public Library, letter dated October 19, 1765.
13. *NYCD*, 7: 760.
14. Stokes, *Iconography*, 4: 750–52, cites a number of these newspaper references.
15. *A Collection of Papers Relating to the Dispute between Great Britain and America, 1764–1775*, ed. John Almon (New York, 1971, reprint of London 1777 ed.), p. 25. General Gage entertained Ruggles, Otis, and Partridge at dinner; see John Richard Alden, *General Gage in America* (Baton Rouge, La., 1948), p. 117.
16. *The Montresor Journals*, ed. G. D. Scull (New York, 1882), 14: 336, 345–46. See also F. L. Engelman, "Cadwallader Colden and the New York Stamp Riots," *William and Mary Quarterly*, 3d s. 10 (1953): 560–79; see *Boston Evening Post*, November 4, 1765, for account of the arrival of the *Edward* in New York.
17. *Engelman*, p. 566. See also *The Letters and Papers of Cadwallader Colden, 1765–1775* (New York, 1923), 7: 56–57.
18. From a manuscript in the Henry E. Huntington Library and Art Gallery, San Marino, California, entitled "Proceedings of

the House of Representatives," H.M. no. 1947, pp. 23–24. Permission to quote the excerpt is gratefully acknowledged. Cf. the document quoted by *Pitkin*, 1: 455–56. It would seem likely that the Commissioners for Trade and Plantations had notice of the Congress before October. On August 2, 1765, Governor Sharpe of Maryland sent a colonial newspaper reporting the forthcoming Congress to Cecil Calvert in England. Officialdom in England was kept posted on colonial developments by numerous informants; for example, on July 11, 1765, Sharpe sent Lord Baltimore a copy of the Virginia Resolves, *Maryland Archives* (Baltimore, Md., 1895), 14: 212, 210.

19. Lawrence Henry Gipson, *The Coming of the Revolution, 1763–1775* (New York, 1954), p. 89.

20. Frothingham, p. 184, suggests that this earlier meeting was held, but he failed to document the information. The October 3 edition of the *New York Post Boy* states, "We hear they have already begun their Conferences, etc." This refers to the informal session held on September 30. A second informal session was also held on October 4, according to William Samuel Johnson, who said he went at 10:00 A.M. to the Congress, where he was introduced to the delegates present, but no official business was conducted. See his Diary in Appendix below.

21. Watts Letter Book, *Mass. Hist. Colls.* Note that Johnson indicates in his Diary that he dined at John Watts's on Thursday, October 24, and no doubt some of the other delegates were present. During these social periods, Watts was able to gather tidbits about the happenings in the Congress.

22. *Adams Works*, 10: 60.

23. *Ibid.*, p. 184. Adams later referred to Otis, Samuel Adams, and John Hancock as the "principal agents of the Revolution." *Old South Leaflets*, no. 179 (Boston, 1907).

24. *Pitkin* 1: 136n.

25. *The Great Historical Sale, The Papers of Caesar Rodney of Del., Thomas Rodney of Del., and Caesar Rodney of Del.*, Catalog no. 1236, Stan V. Henkels, 1304 Walnut St., Philadelphia, June 13, 1919, p. 74. The Delaware Historical Society has a copy of this catalogue, which was first called to my attention by Ruthanna Hindes.

26. *Mass. Journals*, 42: 273. Cotton was paid £26, 4 shillings on February 18, 1766, "as a full Recompence for the Proportion of this Province for his Expenses and Services, as Clerk to

the Committee of the Congress held at New York." *Ibid.*, p. 290. The New Hampshire Assembly on July 11, 1766, contributed £15 to his salary, *N.H. Recs.*, 7: 113. Otis also requested both the Maryland and Georgia Assemblies to contribute. *Maryland Archives*, 61: 29–30; *The Colonial Records of Georgia*, 14: 300–301. Other colonies may also have shared this expense.

27. Coleman's manuscript biography of McKean, citing McKean's letter to Timothy Pickering, January 13, 1804. This precedent of "one colony—one vote" was also followed in the First Continental Congress, although Patrick Henry objected to it. See Edmund Cody Burnett, *The Continental Congress* (New York, 1941), p. 36.

28. *Letters to and from Caesar Rodney*, p. 25.

29. *Ibid.*, pp. 25–26.

30. *Minutes Lower Counties*, pp. 39–40.

31. *Dickinson*, p. 327.

32. *Ibid.*, p. 312.

33. *Ibid.*, p. 331n.

34. Bancroft Transcripts, New York Public Library, letter dated November 2, 1765.

35. *Proceedings*, Massachusetts Historical Society (Boston, 1916), 9: 452–53.

36. *The Political Writings of John Dickinson, Esq.*, ed. John Dickinson (Wilmington, Del., 1801), 1: 93.

37. George Bancroft, *History of the United States of America* (New York, 1886), 3: 153. Bernard Bailyn, *The Ideological Origins of the American Revolution* (Cambridge, Mass., 1967), p. 101, believes that the deeper implication of the Stamp Act was that it was part of the power struggle to force the colonists into a state of feudalism.

38. Bernard Papers, Manuscript, 4: 72, Houghton Library, Harvard University, letter of September 28, 1765, Bernard to Ruggles.

39. *Prologue*, p. 48.

40. *Three Charters of the Virginia Company of London*, Virginia 350th Anniversary Celebration (Williamsburg, Va., 1957), p. 9.

41. From his letter to Garth in *Gibbes*, 1: 8. The same letter with a postscript on the copy he sent to Wiliam Samuel Johnson is given in *The Writings of Christopher Gadsden, 1746–1805*, ed. Richard Walsh (Columbia, N.C., 1966), pp. 65–68.

42. *Dickinson*, pp. 261–62, 357.

43. *Adams Works,* 10 : 61.
44. *Minutes of the Common Council of the City of New York, 1676–1776* (New York, 1905), 6 : 433–34. It is curious that these minutes do not contain any reference to the Stamp Act Congress, which Mayor Cruger was attending.
45. Bancroft Transcripts, New York Public Library, letter dated October 19, 1765.
46. *Gibbes,* 1 : 8–9.
47. A transcript of the report is given in *Pitkin,* 1 : 448–55.
48. R. R. Logan Collection. Dickinson's two earlier drafts, formerly in the collections of the Library Company of Philadelphia (sometimes referred to as the Public Library of Philadelphia), are now also in the custody of the Historical Society of Pennsylvania. Dickinson himself makes reference to the "original draft." *Dickinson's Political Writings,* 1 : 178n. See also David L. Jacobson, *John Dickinson and the Revolution in Pennsylvania, 1764–1776,* University of California Publications in History 78 (1965) : 33–34.
49. Paul Leicester Ford published Dickinson's draft and the final Declaration alongside each other to permit comparisons, *Dickinson,* pp. 183–87. Cf. *Gipson,* 1961, 10 : 330; *Crisis,* p. 108. Ford, however, seems to have overlooked the notation on the document indicating that it was "the original Draft." Ford errs in saying that the Declaration was first published in Almon's 1967 pamphlet; see chapter 4 below.
50. I am aware that other writers have referred to the arguments advanced by some of the delegates, e.g., Frothingham (1886), p. 188; Bancroft (1886), 3 : 150, *Crisis,* pp. 107–12, etc. However, in my synthesis I have gone into greater detail to put the arguments in context.
51. A note in the Chatham Papers, *The English Historical Review* 22 (1907) : 756–58, indicates that a plan had been discussed in England to give the colonies representation in Parliament. even to the extent of enumerating the number of representatives each colony would be permitted.
52. *Gibbes,* 1 : 9.
53. *Journal of the First Congress . . . ,* p. iv. *Pitkin,* 1 : 183n, says it is believed to have been drawn up principally by Johnson.
54. *Dickinson,* pp. 191–96. Groce, *William Samuel Johnson,* p. 58 n23, says that it was more likely that Dickinson prepared the draft than Johnson, who was on the committee, but his only evidence is the clipping in the Dickinson Papers.
55. Tudor, *Life of Otis,* p. 226, is in error in stating that the

Congress did not accept the petition to the House of Commons until October 22.

56. *Gipson, 1961,* 10: 330, intimates that none of the delegates would sign the proceedings and that Cotton was the only one who affixed his name. This is a misinterpretation; the Journal, like any other set of minutes, required only the secretary's signature to attest to its accuracy.

57. *Adams Works,* 2: 180.

58. The *Pennsylvania Gazette,* May 15, 1766, contains his full speech; see also *ibid.,* Feb. 27.

59. *NJCD,* 24: 681.

60. *Dickinson,* p. 475.

61. A transcript appears in *Prologue,* pp. 59–60.

62. *Pennsylvania Gazette. Prologue,* p. 45, gives October 24 as the day of adjournment, which is incorrect.

63. Bancroft, *History,* 3: 155. Bancroft does not document the source, but the quotation occurs in a letter from Dyer to William Samuel Johnson, December 8, 1765, Connecticut Papers, 1759–1776, Bancroft Transcripts, pp. 87–93.

64. Thomas McKean, "Autobiographical Sketch," Manuscript Collections, Historical Society of Pennsylvania, p. 8. I am indebted to Professor G. S. Rowe for first bringing this manuscript to my attention.

65. McKean "Autobiographical Sketch," p. 8.

66. *Mass. Journals,* 42: 227, 254, 271–72, 294 (see William Gordon, *History,* p. 174, who says that Otis was also on the verge of leaving without signing the documents, but Thomas Lynch dissuaded him from doing so. Why Otis would act this way remains a mystery, if the story is correct.)

67. Henry Stoddard Ruggles, *General Timothy Ruggles* (n.p., 1897), says the General was given 10,000 acres in Nova Scotia; see also Clifford K. Shipton, *Sibley's Harvard Graduates* (Boston, 1960), 9: 199–222.

68. *Adams Diary,* 2: 115.

69. *Adams Works,* 10: 61.

70. McKean, "Autobiographical Sketch," pp. 8–9. Cf. *Adams Works,* 10: 60–61.

71. *NJCD,* 24: 681–82. The incident is related by G. S. Rowe, "Thomas McKean and the Coming of the Revolution," *Pennsylvania Magazine of History and Biography* 96 (1972): 3–47. Evidently some effort was later made to excuse Ogden for his conduct, and to present the Stamp Act Congress in an unfavorable light, although nothing came of it. See Rev.

Charles Inglis, letter of December 26, 1765, in "Rodney Letters," ed. Leon de Valinger, Jr., *Delaware History*, 3 (1948) : 111.
72. Halsey, *Descendants of Robert Ogden*. Halsey defends Ogden and introduces evidence that Ogden was in favor of the Congress and urged acceptance of the invitation, but the members refused. *Ibid.*, p. 5.
73. *Boston Post Boy*, April 21, 1766; *Pennsylvania Archives*, 8th s. 7 : 580. The three petitions and the names of the signatories were published in *Boston Post Boy*, April 21, 1766.
74. *Gibbes*, 1 : 7. Barry, *Mr. Rutledge of South Carolina*, pp. 117 and 103, errs in stating that the three delegates returned by vessel, and he gives the wrong date for their arrival in New York.
75. *Minutes Lower Counties*, p. 39. In a letter that he wrote to a certain Mr. Wilmer in December 1765, Caesar Rodney refers to the documents drawn up at the Congress and states that *seven* copies were made of each of the petitions, which is an obvious error. (This letter is found on pp. 58–59 of an article by Harold B. Hancock, "Letters to and from Caesar Rodney," *Delaware History* vol. 12 (1966). This work, cited here only once, should not be confused with Ryden's book by the same title previously cited.)
76. *Pennsylvania Archives*, 8th s. 7 : 5800.
77. *R.I. Recs.*, 6 : 462.
78. *Minutes Lower Counties*.
79. The copies were all made and supplied. See Gadsden's letter, *Gibbes*, 1 : 7. The expense account of the Maryland delegation indicates they spent £1, 10 shillings to express a copy to Virginia.
80. *Mass. Hist. Colls.*, 10 : 581.
81. Paul Leicester Ford in *Dickinson*, p. ix.
82. *Letters to and from Caesar Rodney*, p. 26.
83. *Minutes Lower Counties*, p. 40.
84. *R.I. Recs.*, 6 : 462.

4

The Journal of the Congress

Prefatory Note

The reader has seen that nine complete copies of the Journal of the Proceedings of the Stamp Act Congress, one for each participating delegation, were prepared while the members were in New York. John Cotton, the clerk, made the original version from notes taken while the delegates were in session. Then, as time permitted, he made copies of the original. In order for him to finish the task before adjournment, it was necessary to engage other penmen to make additional transcripts. No doubt it was difficult to find scribes willing to undertake the task because skilled penmen, who were much in demand in New York's legal and commercial offices, were scarce.

The committee assigned to inspect and correct the Journal (McKean, Rutledge, and Robert R. Livingston) read and approved Cotton's original.[1] They probably relied on him to make certain that the copies or "replicas" made for the nine delegations were accurately executed.

After the Congress adjourned, the delegates from Massachusetts, Maryland, and South Carolina fulfilled their obligations to the Congress by having their replicas of the Journal copied for the four colonies not represented at New York. Thus there were an original and twelve contemporary replicas of the Journal. The original was probably taken back to Massachusetts by Cotton, but its whereabouts is not known; it is not in the collections of the Massachusetts State Archives, the Massachusetts Historical Society, nor in any of the libraries where one might logically expect to find the manuscript. Perhaps some day it may be found. In seeking the other replicas, I have had personal or mail contact with responsible historical societies and other agencies in the remaining twelve colonies. Two of the replicas and a transcript of the third have been found, as explained below.

One of the replicas is the copy that Caesar Rodney and Thomas McKean took back from New York to the Assembly of the Lower Counties. The first page reads, "For the Government of the Counties of New Castle, Kent, and Sussex upon Delaware." After McKean and Rodney presented this document to the Assembly in May 1766, it apparently became part of the archives of the Lower Counties along with other papers. When the Assembly adjourned *sine die* (to be succeeded in 1776 by a new Delaware state government and a bicameral legislative body), the replica found its way into the personal papers of Caesar Rodney, who inscribed his name on the second page. This replica will be referred to as the Rodney Journal.

Although many of the official papers were lost, the Rodney Journal, remaining in private hands, was carefully preserved. When Caesar Rodney died in 1784, he devised most of his real estate, and some of his personal property, to his nephew, Caesar A. Rodney, son of his brother Thomas. He willed his letters and other papers to Thomas, and designated him executor of his estate. At Thomas's death Caesar A. Rodney inherited his father's papers, including the Rodney Journal. Following Caesar A. Rodney's death in 1824, the documents remained in the hands of his descendants until 1919, when they were sold at auction in Philadelphia. Among the several purchasers was a New Jersey collector, a student of local history and archaeology named Frank H. Stewart.[2]

In 1948 the Rodney Journal was included in a collection of papers and rare books that Mr. Stewart willed to Glassboro State College, Glassboro, New Jersey. The Rodney Journal is now carefully preserved in the collections of the Savitz Library of that institution.[3]

During the time that Caesar A. Rodney was in possession of his uncle's papers, he loaned the Rodney Journal to his friend Hezekiah Niles, an intensely nationlistic, anti-English editor of a weekly magazine published in Baltimore called *The Weekly Register*.[4] Niles published the Rodney Journal in two installments, the first on Saturday, July 25, 1812, and the second on Saturday, August 1, 1812. In a preface Niles told his readers that he had reason to believe that the Rodney Journal was the only extant contemporary copy of the Journal of the Stamp Act Congress. A loose piece of paper inserted in the Journal contained a list of the members of the Congress in Caesar Rodney's handwriting, and Niles published this with the first installment of the Journal. In 1822 he reprinted both installments in a separate work, also published in Baltimore, entitled *Principles and Acts of the Revolution in America*.

A comparison of the Niles printed versions with the Rodney Journal indicates that Niles arbitrarily altered the spelling where he felt it was needed, and furnished punctuation and capitalization, without indicating where he had done so. But of even greater concern, the Rodney Journal, despite John Cotton's signature attesting to its accuracy, contains numerous textual errors, which have been perpetuated in Niles's printed works.

Niles was unaware that Jonas Green had published the Journal of the Stamp Act Congress at Annapolis in 1766 under the title *Proceedings of the Congress New-York*, a publication that is now extremely rare.[5] Green, a former Deputy-Postmaster, was the official printer of the Province of Maryland, and he printed the text from the replica of the Journal brought back from New York by the Maryland delegates. The Green version also contains an expense account of the Maryland delegation, and a letter dated October 26, 1765, which the Maryland delegates addressed to Charles Garth in London. The latter two documents are not part of the Rodney Journal.

Although the whereabouts of the replica Green used is unknown, a clerk entered a transcript of it in the Minutes of the Lower House of the Maryland Assembly, as ordered May 27, 1766. This transcript, whose existence came to light during the research for this book, has been preserved among the manuscripts in the Hall of Records at Annapolis. It will be referred to as the Maryland Transcript.[9] This transcript has been compared with the Green publication and there are a number of differences, which suggests that Green did not faithfully follow the replica when he set it in type. Like Niles, Green furnished punctuation and capitalization, and corrected misspellings without indicating where he had done so. Of greater concern are discrepancies of a substantive nature in the text between the Niles and Green printed versions, and it is impossible to determine which is correct by comparing the two.

Niles was also unaware that in 1767 John Almon published in London what he purported to be the Journal of the Stamp Act Congress under the title *Authentic Account of the Proceedings of the Congress Held at New-York in 1765 on the Subject of the American Stamp Act*. This account has a number of important omissions, including the letters accrediting the delegations, and the entries of all sessions of the Congress from October 7 to October 19. Almon simply reprinted the Green publication, arbitrarily omitting sections that did not strike him as being significant.

In 1777 Almon published another volume in London entitled *A Collection of Papers Relative to the Dispute Between Great Britain and America 1764–1775*, in which, without alteration, he reprinted his incomplete 1767 version of the Journal.

Another printing of the Journal was made in 1845, a pamphlet edited by Lewis Cruger, published in New York City and bearing the title *Journal of the First Congress of the American Colonies in Opposition to the Tyrannical Acts of the British Parliament.* This is simply a reprint of the Niles 1822 publication and contains the errors found in the Rodney Journal as discussed below, and several others made by the editor.

The experiences of a former United States president in his quest to locate an authoritative copy of the Journal is relevant to the present discussion. After leaving the White House, President John Adams returned to Quincy, Massachusetts, where he devoted his remaining years to a study of history and philosophy. In 1813, at the age of 78, he had an exchange of correspondence about the Stamp Act Congress with Thomas McKean, then in his 80th year. Since Adams had not been a delegate to the Congress, he had to depend upon others to tell him about it. With his background in the First and Second Congresses, Adams could see the Congress of 1765 from the perspective of a contemporary historian evaluating the series of events that led to the break with England and the ultimate struggle for independence.

Years before, when he met McKean and Rodney at the First Continental Congress in Philadelphia, Adams queried both of them about the Stamp Act Congress. On prior occasions he had also discussed the Congress with his good friend James Otis, who told him that a Journal was kept, but Adams had never seen it, and in his retirement he became much interested in finding a copy for study. He wrote McKean in Philadelphia, where the latter was then living, asking whether a copy was available. McKean made careful inquiry and replied that "he had not been able to procure a single copy either in manuscript or print in the United States."[7]

McKean did not know that the replica that he and Rodney brought back from New York was then in the possession of Rodney's nephew, who had permitted Niles to publish it the previous year in *The Weekly Register*. The *Register* then had about 3,000 subscribers, but neither Adams nor McKean was among them. Nor did either man know that the Journal had been published in Annapolis by Green in 1767.

In the course of his inquiries McKean learned that John Almon published the Journal in London in 1767. Under the impression that this was the only available printed version, he obtained a copy of it and reprinted it in Philadelphia at his own expense in order to oblige Adams. He subsequently sent a copy to Adams as a gift.[8]

In the meantime, Caesar A. Rodney, unaware that McKean had been seeking a copy of the Journal for Adams, decided to print at his own expense a memorial edition of the Rodney Journal on fine paper. It was his intention to present a copy to McKean, to whom he erroneously referred as "the last surviving patriot of that illustrious body."[9] He did not know that William Samuel Johnson was still living; in fact, Johnson lived two years longer than McKean, who died in 1817. Something happened to interfere with Rodney's plans, and the memorial edition never materialized, but on August 22, 1813, he mailed to McKean copies of the two issues of *The Weekly Register* in which the installments of the Journal appeared. This was two days after McKean sent Adams a copy of the reprint of Almon's pamphlet.

McKean acknowledged Rodney's letter with thanks, stating that he had never heard of *The Weekly Register,* but was glad to receive the two numbers containing the Journal of the Congress. Then he added, "I had the proceedings of that Body, *not the whole,* reprinted about 2 months ago, from a copy I found in the 1st Vol. of 'American Tracts' contained in the four volume octavo edited by J. Almon in London in

1767. Such an important transaction should not be unknown to the future historian."[10]

The reprint paid for by McKean contained the omissions made by Almon, previously referred to, which explains the three words italicized above. McKean knew that he was supplying Adams with an incomplete account of the proceedings, but it was the best he could obtain.[11] It is also of interest to note McKean's comment that future historians should be aware of this "important transaction."

It has been my good fortune to locate a second replica of the Journal in the Archives of the State of Connecticut. There is little question that this is the copy that the three Connecticut delegates brought back from New York and presented to the Assembly. Along with other official documents relating to the Revolutionary War in the possession of the Assembly, it was preserved by the Secretary of State. In 1845 Sylvester Judd was commissioned to arrange and index these papers, and the Journal was incorporated in one of the many volumes of manuscripts resulting from his efforts.[12]

The finding of the Connecticut replica permits comparisons to be made with the two other primary sources—the Rodney Journal, and the newly found Maryland Transcript. (The Almon publications and the 1845 pamphlet edited by Cruger must be rejected because of their incompleteness, and the Niles and Green printed versions can no longer be regarded as accurate renditions.) It is now evident that the numerous historians who have quoted from the Niles printed versions have been using a faulty reference, and when compared with the Connecticut replica and the Maryland Transcript, the errors stand out boldly.[13] Those cited below are illustrative, but by no means complete:

The Rodney Journal (the basis of the Niles publications) indicates that the last session of the Congress was held on Thursday, October 24, whereas the delegates met for a final time on Friday, October 25. October 8 is given as a Thursday, whereas it was actually a Tuesday. A garbled entry that day reads: "The Congress met according to adjourntment Upon Motion Voted, that the provinces be is adjourned to—Voted that Mr. Justice Livingston, Mr. McKean & Mr. Rutledge be a Committee to inspect the proceedings and Minutes and Correct the same."

The entry should read as follows, as given in the Connecticut replica: "The Congress met according to adjournment—Upon Motion, Voted, that the Provinces be called over every Morning at the time that it is Adjourned to. Voted that Mr. Justice Livingston, Mr. McKean and Mr. Rutledge be a Committee to inspect the proceedings and minutes & correct the same."

In reference to Ruggles's election as chairman, the Rodney Journal states, "on Sorting and Counting the votes *appointed* to have a Majority." The italicized word should be *appeared*. In the address to the King, the phrase *of our government* is used instead of *of your government* and *inconsiderable* is rendered as *in Considerable*," both of which convey different meanings from what the authors intended. The word *bills* is omitted in the following phrase, which also garbles the intended meaning: *money* [bills] *a right enjoyed by the Kingdom of Ireland.*

In the petition to the House of Commons three words have been omitted, and the scribe incorrectly copied a number of others, erroneously using *their* instead of *those* in one sentence, and instead of *these* in another. *Confused* is given instead of *confusion, approbation* instead of *protection, Discharging* instead of *Discharge, Treat* instead of *Entreat*, and *reverence of the Crown* instead of *Revenue of the Crown.* The expression that should read *It gives us also Great pain*, appears as *It always gives us great pain.*

Apart from the errors in substance, the scribe was very careless. *Island* is omitted in the first reference to Rhode Island; Ruggles is given as *Buggles;* Thomas *Cook* appears instead of *Cooch;* and there are numerous inconsistencies in spelling. Niles attempted to correct some of the obvious errors in his printed versions, but since he was working with one replica only, he had no way to check errors of fact. The following passage from the petition to Commons will give the reader the flavor of the Rodney Journal, and how Niles rendered it in the 1812 edition of the *Register*. The original reads as follows, with words distorted by Niles italicized:

> It is als humbly Submitted whether there be not a materal Distinction in Reason and Sound Policy at least between the Necessary Excercise of Parliamentry Jurisdiction in General Acts *for the amendment of the Common Law,* and the Regulation of Trade and Commerce tho' the whole impire and the exersise of that Jurisdiction by imposing Taxes on the Colonies.

Niles rendered the passage as follows and, in his zeal to normalize the spelling, completely changed the meaning by garbling the above italicized phrase:

> It is also humbly submitted whether there be not a material distinction, in reason and sound policy at least, between the necessary exercise of parliamentary jurisdiction in general acts, and the common law, and the regulation of trade, and commerce through the whole empire, and the exercise of that jurisdiction by imposing taxes on the colonies.

The text that follows is an exact transcript of the Connecticut replica. There appeared to be no virtue in making any changes, but rather preserving the original without alteration; the spelling has not been normalized nor punctuation supplied. My few notes or comments are given in brackets. The Rodney Journal and the Connecticut replica were copied by different penmen, and the scribe responsible for the Connecticut replica was also very careless. Perhaps it would be more accurate to refer to him as the "principal" scribe, inasmuch as seven pages of the manuscript appear to be in a different hand. Some of the scribal errors were later corrected in the manuscript, presumably by John Cotton, before affixing his signature. Cotton himself must have read the text hurriedly, because he overlooked a number of errors as well as inconsistencies in spelling and punctuation.

The penman is prone to transpose *i* and *e* in words like *chief* or *grievance*. He consistently misspells *Parliament* and *government*, as well as *together, privilege* and *also*. The reader will have no difficulty finding other errors in spelling when he reads this text. Where a word is consistently misspelled for several pages and then appears correctly, it was probably corrected by Cotton, but the scribe did not rectify the previous errors. Abbreviations such as *Mr.* and *Esqr.* are rarely followed by periods, and the penman terminated many of his sentences with a flourish of the goose quill, a sort of paraph, instead of a period. Where this embellishment occurs I have represented it with a dash, omitting a period.

In several places in the manuscript a symbol is used consisting of the letter *y* with a short horizontal line above it topped with a little curlicue. The *y* appears to be a modification of the character called *thorn*, used in early English literature to represent the sound *th*, and this symbol has been rendered as *ye* ("the").

Finally, the expense account of the Maryland delegates and their letter of October 26, 1765, to Charles Garth have been appended, exactly as the penman recorded them in the Maryland Transcript.[14] These two documents are not part of the Connecticut replica, but they relate directly to the Congress and provide valuable historical information.

NOTES TO PREFATORY NOTE OF CHAPTER 4

1. This was the first committee to be named, which suggests it was considered an important one. Perhaps the committee was instructed to make certain that nothing was recorded that might cause embarrassment to any of the individual delegates.
2. *Letters to and from Caesar Rodney.*

3. I want to express appreciation to Professor Magdalena Houlroyd, Curator of Special Collections at the Savitz Learning Resource Center, for furnishing a photocopy of the Rodney Journal, and also to Glassboro State College for giving unrestricted permission to reproduce it in whole or in part.

4. After two-and-one-half years following publication of the first number on September 11, 1811, the name was changed to *Niles Weekly Register,* and 23½ years later it became *Niles National Register;* see Norbal Neil Luxon, *Niles' Weekly Register, News Magazine of the Nineteenth Century* (Baton Rouge, La., 1947).

5. There is an original copy in the Library of Congress and another in the John Carter Library, Providence, R. I. Fifteen photostatic copies were produced in 1938 by the Massachusetts Historical Society (no. 64 in the Photostat Americana, 2d s.) for fifteen subscribing libraries. See Thomas R. Adams, *American Independence* (Providence, R.I., 1965), p. 32.

6. I am indebted to Gust Skordas, Assistant Archivist, Hall of Records, Annapolis, for his assistance in furnishing a photocopy of the transcript. I also want to acknowledge the cooperation of the Maryland Hall of Records Commission for permission to reproduce it in whole or in part. See *Maryland Archives,* 59: 327 for reference to the transcript and the notation that it had not yet appeared in print. It may be found in the Lower House (manuscript) Journal, 1762–1768, pp. 398–426.

7. *Adams Works,* 10: 60.

8. *Adams Works,* 10: 60.

9. [Anon.], "Caesar Rodney's Ride, July 1776," *Pennsylvania Magazine of History and Biography* 39 (1915): 454.

10. *Ibid.,* p. 456.

11. Kate Heath, Editorial Assistant on the Adams Papers at the Massachusetts Historical Society, advised me February 21, 1973, that a search of the Adams papers failed to find the copy of the Journal that McKean sent Adams. It would be interesting to ascertain what happened to it, and whether other copies were also printed. In *Conn. Recs.,* 12: 410, a footnote states that the Green publication was reprinted in 1813 at the office of the *United States Gazette* in Philadelphia. This must have been the printing that McKean paid for.

12. Mrs. Linda B. Winters, Reference Librarian, History and Genealogy Unit, Connecticut State Library, Hartford, is acknowledged for her assistance in supplying a photocopy

of this manuscript, which is found in Connecticut Archives Revolutionary War, 1st s. 1, beginning with document numbered 22a. I am also indebted to the Connecticut State Library for permission to reproduce it.

13. A zealous collector of early documents and autographs, Dr. Thomas Addis Emmet printed the Niles 1822 version and bound it with original documents and photographs relating to the Stamp Act Congress in a memorial volume entitled *"The Stamp Act Congress of 1765, Autographs of the Members."* The only copy is in the Manuscript Room, New York Public Library. The contents are itemized in the *Calendar of the Emmet Collection of Manuscripts, etc., Relating to American History* (New York, 1900). Despite his obvious care in collecting Stamp Act data, Dr. Emmet was obviously unaware that the Niles version is a faulty one. The Emmet memorial volume contains a rarity on p. 227, an original unused sheet of the stamped paper intended for use in the colonies, with a two-shilling-sixpence embossed stamp in the upper left corner.

14. Dr. Emmet also reprinted this letter in his memorial volume, but incorrectly states that it was sent to Secretary Henry Conway.

THE JOURNAL

Boston June 1765

Sir/

The House of Representatives of this Province, in the present Sessions of the General Court have Unanimously agreed to propose a meeting as soon as may be of Committees from the Houses of Representatives, or Burgesses, of the Several British Colonies on this Continent, to Consult togather on the present Circumstances of the Colonies and the Difficulties to which they are and must be reduced by the Operation of the Acts of Parliment for levying Duties and Taxes on the Colonys, and to consider of a General and United, dutifull loyal and Humble Representation of their Condition to his Majesty and the Parliment and to implore Relief. — The House of Representatives of this Province have allso Voted to propose that such Meeting be at the City of New York, in the Province of New York, on the first Tuesday in October next and have appointed a Committee of three of their Members to attend that service with such as the Other Houses of Representatives, or Burgesses, in the several Colonies may think fit to appoint to meet them, and the Committee of the House of Representatives of this

province are directed to repair to said New York, on said
first Tuesday in October Next Accordingly — If therefore
your Honble House should agree to this proposal, it would
be acceptable that as early Notice of it as possible might be
Transmitted to the Speaker of the House of Representatives
of this Province.

Samuel White Speaker

In Consequence of the foregoing Circular Letter the following Gentlemen met at New York, in the Province of New
York on Monday the Seventh day of October. 1765. —

From the Province of ⎫ James Otis
Massachusetts Bay   ⎬ Oliver Partridge   Esquires
                      ⎭ Timothy Ruggles

Who produced their Appointment as follows Vizt [videlicet,
namely] To James Otis, Oliver Partridge and Timothy Ruggles Esquires
Gentlemen/

The House of Representatives of this Province have appointed You a Committee to meet at New York on the first
Tuesday of October next, such Committees as the other
Houses of Representatives, or Burgesses, in the Several Colonies on this Continent may think fit to Appoint, to Consult
togather on the present Circumstances of the Colonies and
the Difficulties to which they are and must be reduced by
the operation of the late Acts of Parliment — By this Choice,
the House has reposed in you a trust of Singular importance
and has just Reason to expect you will give your utmost
attention to it— In case you should recieve advice that the
Houses of Representatives, or Burgesses, of the other Colonies or any of them agree to send Committees to join you
in this interesting Affair, you are directed to repair to New
York at the time appointed and indeavour to Unite with
them in Sentiment, and Agree upon such Representations
as may tend to preserve our Rights and priveliges: And it
is the Opinion of the House, that no Address or Represen-

tation shall be esteemed the Act of this House unless it is agreed to and Signed by the Major part of their Committee — If it should be said that We are in any manner Represented in Parliment, you must by no means Concede to it, as it is an Opinion, which this House cannot see the least reason to adopt —

Further the House think that such a Representation of the Colonies, as British Subjects are entituled to enjoy would be attended with the Greatest Difficulty, if it is not absolutely impracticable, and therefore you are not to Urge, or consent to any proposal for a Representation if such be made in the Congress — It is the Expectation of the House that a most loyal & dutifull Address to his Majesty and his Parliment will be prepared by the Congress, praying as well for the Removal of the Greivances the Colonies labour under at present, as for the preventing others for the future; which Petitions if drawn up, as far as you shall be able to judge agreeable to the mind of this House, you are empowered to Sign and forward, and you are to lay a Copy of the same before this House, and make report of Your proceedings upon your Return — It is the Hearty prayer of this House that the Congress may be endued with that Wisdom, which is from above, and that their Councils and determinations may be attended with the divine Blessing —

S White Speaker

From the Colony of Rhode Island ⎱ Metcalf Bowler
and Providence plantations ⎰ Henry Ward Esqrs
Who produced the following Appointment — vizt
     By the Honble Samuel Ward Esquire,
     Governor, Captain General, and Commander
S.S. in Cheif of and over the English Colony of
     Rhode Island and Providence Plantations,
     in New England in America —

To Metcalf Bowler, and Henry Ward Esqrs

Greeting/

Whereas, the General Assembly of this Colony have nominated and appointed you, the said Metcalf Bowler and Henry Ward to be Commissioners in behalf of this Colony to Meet such Commissioners as are or shall be appointed by the other British Goverments, in North America, to meet at New York, on the first Tuesday of October next. I do therefore, hereby Authorize empower and Commissionate you the said Metcalf Bowler & Henry Ward forthwith to repair to New York; and there in behalf of this Colony to meet and join with the other Commissioners in Consulting together, on the present Circumstances of the Colonies, and the Difficulties to which they are and must be reduced by the Operation of the Act of Parliment for levying Duties and Taxes, upon the Colonies and to consider of a General and united, dutifull loyal, and humble Representation to his Majesty and the Parliment, and to implore Relief —

And you are allso hereby empowered to conclude, and agree with the other Commissioners, upon such measures as you shall think Necessary and proper for Obtaining Redress of the Grievances of the Colonies, agreeable to the Instructions given you by the General Assembly of this Colony —

Given under My hand and the Seal of the Said Colony this sixteenth day of September 1765 and in the fifth year of his Majestys Reign

By his Honours Command   Samuel Ward
        Henry Ward Secry

From the Colony of   ⎫   Eliphalet Dyer
Connecticut   ⎬   David Rowland   Esquires
                            ⎭   Willm. Saml. Johnson
Who produced the following Appointment viz

At a General Assembly of the Governor and Company of the Colony of Connecticut holden at Hartford (by Special

Order of his honour the Governor of said Colony) on the
19th day of September Anno Domini 1765 —

Whereas it has been proposed that a Congress be attended
by Commissioners from the Several Goverments on this
Continent, to confer upon a General and united, Humble
Loyal and dutifull Representation to his Majesty and the
Parliment of the present Circumstances of the Colonies and
the difficulties to which they are & must be reduced by the
operation of the Act of Parliment for Laying Duties & Taxes
on the Colonies and to implore Releif —

...Resolved, by this Assembly, that Eliphalet Dyer, Willm.
Saml. Johnson and David Rowland Esquires or any two of
them be and hereby are appointed Commissioners on Behalf
of this Colony to repair to New York to attend the proposed
Congress in the Matters above Referrd to, and his honour
is hereby desired to Commissionate them Accordingly

                    A True Copy Examd
                    by George Wyllys Secry

At a General Assembly of the Governor and Company of
the Colony of Connecticut, holden at Hartford (by Special
Order of his honour the Governor of Said Colony) on the
19th day of Septemr Anno Dom 1765

Instructions to the Commissioners of this Colony appointed
to meet Commissioners from the other Colonies at New York
on the first Tuesday of October Next
Gentlemen

You are to repair to the said City of New York, at the
said time, or at the time, which according to the Intelligence
You may Recieve of the Convening of the other Commissioners it may appear to You Seasonable and best, to consult
togather with them on the present Circumstances of the
Colonies and the Difficulties to which they are and must be
reduced by the Operation of the Acts of Parliment for
laying duties and Taxes on the Colonies, and to Consider of,
and propose a general and United, dutifull loyal and Humble
Representation of their Condition to his Majesty and the

parliment and to implore Relief —

In your proceedings you are to take care that you form no such Junction with the other Commissioners as will Subject you to the Major Vote of the Commissioners present —

You are to inform the Governor and General Assembly at the Sessions in October Next of all such proceedings as shall appear to you needfull and Convenient to be Communicated for Consideration and to observe all such further Instructions as you may Recieve —

And you are to report your doings with the doings of the Commissioners at such meeting to the General Assembly of this Colony for Acceptance and approbation

A true Copy Examd
by George Wyllys Secry

S.S.   Thomas Fitch Esqr Governor and Commander in Chief of his Majestys Colony of Connecticut in New England in America —

To Eliphalet Dyer, David Rowland,& William Saml Johnson, Esquires

Greeting

Whereas the General Assembly of the said Colony of Connecticut, at their Sessions holden at Hartford, on the nineteenth day of this Instant September nominated and appointed You, or any two of you, to be Commissioners, on behalf of this Colony, to repair to New York to attend a Congress, proposed to be held there by Commissioners from the several Goverments, on this Continent, to Confer upon a general and united humble loyal and Dutifull Representation to his Majesty and the Parliment of the present Circumstances of the Colonies and the Difficulties to which they are and must be Reduced by the Operation of the Acts of Parliment for levying duties and Taxes on the Colonies and to implore Relief &c and have desired Me to Commission you Accordingly —

I do therefore, reposeing a special Trust and Confidence in

your loyalty Ability and good Conduct, hereby Constitute, Authorize and Commission you the said Eliphalet Dyer, David Rowland, and Willm Samuel Johnson Esquires (or any two of you) for and on behalf of this Colony to repair to the said City of New York, on the first day of October next, or at the time, which according to the inteligence you may Recieve of the Convening of the other Comissioners may appear to you seasonable and best, to Confer and Consult with them or such of them as shall be present, upon and concerning the Matters and things before Mentioned, for the purposes aforesaid wherein You are to Observe such Instructions as You have recieved, or shall further Receive from the General Assembly of the said Colony of Connecticut agreable to the important trust reposed in You

Given under my hand and the Public
seal of the said Colony of Connecticut, within
the same, the twenty first day of
September in the fifth year of the
Reign of Our Soverign Lord George the
third of great Britain France and
Ireland King defender of the faith &c
Anno Domini one thousand seven hundred
and sixty five

Thomas Fitch

By his honours Command

George Wyllys Secry

From the Colony
of New York

} Robert R. Livingston
John Cruger
Philip Livingston   Esqrs
Willm Byard
Leonard Lispenard

Appeared and informed the Congress that since the Receipt of the above letter from the Speaker of the House of Representatives of Massachusetts Bay, the General Assembly of New York have not had an opportunity of meeting but that they Confidently expect from the General Sense of the People, and such of the Representatives as they have had an Opportunity of Speaking to that when the Assembly do meet (which will probably be verry soon) the Congress will be approved and a Regular Committee for the purpose Appointed, in the mean time they think themselves in some measure Authorized to meet the Congress by the following Votes Vizt — Extract from the Votes and proceedings of the General Assembly for the Colony of New York —

Die Sabati 9h. A.M. the 4th April 1761 Mr. Speaker represented to this House that his situation in the Country rendred it vastly inconvenient, to him alone, to Correspond with the Agent of this Colony, at the Court of Great Britain, and more especially so during the Recess of the House

Ordered, that the Members of the City of New York, or the Major part of them, be a Committee of Correspondence to Correspond with the Agent of this Colony at the Court of Great Britain during the Recess of the House, concerning the public Affairs of this Colony and that they lay before the House, copies of all such letters, as they may write to him, and allso all such letters, and allso all such letters and advices, as they may recieve from him respecting the same —

Die Jovis 9h. A.M. the 9th December 1762. Alderman Livingston from the Committee appointed to Correspond with the Agent of this Colony, at the Court of Great Britain; acquainted the House that the Committee concieved it expedient that one or more Members should be added to the said Committee to Correspond with the said Agent about the affairs of this Colony — Ordered that Robert R. Livingston Esqr be added to and made one of the said Committee of Correspondence —

Die Jovis 9h A.M. the 18th October 1764 Ordered that the said Committee appointed to Correspond with the said Agent, be allso a Committee during the Recess of the House, to write to and Correspond with the several Assemblies or

Committees of Assemblies on this Continint on the Subject matter of the Act commonly called the Sugar Act, of the Act restraining paper Bills of Credit, in the Colonies, from being a legal tender, and of the Several acts of Parliment lately passed with relation to the Trade of the Northern Colonies: And also on the Subject of the impending dangers which threaten the Colonies of being taxed by laws to be passed in Great Britain —

Extracted from, compared and examined with the Records of the proceedings of the General Assembly for the Colony of New York by   Abrm Lott Clk —

From the Colony   ⎫   Robert Ogden
of New Jersey   ⎬   Hendrick Fisher   Eqrs
                       ⎭   Joseph Borden

Who produced the following Appointment Vizt
At a meeting of a large Number of the Representatives of the Colony of New Jersey at the House of Robert Sprowle October ye third 1765 —
At the desire of the Speaker of the House of Representatives as aforesaid — and at the earnest Request of Many of Our Constituents to consider of some method for humbly loyaly and dutifully joining in a Petition to his Majesty that he would be graciously pleased to recommend it to the Parliment of Great Britain, to Redress our Grievances by repealing several of the late Acts of Parliment Affecting the Northern Colonies, particularly that called the Stamp Act —

Robert Ogden Esqr Hendrick Fisher Esqr and Joseph Borden Esqr were desired to attend the Congress now met at New York and join in the Measures there to be Concluded on for the purposes aforesaid, and to make report of their proceedings therein, at the next meeting of General Assembly

Signed by Order
Jno Lawrence

From the Province of ⎫   John Dickinson
Pennsilvania   ⎬   John Morton   Esqrs
                      ⎭   George Bryan

Who produced the following Appointment
In Assembly September 11th 1765 A.M. The House resumed
the Consideration of their Resolution of Yesterday, to appoint a Committee of three or more of their Members to
attend the General Congress of Committees from the several
Assemblies on this Continent, to be held at New York on
the first of October next, and after some time spent therein — Resolved That Mr. Speaker, Mr Dickinson, Mr Bryan
& Mr Morton be, and they are hereby Nominated and appointed to that service — A true Extract from the Journals,
Chas Moore

Clk of Assembly

Extracts from the Journals of the House of Representatives
for the Province of Pensilvania —

Wednesday Sept 11th 1765 AM
The Committee appointed to prepare instructions for the
deputies nominated by this House to attend the proposed
Congress, at New York on the first of next Month reported
an Essay for that purpose which they presented to the
Chair and the same being Read and agreed to, by the House,
follows in these Words Vizt —

Instructions to the Committee appointed to meet the
Committees of the other British Continental Colonies at
New York —

It is directed by the House that you shall with the Committees that have been or shall be appointed by the several
British Colonies on this Continent to meet at New York,
consult togather on the present Circumstances of the Colonies and the Difficulties they are and must be Reduced to,
by the late Acts of Parliment for levying Duties and Taxes
upon them, and join with the Said Committees, in loyal and
dutifull Addresses to the King, and the two Houses of Parliment humbly Representing the Condition of these Colonies

and imploring Relief by a Repeal of the said Acts; and you are Strictly required to take Care that such Addresses in which you join are drawn up in the most decent and Respectful terms, so as to Avoid every Expression that can give the least Occassion of Offence to his Majesty or to either House of Parliment —

You are allso directed to make a Report of your proceedings herein to the Succeeding Assembly —

A true Extract from the Journals

Sept 26, 1765   Chas Moore Clk of Assembly

From the Government of   ⎫   Caesar Rodney   Esqs
the Counties of New Castle   ⎬   Thos McKean
Kent, and Sussex upon Delaware ⎭
Whose appointments are as follows vizt —

Caesar Rodney and Thomas McKean Esqrs appeared from the Goverments of the Counties of New Castle Kent and Sussex upon Delaware, and informed this Congress that the Representatives of the said Goverment could not meet in General Assembly, after the above Letter was wrote and before the first day of this Instant, that the said Assembly consists of only eighteen Members fiveteen of whome have appointed the other three to attend here — by three several Instruments of Writing, which are in these Words. To Wit.

To all to whome these presents shall come — Know Ye — That we the Subscribers five of the Representatives of the freemen of the Goverment of the Counties of New Castle, Kent & Sussex upon Delaware, Sensible of the weighty and oppressive Taxes imposed upon the Good people of this Goverment, by divers late Acts of Parliment, and of the great Infringement of the liberties and just established Rights of all his Majestys Colonies on this Continent, Occasioned by the late measures in England and being of opinion that the method proposed by the Honble House of Assembly of the Province of Massasa Bay is the Most likely to Obtain a Redress of these Grievances and takeing into

Consideration the Misfortune, we at present labour Under in not haveing it in our Power to Convene as a House, and in a Regular manner to appoint a Committee. Yet zealous for the hapiness of Our Constituents, think it Our duty in this way to serve them as much as in Us lies (Assured of the Hearty Approbation of any future House of Assembly of this Goverment) and therefore do hereby Nominate and appoint Jacob Kollock Thomas McKean & Caesar Rodney Esqrs three of the Representatives of the same Goverment, A Committee to repair to the City of New York on the first day of October next, and there to Join with the Committees sent by the other Provinces, in one United and loyal Petition to his Majesty and Remonstrance to the Honourable House of Commons of Great Britain against the aforesaid Acts of Parliment, Therein dutifully yet most firmly Asserting the Colonies Rights of Exclusion from Parlimentary Taxation and praying that they may not in any Instance be Stripped of the Ancient and most valuable Privelige of a Tryal by their Peers and most humbly imploring Relief —

In Testimony whereof we have hereunto sett our hands at New Castle the twenty first day of September Annoqu: Domini 1765

> Evan Rice
> Thomas Cooch
> Willm Armstrong
> George Munro
> John Evans

Kent County to wit

We whose names are hereunder written Members of the General Assembly of the Goverment of the Counties of New Castle Kent & Sussex upon Delaware for the said County of Kent; tho sensible of the impropriety of Assuming the Functions of Assembly Men, during the Recess of Our House, Yet Zealous to Concur in any Measures which may be productive of Advantage to this Goverment and the other

British Colonies on the Continent of America in general —
Have appointed and as much as in us lies, do appoint Jacob
Kollock Esqr, Caesar Rodney Esqr and Thomas McKean
Esqr members of said Assembly to be a Committee, to meet
with the other Committees allready appointed or to be appointed by the several and Respective Assemblies, of the
said other Colonies, at the City of New York, on the first
Tuesday in October next, in Conjunction with the said other
Committees, to Consider of the present distressfull Circumstances of the said Colonies, Occasioned in some Measure
as we Apprehend, by several late Acts of Parliment, and
to join with them, in an humble Address to his most Gracious Majesty, and the Parliment of Great Britain for
Redress of our Grievances, or in any other Expedient, that
shall be agreed on by the said Committees which may tend
to promote the Utility and Wellfare of the British Dominions in America

Sept 13th 1765   John Vining
                                 John Caton
                                 Jno Barnes
                                 Willm Killen
                                 Vincent Lookerman

Sussex County to wit

We whose Names are hereunder written Members of the
General Assembly of the Goverment of the Counties of New
Castle, Kent and Sussex upon Delaware for the said County
of Sussex though sensible of the impropriety of Assumeing
the Functions of Assembly Men during the Recess of Our
House; Yet Zealous to Concur in any measures which may be
productive of Advantages to this Goverment, and the other
British Colonies on the Continent of America in general, have
appointed, and as much as in Us lies, do appoint Jacob Kollock
Esqr Caesar Rodney Esqr & Thomas McKean Esqr Members
of the said Assembly, to be a Committee, to meet with the
other Committees, allready appointed, or to be Appointed by

the several and respective Assemblies of the said other Colonies at the City of New York on the first Tuesday in October next, in conjunction with the said other Committees, to Consider of the present distressfull Circumstances of the said Colonies occasioned in some measure as we apprehend by several late Acts of Parliment & to join with them in an humble Address to his most Gracious Majesty,and the Parliment of Great Britain for Redress of Our Grievances or in any other Expedient that shall be agreed on by the said Committee which may tend to promote the Utility and Wellfare of the British Dominions in America

Sept 17th 1765.

> David Hall
> Benjin Burton
> Levin Crapper
> Thos Robinson
> Jacob Kollock junr

From the Province of Maryland } Willm Murdock
Edward Tilghman Esqrs
Thomas Ringgold

Instructions from the Honourable the lower House of Assembly of the Province of Maryland —

To William Murdock, Edward Tilghman & Thomas Ringgold Esquires A committee appointed to Join the several Committees, from the several Colonies in America at New York

Gentlemen

You are to repair imediately to the City of New York, in the Province of New York and there join with the Committees from the Houses of Representatives of the other Colonies in a General and United dutifull, loyal and humble Representation to his Majesty and the British Parliment, of the Circumstances and Condition of the British Colonies and Plantations and to pray Relief — from the Burthens and Restraints lately laid on their Trade, and Commerce,

and Especially from the Taxes imposed by an Act of the
last Sessions of Parliment, Granting and applying certain
Stamp duties, and other Duties in the British Colonies, and
plantations, in America — Whereby they are deprived in
some Instances of that invaluable privelege of English Men
and British Subjects tryals by Juries, that you take Care
that such Representation shall humbly and decently, but
expressly Contain an Assertion of the Rights of the Colonists
to be exempt from all and every Taxation and imposition
upon their persons and Properties, to which they do not
consent in a Legislative way, either by themselves or their
Representatives, by them freely Chosen, and appointed

Signed by Order of the House
Robt Lloyd Speaker

From the Province of ⎫ Thomas Lynch
South Carolina   ⎬ Christopher Gadsen [Gadsden] Esqrs
                     ⎭ John Rutledge
Who produced the following appointment

Thursday ye 25th July 1765
The House (according to Order) took into Consideration the
letter from the Speaker of the House of Representatives of
the Massachusetts Bay, laid before them on Friday last —
And a debate arising thereon, and some time spent there-
in —
Ordered That the said letter be Referred to a Committee of
the following Gentlemen Vizt Capt Gadsen [Gadsden], Mr
Wright, Mr Galliard, Mr Wragg, Mr Parsons, Mr Pinckney,
Coln [Colonel] Laurens Mr Rutledge, Mr Manigault, and
Mr Drayton

Friday ye 26th day of July 1765
Capt Gadsden Reported from the Committee appointed to
Consider of the letter sent from the Speaker of the House
of Representatives of the Province of the Massas Bay to
the Speaker of this House and to report their Opinions

thereupon of the Expediency & Utility of the Measures, therein proposed and the best Means to Effect the Relief therein Mentioned —

That they are of opinion the measures therein proposed is prudent and Necessary and therefore Recommend to the House to send a Committee, to meet the Committees, from the Houses of Representatives, or Burgesses of the Several British Colonies on this Continent at New York the first Tuesday in October Next —

That the said Committee be Ordered to Consult there, with those other Committees on the present Circumstances of the Colonies, and the Difficulties which they are and must be reduced to by the Operation of the Acts of Parliment for levying, duties and Taxes on the Colonies, and to consider of a General, United dutifull loyal, and humble Representation of their Condition to his Majesty and the parliment and to implore Relief

That the Result of their Consultation shall at their Return be imediately laid before the House to be Confirmed or not, as the House may think proper — And the said Report being delivered in at the Clerks Table and Read a second time — The Question was finally put, that the House do Agree to the first, second and third Paragraphs of the said Report — It was resolved in the Affirmative Friday ye 2d of August 1765 — Motion being Made

Resolved that this House will provide a Sum sufficient to defray the Charges and expences of a Committee of three Gentlemen, on Account their going to, Continuing at, and returning from the Meeting of the Several Committees, proposed to Assemble at New York on the first Tuesday in October Next, to Consult there with those other Committees on the present Circumstances of the Colonies and the Difficulties which they are and must be reduced to, by the Operation of the Acts of Parliment, for levying duties and Taxes on the Colonies, and to consider of a General, United, dutifull loyal, and Humble Representation of their Condition to his Majesty, and the Parliment, and to implore Relief —

Ordered, That the public Treasurer do advance out of any Monies in his hands, to the said Committee a sum not Exceeding Six hundred pounds sterling, for the purpose aforesaid —

Resolved that this House will Reimburse the Treasurer the said sum

Ordered, That the following Gentlemen be appointed a Committee for the purposes aforesaid Vizt Mr Thomas Lynch, Mr Christopher Gadsden [the scribe rendered it Gadsen, but it had been corrected, presumably by John Cotton] Mr. John Rutledge —

Thursday ye 8th Aug 1765

Ordered,

That the Speaker do inform Thos Lynch Christopher Gadsden [again corrected] & John Rutledge Esquires that they are appointed a Committee to meet the Committees of the several other Colonies on this Continent on the first Tuesday in October next, at New York and that he do acquaint them it is the desire of the House that they repair to New York on the said first Tuesday in October Next, for the purposes Mentioned in the Report of the Committee, as agreed to by this House on Friday the 26th day of July last —

Ordered

That three Copies of the proceedings of this House rellative to the said matter, be made out and Signed by the Speaker, and that he deliver one of the said Copies to each of the said Gentlemen

Raw[lins] Lowndes Speaker

[In the following proceedings, I have made indentations for paragraphs to facilitate reading the entries.]

[Monday, October 7, 1765]

Then the said Committee[s] proceeded to Chuse a Chairman by Ballot, and Timothy Ruggles Esqr, on sorting and counting the Votes, appeared to have a Majority and thereupon was placed in the Chair —

Resolved, Nemine Contrade [nemine contradicente, "without dissent"] that Mr John Cotton be Clerk to this Congress, during the Continuance thereof —

Then the Congress took into Consideration the several Appointments of the Committees from New York, New Jersey, and the Goverment of the lower Counties on Delaware and —

Resolved , Nem. Conte that the same are suffecient to Quallify the Gentlemen therein named to sit in this Congress —

Resolved also, that the Committee of each Colony shall have one Voice only, in determining any Questions that shall arise in this Congress.

Then the Congress adjourned till tomorrow Morning at 9 OClock

Tuesday Octor 8th 1765 A.M.

The Congress met according to adjournment —

Upon Motion, Voted, that the Provinces be called over every Morning at the time that it is Adjourned to.

Voted that Mr Justice Livingston, Mr McKean and Mr Rutledge be a Committee to inspect the proceedings and minutes & Correct the same —

Then the Congress took into Consideration the Rights & Privileges of ye British American Colonists with the several Inconveniences and hardships to which they are and must be subjected by the Operation of several late Acts of Parliment, particularly by the Act called the Stamp Act, and after some time spent therein, the same was postponed for further Consideration.

Then the Congress Adjourned to tomorrow 11 O Clock

Wednesday Octor 9th 1765 A.M.
Then the Congress met according to adjournment
The Congress Resumed the Consideration of the Rights
and Privilages of the British American Colonists &c the
same was Referrd after sundry debates, for further Consideration —
Then the Congress Adjourned until tomorrow Morning
11 o'Clock

Thursday Octor 10th 1765 A.M.
The Congress met according to Adjournment & Resumed
&c as yesterday
And then Adjourned to 10 OClock tomorrow Morning

Friday Octor 11th 1765 A.M.
The Congress met according to adjournment & Resumed
&c as yesterday
And then Adjourned to 10 OClock tomorrow Morning

Saterday Octor 12th 1765 A.M.
The Congress met according to Adjournment and Re-
sumed &c as yesterday
And then Adjourned to Monday Morning next 10 OClock

Monday Octor 14th 1765 A.M.
The Congress met according to Adjournment and resumed &c as on Saterday last — and then Adjourned to
tomorrow morning at 9 OClock

Tuesday Octor 15th 1765 A.M.
The Congress met according to adjournment, and Resumed &c as yesterday — and then Adjourned to tomorrow
morning at 9 OClock —

Wednesday Octor 16th 1765 A.M.
The Congress met according to Adjournment, and Resumed &c — as yesterday — and then Adjourned to tomorrow Morning 9 OClock

Thursday Octor 17th 1765 A.M.
The Congress met according to Adjournment, and Resumed &c as yesterday. and then Adjourned to tomorrow Morning 9 OClock

Friday Octor 18th 1765 A.M.
The Congress met, according to Adjournment & Resumed &c as yesterday
Adjourned to tomorrow Morning 9OClock.

Saterday Octor 19th 1765 A.M.
The Congress met according to Adjournment and Resumed &c as Yesterday — And upon Mature Deliberation agreed to the following Declarations of the Rights & Grievances of the Colonists, in America which were ordered to be inserted

The Members of this Congress sinceerly devoted with the warmest Sentiments, of Affection and Duty to his Majestys Person & Goverment invoilably [inviolably] attached to the present happy Establishment of the Protestant Succession, and with Minds deeply impressed by a Sense of the present, and impending Misfortunes of the British Colonies on this Continent, haveing Considered as Maturely as time will permit, the Circumstances of the said Colonies esteem it our indispensable Duty to make the following Declarations of Our Humble Opinion respecting the most essential Rights, and Liberties of the Colonists, and of the Grievances, under which they labour, by Reason of Several late Acts of Parliment.

1st That his Majesty's Subjects in these Colonies Owe

the same Allegiance to the Crown of Great Britain, that is Owing from his Subjects born within the Realm, and all due Subordination to that August Body the Parliment of Great Britain.

2d That his Majestys liege Subjects in these Colonies are intituld to all the Inherent Rights and liberties of his Natural Bornd Subjects, within the Kingdom of Great Britain.

3d That it is inseperably essential to the Freedom of a People, and the Undoubted Right of Englishmen, that no Taxes be imposed on them, but with their own Consent, given personally or by their Representatives.

4th That the People of these Colonies are not and from their local Circumstances cannot be Represented in the House of Commons in Great Britain.

5th That the only Representatives of the People of these Colonies are persons chosen therein, by themselves & that no Taxes ever have been or can be constitutionally imposed on them but by their respective Legislatures.

6th That all Supplies to the Crown, being free Gifts of the People, it is unreasonable, and inconsistent with the principles and Spirit of the British Constitution, for the People of Great Britain, to Grant to his Majesty, the property of the Colonists.

7th That Tryal by Jury is the inherent and invaluable Right of every British Subject, in these Colonies.

8th That the late Act of Parliment, intituled, "An Act for Granting and applying certain Stamp Duties, and other Duties in the British Colonies and Plantations in America

&c by imposing Taxes on the Inhabitants of these Colonies, and the said Act, and several other Acts, by extending the Jurisdiction of the Courts of Admiralty, beyond its Ancient limits, have a Manifest tendency to Subvert the Rights, and liberties of the Colonists.

9th That the Duties imposed by several late Acts of Parliment from the peculiar Circumstances of these Colonies, will be extreamly Burthensome & Grevious; and from the Scarcity of Specie, the Payment of them absolutely impracticable.

10th That as the profits of the Trade of these Colonies ultimately center in Great Britain, to pay for the Manufactures which they are Obliged to take from thence, they eventually contribute very largely to all Supplies Granted there to the Crown.

11th That the Restrictions imposed by several late Acts of Parliment on the Trade of these Colonies, will render them unable to purchase the Manufactures of Great Britain.

12th That the Encrease Prosperity and hapiness of these Colonies, depend on the full and free Enjoyment of their Rights and Liberties, and an Intercourse with Great Britain mutually Affectionate and Advantageous.

13th That it is the Right of the British Subjects in these Colonies to Petition the King, or either House of Parliment.

Lastly That it is the indispensable duty of these Colonies to the best of Soverigns, to the Mother Country, and to themselves, to endeavour by a loyal and dutifull Address to his Majesty, and humble Applications to both Houses of Parliment, to procure the Repeal of the Act for Granting and applying certain Stamp Duties, of all Clauses of any other Acts of Parliment, whereby the Jurisdiction of the Admiralty is extended as aforesaid, and of the other late Acts for the Restriction of American Commerce.

Upon Motion Voted, That Robert R. Livingston, Wm Samuel Johnson, and William Murdock Esqrs be a Committee to prepare an address to his Majesty and lay the same before the Congress, on Monday next.

Voted allso that John Rutledge, Edward Tilghman and Philip Livingston Esqrs be a Committee to prepare a Memorial and Petition to the Lords in Parliment, and lay the same before the Congress on Monday Next. [Note that this instrument was termed "a Memorial and Petition."]

Voted also, that Thomas Lynch, James Otis and Thomas McKean Esqrs be a Committee to prepare a Petition to the House of Commons of Great Britain, and lay the same before the Congress on Monday next. Then the Congress Adjourned to Monday next at 12 OClock.

Monday Octor 21th 1765 A.M.
The Congress met according to Adjournment.

The Committee Appointed to prepare and bring in an Address to his Majesty, did Report they had Essayed a draught for that purpose, which they laid on the Table and humbly Submitted to the Correction of the Congress.

The Said Address was read, and after sundry Amendments, the same was approved of by the Congress, and Ordered to be Engrossed.

The Committee appointed to prepare and bring in a Memorial & Petition to the Lords in Parliment did Report that they had Essayed a Draught for that purpose, which they laid on the Table, and humbly submitted to the Correction of the Congress.

The Said Address was read and after sundry amendments the same was approved of by the Congress, and Ordered to be Engrossed.

The Committee appointed to prepare and bring in a Petition to the House of Commons of Great Britain did Report that they had Essayed a Draught for that purpose, which they laid on the Table, and humbly Submitted to the Correction of the Congress.

The Said Address was read, and after sundry Amendments the same was approved of by the Congress, and Ordered to be Engrossed.

The Congress Adjourned till tomorrow Morning at 9OClock

Tuesday Octo. 22, 1765 AM The Congress Met according to adjournment The address to his Majesty being Engrossed was read & Compared & is as follows viz–

To the King's most Exulent Majesty

The Petition of the Freeholders and other Inhabitants of the Massachusetts Bay, Rhode Island & Providence Plantations, [a blank space follows] New Jersey, Pensylvania, The Goverment of the Counties of New Castle, Kent & Sussex upon Delaware, Province of Maryland,

Most Humbly Sheweth

That the Inhabitants of these Colonies Unanimously Devoted with the warmest Sentiments of Duty and Affection to Your Majestys Sacred person and Goverment Inviolably Attached to the present happy Establishment of the Protestant Succession in Your Illustrious House and deeply sensible of Your Royal attention to their Prosperity and Happiness, humbly beg leave to approach the Throne, by Representing to your Majesty That these Colonies Were originally planted by Subjects of the British Crown, who animated with the Spirit of Liberty encouraged by Your Majestys Royal Predecessors and confideing in the Public faith for the Enjoyment of all the Rights & Liberties Essential to Freedom Emigrated from their native Country to this Continent and by their Successfull perseverance in the Midst of Inumerable Dangers and Difficulties togather with a profusion of their Blood, and Treasure have happily added these Vast and valuable Dominions to the Empire of Great Britain.

That for the Enjoyment of these Rights and Liberties several Goverments where [were] early formed in the said Colonies with full power of Legislation agreable to the principles of the English Constitution.

That under those Governments these Liberties thus Vested in their Ancestors and transmitted to their Posterity have been excercised and Enjoyed and by the Inestimable Blessings thereof under the favour of Allmighty God, the Inhospitable Desarts of America have been converted into Flourishing Countries. Science, Humanity, and the Knowledge of Divine Truths diffused through Remote Regions of Ignorance, Infidelity, and Barbarism, the Number of British Subjects wonderfully Increased and the Wealth and Power of Great Britain proportionably Augmented.

That by means of these Settlements and the unparraleled Success of your Majesty's Arms A Foundation is now laid for Rendering the British Empire the Most Extensive and Powerfull of any Reccorded in History Our Connection with this Empire we esteem Our greatest Happiness, and Security and humbly Concieve, it may now be so Established by Your Royal Wisdom as to endure to the latest Period of Time. This with most Humble Submission to Your Majesty We apprehend will be most Efectually accomplished by fixing the Pillars thereof on Liberty and Justice and Secureing the Inherent Rights and Liberties of Your Subjects here upon the Principles of the English Constitution. To this Constitution these two principles are Essential, the Right of Your faithfull Subjects freely to Grant to Your Majesty such Aids as are Required for the Support of Your Government over them and other Public Exigencies, And Tryals by their Peers. By the one they are Secured from unreasonable Impositions, and by the other from Arbitrary decisions of the Executive Power.

The continuation of these Liberties to the Inhabitants of America, we ardently implore as absolutely Necessary to Unite the several parts of Your wide extended Dominions in that Harmony so essential to the Preservation & happiness of the Whole. Protected in these Liberties the Emoluments Great Britain Recieves from Us however great at present are inconsiderable compared with those She has the fairest Prospect of Aquiring. By this Protection She will for ever secure to Herselfe the Advantage of Conveying to all Europe the Merchandizes which America furnishes, and of Supplying through the same Channel whatever is wanted from thence. Here opens a Boundless Source of Wealth and Naval strength yet these Imense Advantages, by the Abridgment of those Invaluable Rights and Liberties, by which Our Growth has been Nourished, are in danger of being for ever lost, and Our Subordinate Legislatures in Effect rendered Useless by the late Acts of Parliment imposeing Duties and Taxes on these Colonies and extending the Jurisdiction of the Courts of Admiralty here beyond its Ancient Limits; Statutes by which Your Majestie's Commons in Britain undertake, absolutely to dispose of the Property of their fellow Subjects in America, without their Consent and for the enforceing Whereof they are Subjected to the Determination of a Single Judge in a Court unrestrained by the Wise Rules of the Common Law the Birthright of Englishmen and the safegaurd of their Persons and Properties.

The invaluable Right of Taxing Ourselves and Tryal by Our Peers, of which We implore Your Majestys Protection are not we most humbly Concieve Unconstitutional but Confirmed by the Great Charter of English Liberty. On the first of these Rights the Honourable the House of Commons found their Practice of Originateing Money Bills, A Right Enjoyed by the Kingdom of Ireland by the Clergy of England until Relinquished by themselves, A Right in-fine [in brief] which all other your Majestys English Subjects both within and without the Realm have hitherto enjoyed.

With Hearts therefore impressed with the most Indelable Characters of Gratitude to Your Majesty and to the Memory of the Kings of Your Illustrious House whose Reigns have been Signally distinguished By their Auspicious Influence on the Prosperity of the British Dominions and convinced by the most Affecting Proofs of Your Majesties Paternal Love to all Your People however distant, and Your Unceasing and Benevolent desires to promote their Happiness. We most humbly Beseech Your Majesty that You will be Graciously pleased to take into Your Royal Consideration the distresses of Your faithfull Subjects on this Continent, and to lay the same before Your Majestys Parliment and to afford them such Relief as in Your Royal Wisdom their Unhappy Circumstances shall be judged to require And your petitioners as in Duty bound will pray.

The Memorial to the Lords in Parliament being Engrossed was read and compared , and is as follows — Vizt

To the Right Honourable the Lords Spiritual and Temporal of Great Britain in Parliment Assembled.
The Memorial [Note that the word Petition has been omitted.] of the Freeholders and other Inhabitants of the Massachusetts Bay, Rhode Island and Providence Plantations [blank space] New Jersey, Pensilvania, The Goverment of the Counties of New Castle Kent and Sussex Upon Delaware Province of Maryland.

Most Humbly Sheweth,
That his Majestys leige Subjects in his American Colonies through they Acknowledge a due Subordination to that August Body the British Parliment, are intituled in the Opinion of Your Memorialists to all the Inherent Rights

and Liberties of the Natives of Great Britain and have ever Since the settlement of the Said Colonies exercised those Rights and Liberties as far as their local Circumstances would Permit.

That your Memorialists humbly concieve one of the most Essential Rights of these Colonists which they have ever till lately uninterruptedly enjoyed to be Tryal by Jury.

That Your Memorialists also humbly concieve another of these essential Rights to be the exemption from all Taxes but Such as are imposed on the People by the several Legislatures in these Colonies which Right also they have till of late freely enjoyed. But your Memorialists humbly beg leave to represent to your Lordships that the Act for granting certain Stamp duties in the British Colonies in America &c fills his Majesties American Subjects with the deepest Concern as it tends to deprive them of the two Fundamental and invaluable Rights and Liberties above Mentioned and that several other late Acts of Parliament which extend the Jurisdiction and Powers of Courts of Admiralty in the Plantations beyond their Limits in Great Britain thereby make an unnecessary and unhappy distinction as to the modes of Trial between Us and Our fellow Subjects there, by whome we never have been excelled in Duty and Loyalty to Our Soverign

That from the Natural connection between Great Britain and America, the perpetual continuance of which Your Memorialists most ardently desire they Concieve that nothing can conduce more to the Interest of Both than the Colonists free Enjoyment of their Rights and Liberties and an Affictionate Intercourse between Great Britain and them. But your Memorialists (not waving their Claim to these Rights of which with the most becomeing veneration and deference to the Wisdom and Justice of Your Lordships they apprehend they cannot reasonably be deprived) Humbly Represent that from the peculiar circumstances of these Colonies the Duties imposed by the aforesaid Act and several other late Acts of Parliment are extreamly Grevious and Burthensome and the payment of the said Duties will very soon for want of Specie become Absolutely impracticable and that the Restrictions on Trade by the said Acts will not only greatly distress the Colonies but must be extreamly detrimental to the Trade and true interest of Great Britain.

Your memorialists therefore impressed with a just Sense of the Unfortunate Circumstances of the Colonies the impending distructive Consequences which must necessarily ensue from the Execution of those Acts, And Animated with the warmest Sentimints of filial Affection for their Mother Country most earnestly and Humbly intreat that Your Lordships will be pleased to hear their Council in Support of this Memorial and take the premises into Your most Serious Consideration and that Your Lordships will also be thereupon pleased to pursue such measures for Restoreing the Just Rights and Liberties of the Colonies and preserveing them for ever inviolate for Redressing their present and preventing future Grievances thereby promoteing the United Interest of Great Britain and America, as to your Lordships in Your great wisdom Shall seem most conducive and Effectual to that important End. And Your Memorialists [as in Duty bound] will [ever] pray.

The Congress adjourned to tomorrow morning at 9 o'Clock

Wednesday 23. October 1765. AM —
The Congress Met According to Adjournment
The Petition to the House of Commons being Engrossed was read & Compared & is as follows Viz. —
To the Honourable the Knights Citizens & Burgesses
In Great Brittain in Parliament Assembled
The Petition of his Majesty's Dutiful and Loyal Subjects
The Freeholders & other Inhabitants of the Colonies of the
Massachusetts Bay Road Island & Providence Plantations

[blank space] New Jersey Pennsylvania the Goverment of the Counties of New Castle Kent & Sussex upon Delaware Maryland

Most Humbly Sheweth

That the Severel late Acts of Parliament imposing divers Duties & Taxes on the Colonies and laying the Trade & Commerce thereof under very burthensome Restrictions But Above All the Act for Granting & applying certain Stamp Duties &c in America have filled them with the deepest Concern and Surprize And they Humbly conceive the Execution of them will be Attended with consequences very Injurious to the Commercial Interest of Great Britain & her Colony's and must terminate in the Eventual ruin of the Latter

Your Petitioners therefore most Ardently implore the Attention of the Honorable House to the United & Dutiful representation of their Circumstances & to their earnest Supplications for Relief from those Regulations that have already involved this Continent in Anxiety Confusion & Distress

We most Sincerely Recognize our Allegience to the Crown and Acknowledge all due Subordination to the Parliament of Great Britain & shall always retain the most grateful sense of their Assistance & protection. It is from & Under the English Constitution we derive all our Civil & Religious Rights & Liberties, We glory in being Subjects of the best of Kings and having been Born Under the most perfect Form of Government But it is with Most Ineffible & Humiliating Sorrow that we find ourselves of late deprived of the Right of Granting our own property for his Majestys service to which our Lives & fortunes are intirely devoted, and to which on his Royal Requisitions we ever been ready to contribute to the utmost of our Abilities.

We have also the Misfortune to find that all the Penaltys & forfeitures mentioned in the Stamp Act & in divers late

Acts of Trade extending to the plantations are at ye Election of the Informer recoverable in any Court of Admiralty in America. This as the Newly erected Court of Admiralty has a General Jurisdiction over all British America renders his Majesty's Subjects in these Colonies liable to be carried at an immense expense from one end of the Continent to the other.

It gives us also great pain to see a manifest distinction made therein between the Subjects of our Mother Country & those in the Colonies in that the like penalties & forfeitures recoverable there only in his Majestys Court of Record are made Cognizable here by a Court of Admiralty by this means we seem to be in effect unhappily deprived of two priviledges essential to Freedom & which all Englishmen have considered as their best Birthrights —

That of being free from all taxes but such as they have Consented to in person or by their representatives & of Trial by their Peers.

Your Petitioners further shew that the remote Scituation & other Circumstances of the Colonies render it impracticable that they should be represented but in their respective subordinate Legislatures and they humbly Concieve that the Parliament Adhering Strictly to the principles of the Constitution have never hitherto taxed any but those who are actually therein represented for this reason we humbly Apprehend they never have Taxed Ireland or any other of the Subjects without the realm. But were it ever so clear that the Colonies might in Law be reasonably deemed to be represented in the Honlbe. House of Commons yet we conceive that very good reasons from inconvenience from the principles of true policy and from the Spirit of the British Constitution may be adduced to show that it would be for the real Interest of Great Britain as well as her Colonies. That the late regulations Should be rescinded and the several Acts of Parliament imposing Duties & Taxes on the Colonies & extending the Jurisdiction of the Courts of

Admiralty here beyond their Antient Limits should be repealed.

We shall not attempt a minute detail of all the reasons which the Wisdom of the Honble. House may suggest on this Occasion but would humbly Submit the following particulars to their Consideration

That money is already become very scarce in these Colonies and is still decreasing by the necessary exportation of Specie from the Continent for the discharge of our Debts to Brittish Merchants. That an immensly heavy debt is yet due from the Colonies for British Manufactures & that they are still heavily burthened with Taxes to discharge the Arreages [arrearages] due for aids granted by them in the late War

That the Ballance of Trade will ever be much against the Colonies & in favor of Great Britain whilst we consume her Manufactures the demand for which must ever increase in proportion to the Number of Inhabitants setled here with the means of purchasing them. We therefore humbly Conceive it to be the Interest of Great Britain to increase rather than diminish those means as the profits of all the Trade of the Colonies Ultimately center there to pay for her Manufactures as we are not allowed to purchase Elsewhere, and by the Consumption of which at the Advanced prices the British Taxes Oblige the Makers & Venders to set on them we eventually contribute very largely to the revenue of the Crown —

That from the Nature of American business the Multiplicity of Suits & papers used in matters of Small Value in a Country where freeholds are so minutely divided & property so frequently transferred a Stamp Duty must ever be very burthensome & Unequal

That it is extreamly improbable that the Honble House of Commons should at all times be thoroughly Acquainted with our Condition & all facts requisite to a Just & Equal Taxation of the Colonies

It is also humbly Submitted whether there be not a Material distinction in reason & Sound policy at least between the Necessary exercise of parliamentary Jurisdiction in General Acts for the Amendment of the Common Law & the regulation of Trade & Commerce thro[ugh] the whole Empire & the exercise of that Jurisdiction by imposing Taxes on the Colonies

That the severel Subordinate provincial Legislatures have been moulded into forms as nearly resembling that of the Mother Country as by his Majestys Royal predecessors was thot Convenient and these Legislatures seem to have been wisely & graciously Established that the Subjects in the Colonies might under the due administration thereof enjoy the happy fruits of the British Government which in their present Circumstances they cannot be so fully & clearly availed of any other way

Under these forms of Government we & our Ancestors have been born or settled & have had our Lives Liberties & properties protected. The people here as every where else retain fondness for their Old Customs & Usages & we trust that his Majestys Service & the Interest of the Nation so far from being obstructed have been Vastly promoted by the provincial Legislatures.

That we Esteem our Connection with & dependance on Great Britain as one of our greatest blessings & apprehend the latter will appear to be Sufficiently secure when it is Considered that the Inhabitants in the Colonies have the most unbounded Affection for his Majesty's person Family & Government as well as for the Mother Country and that their Subordination to the Parliament is Universally Acknowledged

We therefore most humbly Intreat that the Honble House would be pleased to hear our Council in Support of this Petition and take our distressed & deplorable Case into their serious Consideration & that the Acts & Clauses of Acts so greviously restraining our Trade & Commerce Imposing Duties & Taxes on our property & extending the Jurisdiction of the Court of Admiralty beyond its Antient Limits may be repealed or that the Honourable House would Otherwise releive your petitioners as in your great Wisdom & Goodness shall seem meet And your petitioners as in duty bound shall ever pray —

The Congress Adjourned to tomorrow morning 10 o'Clock AM

Thursday Octo. 24 1765. the Congress met According to Adjournment

The Congress took Into Consideration the manner in which their several Petitions should be preferred and solicited in Great Britain, and thereupon came to the following Determination — Vizt

It is recommended by the Congress to the several Colonies to appoint Special Agents for soliciting Relief from their present [the word great occurs here in both the Rodney Journal and the Maryland Transcript] Grievances and unite their utmost Interest and Endeavours for that Purpose —

Voted unanimously, that the Clerk of this Congress Sign the Minutes of their Proceedings and deliver a Copy, for the use of each Colony and Province–

By Order of the Congress–

John Cotton Clerk

[A messenger from the Georgia Assembly delivered a letter while the Congress was in session and the following is a copy of that entered into the records. It is transcribed as it appears in the Connecticut replica of the Journal.]

Savannah in Georgia Septr:6th, 1765.

Sir,

Your Letter dated in June last acquainting me that the House of Representatives of your Province had unanimously agreed to propose a meeting at the City of New York of Committees from the Houses of Representatives of the Several British Colonies on this Continent on the first Tuesday in October next to consult together on the present circumstances of the Colonies and the difficulties to which they are and must be reduced by the Operation of the Acts of Parliament for laying duties and Taxes on the Colonies and to Consider of an Humble representation of their Condition to his majesty and the Parliament and to Implore Releif came to hand at an unlucky Season it being in the recess of the General Assembly of this Province. Nevertheless Immediately upon the receipt of your Letter I dispatched Expresses to the Several Represtatives of the Province Acquainting them with the purport thereof and requesting them to meet at this place without delay, and accordingly they met here on Monday last to the number of Sixteen being a Large majority of the representatives of this Province the whole Consisting of Twenty five persons, but His Excelly. our Governor being applyd to did not think it Expedient to call them together on the Occasion which is the reason of their not sending a Committee as proposed by your House for you may be assured, Sir, that no representatives on this Continent can more Sincerely Concur in the measures proposed than do the representatives of this Province now met together neither can any People as Individuals more warmly espouse the Common Cause of the Colonies Than do the people of this Province.

The Gentlemen now present request it as a favour you'l be pleased to send me a Copy of Such representation as [may] be Agreed upon by the Several Committees at New York and acquaint me how and in what manner the Same is to be lain before the King and Parliament whether by any person particularly authorised for that purpose or by the Colony Agents.

The General Assembly of this Province Stands Prorogued

to the Twenty second day of October next which is the time it Generally meets for the dispatch of the Ordinary Business of the Province and I doubt not the Representatives of this Province will then in their Legislative Capacity take under Consideration the Grievances so Justly Complained of and Transmit their Sense of the Same to Great Brittain in Such way as may seem best Calculated to Obtain redress and so as to Convince the Sister Colonies of their Inviolable attachment to the Common Cause.

I am Sir
Your most Obedt. &
most hum[b]l[e] Servt.
[Alexander Wylly]

[The signature, absent above, appears in the Rodney Journal as "Alex; Wylly" and in the Maryland Transcript as "Alexr. Willy." The Rodney Journal contains a line, found in neither the Connecticut replica nor the Maryland Transcript, which reads: "A Copy of A Letter Recd. from Georgia During the Setting of the Congress."]

[A line in the Rodney Journal, but not in the Connecticut replica nor the Maryland Transcript, is inserted here, reading as follows: "A Copy of the proceedings of the province of New Hampshire as Transmitted to the Congress"]

To Samuel White Esqr Speaker of the House of Representatives of Massachusets Bay at Boston in New England

Province of   In the House of
Newhampsr [New Hampshire]   Represent[ative]s
                               June 29th, 1765

Mr. Speaker laid before the House a letter from the Honourable Speaker of the Honourable House of Representatives of the Province of the Massachusetts Bay to the

Speaker of this Assembly proposing a meeting of Committees from the several Assemblies of the British Colonies on the Continent at New York to consider of a General United dutifull Loyal and Humble Representation of Our Circumstances and for Imploring his Majesty and the Parliament for Relief.

Which being Read

Resolved, that notwithstanding We are sensible such Representation ought to be made and approve of the proposed method for Obtaining thereof Yet the present Situation of our Governmental Affairs will not permit us to appoint a Committee to attend such meeting but shall be ready to Join in any Address to his Majesty and the Parliment We may be honoured with the Knowledge of probable to answer the proposed End.

A Clarkson Clerk

The two foregoing Letters are true Copies of the Original
Attest: John Cotton Clerk [his signature]

[The Rodney Journal ends at this point, and the following entry covering the final day of the Congress is missing, but occurs in the Maryland Transcript.]

Adjourned to tomorrow morning 9 o'clock

Friday October 25, 1765

The Congress met according to adjournment

Time not permitting the Clerk to make Copies at large of the Proceedings of the Congress for all the Colonies they think it proper shoud be furnished therewith.

Resolved that the Gentlemen from Massachusetts Bay be requested to send a copy thereof to the Colony of New Hampshire, the Gentlemen from Maryland to Virginia and the Gentlemen of So. Carolina to Georgia and North Carolina —

Sign'd by Order
Jno: Cotton Clerk [his signature]
[According to William Samuel Johnson's Diary, the Congress did not break up until 3:00; see Appendix. The Connecticut replica ends here. The two documents that follow appear in the Maryland Transcript but were not part of the official Journal. Both are reprinted here because of their relevance; the letter dated October 26, 1765, is particularly informative.]

An Account of the Disposition of the £500 granted by Ordinance and received of the Treasurer by William Murdock Edward Tilghman and Thomas Ringgold.

To Cash paid the whole Expences of the Committee to New York, there and back again	138. 14. 1
To Cash paid Express to New York to give Notice of our Coming	15
To paid for Express to send a Copy of our Proceedings to the Speaker of Virginia	1. 10
To paid for a Bill of Exchange to remit to Charles Garth Esqr. with the Address and Petitions 150. Sterling at 65 per cent exchange	247. 10
Cash remaining in hand 127 Pistoles and 18/8	172. 7. 8
	£575. 1. 9

By Cash received of the Treasurer in Gold £500 at 5/6 per dwt as follows

409 Spanish Pistoles at 27/s	£532. 3. 0
5 half Johannes at 57/6	14. 7. 6
4 French Pistoles at 26/6	5. 6. 0
1 Moidore	2. 3. 6
1½ Do [ditto]	1. 1. 9
	£575. 1. 9

[The foreign coins cited above were all of gold. Johannes and Moidores were Portugese coins also used in Brazil. The scarcity of English specie in the colonies necessitated the use of foreign money.]

Oct[obe]r 26th. 1765
[Letter to Charles Garth in London dispatched by the Maryland delegates while they were still in New York]

Sir,

We had the Honour to be appointed by the House of Representatives of the Province of Maryland a Committee to meet Committees of the Members of Assembly of the other Colonies on this Continent at New York the first of this Instant to join in a general and united Dutifull Loyal and humble Representation of the Condition of those Colonies to his Majesty and the Parliament and to implore Relief from their grievous Burthens lately laid upon our Trade and the Taxes and Duties lately imposed on us especially by the Stamp Act.

Accordingly Members from Nine Colonies met, to wit, from the Massachusetts Bay Connecticutt, Rhode Island, and Providence Plantations, New York, New Jersey, Pensylvania, The Government of the Counties of New Castle Kent and Sussex upon Delaware, Maryland and South Carolina, but as you'll find the Address &c Signed only by Members from Six of those Colonies it may be proper to acquaint you with the Reasons why they did not all Sign, tho they all concurred with the Proceedings.

The Lieutenant Governor of New York Prorogued their Assembly from Time to Time so that their House had not an Opportunity of appointing Members with full Powers to join and Sign the Address &c Yet the Assembly of New York having at their last Meeting appointed five of their Members as a Committee not only to Correspond with their Agent at home but also during the Recess of the House to write to and Correspond with the Several Assemblies of Committees of Assemblies on this Continent on the Subject matter of the several late Acts of Parliament so grievous and Dangerous to their Colonies it was thought proper to admit this Committee to join in the Conferences and they agreed to what was done and promised to use their Endeavours with their Assembly to concur also whenever they should be permitted to meet.

The South Carolina Assembly not rightly viewing the Proposal (which Originally came from the Assembly of the Government of the Massachusetts Bay) as it was intended that the several Committees when met should frame and Sign an Address to his Majesty and Memorial and Petition to the Parliament to be immediately dispatched by the Congress: Instructed their Members (M[essieu]rs Lynch, Rutledge and Gadsden) to return their Proceedings to them for Approbation The Connecticut Assembly made the same Restrictions in their Instructions. The Assembly also of New Hampshire wrote that they had resolved that notwithstanding they were sensible such a Representation ought to be made, and approved of the proposed Method of obtaining thereof, yet the present Scituation of their Governmental Affairs would not permit them to appoint a Committee to attend such Meeting but should be ready to join in any Address to his Majesty and the Parliament they might be honoured with the Knowledge of, Probable to answer the proposed End: And the Speaker of the Assembly of Georgia wrote that a Majority of their Members had applyed to the Governor to call their Assembly and he did not think it expedient which was the reason they did not send a Committee as proposed, but requested Us to transmit a Copy of our Proceedings to them (which will be done) and that their Assembly woud meet about this Time, and he did not doubt but they shoud Act so as to convince the Sister Colonies of their inviolable Attachments to the common Cause: We also understood the North Carolina, and we know the Virginia Assembly was Prorogued whereby they coud not have the Opportunity of joining us: So that we doubt not but the Colonies who have not Signed will very Speedily Transmitt Similar Addresses &c. if their Assembly's shoud not be hinered from Meeting And to this Purpose We hope you'll soon hear from the Assembly of South Carolina. By the Gentlemen of that Colony we were favoured with a Sight of your late Letters and informed of your careful and Spirited Conduct with regard to the Interests of that Colony and that together with your declaration which we find in those Letters that you enjoy an independant Seat in the British Parliament, induced us (as we have no established Agent at present for this Province nor have yet been able to obtain a Law to Tax ourselves for that Purpose) to trouble you with our Request that you will present the Inclosed Address to his Majesty and Memorial and Petition to the House[s] of Parliament, and exert your utmost Interest and abilities in behalf of this poor distressed Country and of this Province in Particular.

We hope as there is a Change in the Ministry and as the Gentlemen in the House of Commons may at their next Meeting take a more enlarged View of the true Interest of Great Britain and her Colonies they will find it to be in Supporting the Rights and encouraging the Trade of the latter, and that the Happiness of the Mother Country and her Colonies must be inseperable and that we shall obtain Relief.

The Several Committees agreed to Recommend it to their respective Colonies to appoint special Agents on this occasion and to instruct them to unite their utmost Interests and Endeavours for that Purpose; One Address &c. was Transmitted by the Gentlemen of the Massachusetts Government immediately to their Agent Mr. Jackson, we understood and We expect the other Colonies will have Duplicates sent to their Agents and we hope will all Unite in Expence and Instructions to have able Counsel before both the Lords and Commons, as our Petitions Pray.

We were intrusted with the Disposition of some Money upon this Occasion and inclose you a Bill of Exchange on Messrs. Capel and Osgood Hanbury for One hundred and fifty Pounds Sterling as a Compensation for your Trouble and Expence in this Affair. We doubt not our Assembly will approve of what we do in this matter, and as they are to Meet the last of this Month we shall lay our Proceedings before them and 'tis probable they will write you more fully and furnish you with Such further Instructions and Arguments as may appear to them to be proper to be given and urged on this Occasion in behalf of the Colonies —

We are your most Obedt. Servts.

[William Murdock, Thomas Ringgold, Edward Tilghman]

5

Aftermath

As agreed on at the Congress, the delegates from New York, Connecticut, and South Carolina, who had not signed the petitions, presented the three documents to their Assemblies for approval when they returned home to their respective colonies. It is of interest to examine what action was taken by the three legislative bodies.

New York
The New York Assembly was situated in a hotbed of dissension, not only as a result of the furore caused by the Sons of Liberty after the arrival of the stamped paper, but because of the troop activity at Fort George, which further contributed to the tension. A Congress of delegates from nine colonies meeting daily at the City Hall and gathering in the inns and coffee houses also tended to reinforce the opposition of the city's merchants and lawyers. On November 25, less than a month after the Congress dispersed, seventeen hundred New York City freemen and freeholders petitioned their representatives in the Assembly to take immediate action opposing the Stamp Act. Unaware of the contents of the documents drawn up at the Congress, they urged the Assembly to issue a declaration of rights including trial by jury and exemption "from Parliamentary internal taxation."[1]

The members of the Assembly recognized that their approval of the Declaration of Rights and the petitions drawn up at the Congress would meet the demands of their New York City constituents. Not only had they agreed to observe secrecy regarding the content of the documents, but a number of members did not approve of the phraseology of the petitions although not disagreeing in substance with their contents. After long discussion it was decided in the Lower House to rewrite the three petitions, and numerous revisions were made, which the Assembly approved on December 11. The words *address* and *memorial* were discarded, and the three instruments were drawn up as separate *petitions,* one addressed to the King, one to the Lords Spiritual and Temporal, and the third to Commons. All three petitions were signed by Speaker William Nicoll, and the members agreed to engage John Sergeant of London as a special agent to act in conjunction with Robert Charles, New York's appointed agent in England, to deliver the petitions and solicit relief for the grievances.[2] Thus, the New York colony acted unilaterally and independently of the Congress in its protests to King and Parliament.

On December 18, the New York Assembly also issued its own resolves, the language differing in many respects from the Declaration of Rights approved by the Stamp Act Congress, although incorporating the same general political philosophy.[3]

Connecticut

After the Connecticut Assembly listened to a reading of the three petitions by their delegates, some of the members wanted to withhold approval. They too objected to the phraseology, and had reservation about the references to "due subordination" in the petitions addressed to the two Houses of Parliament. But, as William Samuel Johnson said in a letter he wrote to Robert Ogden, they did not want "to imply a disunion, or want of Zeal or firmness in the Common

Cause they were by a great Majority approved without any alteration & ordered to be signed & forthwith forwarded to our agent Mr. Jackson. . . . "[4]

Johnson, Dyer, and Rowland were then authorized by the Assembly to affix their signatures to the petitions below the signatures of the other thirteen signatories. The Assembly then requested Governor Fitch to forward the documents to Richard Jackson in London, which he did, with a covering letter asking Jackson to present the petitions at Whitehall without delay. To impress Jackson with the importance of the petitions, the Assembly wrote him a separate letter urging that he exert his best efforts, and cooperate with the other colonial agents in seeking repeal of the Stamp Act and other objectionable tax measures enacted by Parliament.[5]

William Samuel Johnson had reservations about Jackson's competence to handle the assignment, and in a letter to Christopher Gadsden he wrote, "Happy would it be for us if we had an Agent as vigilant, assiduous & Zealous in the cause of the Colonies as you are blessed with [i.e., Charles Garth]. . . . I can not but hope he [Jackson] will exert himself upon this occasion since as he cannot but be sensible that if he does not he must lose all reputation with us, as well as incur the utmost displeasure of his Constituents."[6] When Johnson went to England two years later to represent Connecticut, he met and became friendly with Jackson, who was then counsel for the South Sea Company and Cambridge University. He learned to respect Jackson, a brilliant barrister held in such high esteem that his colleagues called him the "Omniscient Jackson."[7]

The Connecticut Assembly, after dealing with the petitions of the Congress, passed its own series of resolves on October 25, 1765.[8]

South Carolina
At a meeting of the South Carolina Commons House on

November 25, 1765, Christopher Gadsden made a report on what had taken place at the New York Congress, and presented the texts of the three petitions for approval. A vote was then called; the House approved the instruments with only one dissenting vote, and authorized Speaker Peter Manigault to affix his signatures to them. The three documents were then dispatched to Garth on the vessel *Charming Charlotte,* then preparing to sail from Charleston Harbor to England. The reader will recall that almost a month before, the Maryland delegation had already sent copies of the same petitions from New York to Garth.

"The next day [November 26]," Gadsden wrote, "the House did us the honor to give us their thanks by the Speaker signifying their approbation of our whole conduct in the most ample and obliging manner." Gadsden was then appointed chairman of a committee to draw up South Carolina's set of resolves. The House approved these resolves on November 29 and ordered them published.[9]

As an added touch, which occurred some time after the Stamp Act was repealed, the Commons House appointed a committee to wait on Gadsden, Lynch, and Rutledge to ascertain if they would sit for their portraits at the colony's expense "as a Memorial to the great service they performed for their country at the Congress in October." The intention was to hang the paintings in the Commons House, although I have found no evidence that the paintings were ever executed.[10]

Of the four colonies not represented at the Congress, subsequent action on the petitions was taken only by two of them, as indicated below.

Georgia
On November 25, 1765, the Georgia Assembly received

copies of the petitions and the Journal from the South
Carolina delegation, and at a session of the Common House
on December 14 the petitions were read and promptly approved. A resolution was then passed authorizing Speaker
Wylly to sign the documents and forward them to Charles
Garth for presentation to King and Parliament.[11] The House
appropriated £50 for Garth's fee, which was considerably less
than the fees paid him by the other colonies he represented,
but Georgia, having a very small white population was not
an affluent colony.

New Hampshire

On November 22, 1765, Speaker Henry Sherburne laid
before the New Hampshire Lower House the proceedings of
the Stamp Act Congress, including the Declaration of Rights
and the three petitions. The question as to what course of
action should be taken was discussed, and the members
voted unanimously "That this House do fully Approve and
Heartily Joyn in the Resolves and several Petitions agreed
upon by the General Congress. . . . " A committee of three
members, including the Speaker, was empowered to sign the
petitions, which were then forwarded to Barlow Trecothick
and John Wentworth, New Hampshire's agents in London.
The agents were instructed to use their "utmost Endeavors"
to obtain the favor and compassion of King and Parliament
toward his majesty's faithful and dutiful subjects.[12]

The enthusiastic support the House gave to the actions of
the Congress was enough to silence any criticism of the
colony's failure to send delegates to New York.

North Carolina

Governor Tryon continued to prevent the North Carolina
Assembly from meeting by the series of prorogues he issued,

and the members were not able to assemble and act on the petitions that the South Carolina delegation had copied and sent to the Speaker. On December 21, 1765, Tryon dissolved the Assembly, and suggested that he would call the members into session on April 22, 1766. He failed to do so, and did not summon them until November 3, 1766. By then the Stamp Act had been repealed. At this late date there was no reason for the House to do anything with the petitions the Speaker had received six months before. On November 6 the members of the House gently rebuked Tryon in these words: "This House is truly sorry, Sir, that any reason whatsoever, should have prevented your meeting this Assembly till this time."[13] Thus, North Carolina did not sign the petitions drawn up at the Congress, nor did it originate its own petitions to King and Parliament.

Virginia
It was the same story in Virginia. After a succession of recesses Governor Fauquier called the House of Burgesses into session on November 6, 1766. He blithely excused himself for not convening the members earlier, by telling them:

"Not having any pressing Occasion for my meeting you in General Assembly before this time, I have followed the Bent of my own Inclinations, which have always been to create as little Expense to the Country and as little Trouble to yourselves, as the Circumstances of the times would permit me." He added that since the Stamp Act was no longer in effect, "Your Grievances have been redressed, the Act you thought oppressive repealed, and every Indulgence in Commerce which you should with reason expect, or even desire, have been granted you."[14]

The Burgesses then officially thanked the Governor in a formal address full of extravagant praise, approved on November 12, in which they assured him that they "declare

our constant Readiness to devote our Lives and Fortunes
in Defence of his [the King's] sacred Person, Crown and
Dignity against all his Enemies."[15]

What about the three petitions in the hands of the Speaker
still awaiting action? Inasmuch as the Stamp Act was now
a bad memory, the documents were simply tabled, which
was the most convenient way to dispose of papers that had
then outlived their usefulness.

Massachusetts, Pennsylvania, Maryland, New Jersey, Rhode Island, Lower Counties

Further action by the six colonies whose delegates had
signed the petitions in New York was unnecessary, since the
Massachusetts delegates had already sent the signed petitions
to Richard Jackson in London. Nevertheless, the reactions
of the several Assemblies are worth noting.

When the Massachusetts delegates returned to Boston,
James Otis made a report to the House on November 1 and
the members officially extended their thanks to the delegation.
The House later authorized the printing of the three petitions
in their official journal. The members also authorized the
payment of £200 to Richard Jackson and his co-agent, Dennys
(Dennis) De Berdt, a colonial merchant of Dutch descent,
to compensate them for presenting the petitions.[16]

Since Dickinson and Bryan were not reelected to the
Pennsylvania Assembly, Morton made the report to the
Pennsylvania Lower House on January 7, 1766, and delivered a set of the signed petitions and a copy of the Journal
of the Congress. The House heard the petitions read and the
texts were entered into the journal. It was then ordered
that the three petitions be transmitted by the Committee of
Correspondence to Pennsylvania's agents in London (one
of whom was Richard Jackson) at the earliest opportunity.[17]
The members also extended their formal thanks to the dele-

gates, which Morton acknowledged in their behalf, by stating that they "esteem the Approbation of this Honourable House the best reward of their Endeavours to serve the Public."[18]

The three Maryland delegates had taken independent action on October 26, the day after the Congress adjourned, without waiting for the endorsement of their Assembly. Maryland did not have an agent in London, and during the Congress her delegates talked over the matter with the South Carolina representatives. Based on the recommendations given Charles Garth, a barrister in his early thirties and a member of Parliament, who had represented South Carolina in London since 1762, the Maryland delegates addressed a letter to him. They requested that he present the signed petitions on behalf of Maryland to the King and both Houses of Parliament. For this service they enclosed a bill of exchange in the amount of £150 sterling, which they deducted from the expense funds allotted them by the Maryland Assembly for the New York trip. (See letter to Garth in Journal above, chap. 4). Incidentally, Garth had been paid £200 in sterling annually by South Carolina, with his expenses reimbursed, and when he was asked to handle a special mission he was usually given an additional fee.

Upon their return to Annapolis from New York, Tilghman, Murdock, and Ringgold were present at a session of the Lower House of the Maryland Assembly on November 5, 1765. They delivered a copy of the Journal of the Congress, which was read aloud and placed in the custody of the Speaker, Robert Lloyd. Tilghman introduced a bill that was favorably received, authorizing the support of an agent in England. He explained that the delegates had written Garth before leaving New York, asking him to accept the appointment. The other members had no objection to Garth's appointment.

On November 27 the three delegates submitted the expense accounts of the New York trip, which the House unanimously approved, and authorized the Speaker to thank them "for their conduct in the Execution of the Trust reposed in them by this House at the late Congress at New York." A committee was then appointed to dispatch a second set of the petitions to Garth and to advise him officially that the House fully concurred with the action of the Congress at New York and the conduct of the Maryland representatives.[19]

On November 29, 1765, Hendrick Fisher reported to the New Jersey Lower House what had occurred at New York, presenting copies of the Journal, the Declaration, and the three petitions. The House voted unanimous approval of the documents, and extended their thanks to Fisher and Borden (not to Ogden) "for their faithful and judicious discharge of the trust reposed in them."[20]

The next day the members passed a separate set of resolves, containing many of the points that were included in the Declaration of Rights.[21]

The two Rhode Island delegates, Bowler and Ward, made their report to the General Assembly of Rhode Island and Providence Plantations on October 30, 1765. The members approved the report, and requested and empowered Governor Samuel Ward to send copies of the three signed petitions to Joseph Sherwood, the Rhode Island agent in London (also the agent for New Jersey), and requested that Sherwood be directed "to join with other agents in enforcing the said addresses." Governor Ward wrote Sherwood on November 7, and Sherwood was paid £200 to handle the petitions.[22]

Rodney and McKean returned to New Castle after the October 1765 session of the Assembly of the Lower Counties had adjourned, but they made their report at a May 1766 adjourned session. The members of the Assembly unanimously approved the Journal of the Congress, the Declaration of Rights, the three petitions, and the conduct of the two representatives. They voted them their official thanks "for their faithful and judicious Discharge of the Trust in them reposed, and that this House will make them a generous

Allowance for their great Care and Expence in attending the Service aforesaid."[23]

In summation, the petitions were signed at New York by thirteen representatives of six colonies: Massachusetts, Maryland, New Jersey, Pennsylvania, Rhode Island, and the Lower Counties, and were sent to England by the Massachusetts delegates.

Following adjournment of the Congress, Connecticut, South Carolina, New Hampshire, and Georgia signed the petitions and sent them to their respective agents in England. The New York Assembly drew up its own petitions, which were forwarded to the colony's London agent for presentation to King and Parliament. Virginia and North Carolina did not sign the documents, nor did the Assemblies of these two colonies feel it necessary to draw up their own petitions.

What happened when this plethora of petitions was received by the colonial agents in London? Were they delivered to the King and the Houses of Parliament as intended? If so, did they influence Parliament's decisions? It is not necessary to search further in contemporary English records than the papers of the two most prominent colonial agents, Charles Garth and Richard Jackson, to learn what happened. The petitions sent to Jackson were handled by his 72-year-old associate and co-agent, Dennis DeBerdt. Jackson represented Connecticut, Pennsylvania, and Massachusetts; DeBerdt received a fee from Massachusetts, but not from the other two colonies.

Charles Garth, who represented South Carolina, Maryland, and Georgia, was present as a member of the House of Commons during the debates in the closed sessions of the House. Thus, his reports of what occurred are authoritative. Although not a member of Parliament, DeBerdt had excellent political contacts, and when he received the petitions and letter of instructions that the Massachusetts delegates had sent to Jackson from New York when the Congress adjourned, he knew what steps to take. He promptly delivered the address to the King to Secretary of State General Conway, a friend of the colonies, who had opposed the Stamp Act when it was first introduced. Conway agreed to present the address to His Majesty, George III.

DeBerdt then gave the petition for the House of Commons to George Cooke, a member of Commons, who was also friendly to the colonies and who had considerable political influence in Parliament. Cooke assured him that he would do his utmost to introduce it in the House when the members reconvened on January 14, 1766. There had been a short session beginning December 17 (which recessed on December 20), at which time the Stamp Act was discussed but no action taken.

DeBerdt next paid a call on his good friend the Earl of Dartmouth, President of the Lords Commissioners for Trade and Plantations (also called the Board of Trade), to ask him if he would deliver the memorial to the House of Lords. After examining the document Lord Dartmouth refused to do so. He told DeBerdt that the Lords would not receive a "memorial" from the colonies, because the word had diplomatic connotations that the Lords could not accept.[24] There the matter rested. Although Dartmouth did not officially accept the memorial, he was well aware of its contents, and probably informed his colleagues.

On January 28, 1766, which was about two months after DeBerdt delivered the petitions, Charles Garth received the letter dated October 26, 1765, along with the petitions that the Maryland delegates sent him from New York. What caused the delay in the delivery of these documents is not known. A few days later Garth received letters of instructions and similar petitions from South Carolina and Georgia. Garth promptly made an appointment with Secretary Conway, who was already familiar with the contents of the petitions as a result of DeBerdt's call. He had also received a letter that Governor Ward of Rhode Island had written him on November 6 expressing the hope that "the united addresses of the colonies will be graciously received and granted."[25]

Conway accepted the address to be laid before the King, identical with the document given him by DeBerdt except for the additional signatures. But in view of what had happened in the House of Commons the previous day when George Cooke introduced the petition (see below), Conway advised Garth that it would be unwise and unnecessary to introduce in Commons a second petition identical with one that had already been presented.

Garth accepted Conway's advice, making no effort to introduce the petition to Commons. However, he took the memorial intended for the House of Lords to Lord Dartmouth, who reiterated what he told DeBerdt, that is, that the Lords considered a memorial from the colonies an inappropriate instrument and would not receive it. It is apparent that Dartmouth was looking for an excuse not to introduce any document in the House of Lords that originated in the Stamp Act Congress. He knew that both Commons and Lords were then debating the Stamp Act in their closed sessions. During the Christmas recess he had been present at a meeting in Lord Rockingham's London home, where the Stamp Act was thoroughly discussed and various ways of amending it were considered. He was fully aware that Rockingham, who had inherited the Act from Grenville, favored its outright repeal as soon as possible. The ministry was in a weak position at home and could not afford to take forceful action in the colonies. Dartmouth believed that additional pressures put on Parliament from a Congress that had met without approval would do more harm than good. If repeal were to be accomplished, the petitions of an illicit Congress should not be associated with it, because neither Lords nor Commons should be placed in a position of acknowledging the existence of such body.[26]

Secretary Conway also shared Dartmouth's view that no

impression should be left that Parliament had been intimidated into repealing legislation it had passed the previous year, in order to appease colonial subjects who refused to obey it. Conway was reported as saying that the Act should be repealed, "but there was some difficulty about coming off with honor, and that America would boast she had conquered Britain. . . . "[27]

Garth was disappointed when Dartmouth rejected the memorial to the Lords, but he was more persistent and more resourceful than the elderly DeBerdt. After reflecting on the situation, which to him seemed to have reached an impasse because of the inept use of a diplomatic term and not because of the contents of the document, he decided on a new tack. He composed what he termed a *petition* addressed to the Lords on behalf of Maryland, South Carolina, and Georgia to serve as a sort of covering letter for the memorial. He delivered the petition and its pertinent attachment to Lord Dartmouth, who evidently could not think of any valid reason for not accepting it. What Dartmouth did with the document is not known, but the House of Lords was never called upon to act on it.

The whole situation in Parliament was fraught with potential repercussions, none of which would benefit the empire. If the members agreed to redress the grievances of the colonists as an official acknowledgment of their petitions, protocol demanded that colonial violators of the Stamp Act must be brought to justice. Not to punish lawbreakers would be an affront to Parliament and a mockery to English jurisprudence. Rockingham, Dartmouth, and Conway knew that to attempt to bring thousands of Sons of Liberty rioters into the colonial courts for trial was next to impossible, and would cause further discord, which would widen the breach they were trying to close. Enforcement of the Act might also cause an uprising in England among unemployed workmen and seamen who supported the colonies. This would require the use of armed forces in both England and America, and Parliament would have a Civil War on its hands. If war broke out, there was a likelihood that France and Spain would come to the aid of the colonies, in which case Britain would face a real crisis. The opposite course of action was to yield to colonial pressures, which would weaken Parliament's authority.

Lord Dartmouth had found a technicality whereby the Lords could escape recognizing the protests of the Stamp Act Congress, and Secretary Conway was doing his utmost to find a similar excuse to keep the petition from formally coming before Commons. When George Cooke told Conway that he intended to introduce the petition, the latter did his best to dissuade him, but Cooke went ahead despite Conway's objections.²⁸ When Cooke took the floor he read the petition aloud, making appropriate comments about the contents. The document was not new to most of the members, since the colonial agents all had copies in their possession, and had doubtless discussed it among themselves when they gathered in their favorite coffee house to exchange views, as they frequently did. The agents, in turn, having direct contact with British officialdom, had laid the foundation for repeal by pressing members of Parliament, as well as London merchants, for their support. The reading of the petition by no means meant that the House officially received it for disposition, because there was strong opposition against doing so.

The procedure was for a member to introduce a petition if the House consented to hear it. If the members decided to act on it, it was then brought to the table and read aloud in its entirety by the Clerk of the House. It was well known that the ministry was studiously avoiding the recognition of any petition that questioned Parliament's right to tax the colonies, and the House needed an excuse for not taking action that would *per se* admit such recognition. This prompted a discussion of the technicalities that could be invoked to avoid acknowledging the petition and blocking its introduction.

One argument was that it had not been submitted in proper and legal form since it purported to come from "the Freeholders and Inhabitants" of six of the colonies, but it bore the signatures of only a few colonial leaders. To be admissible, it was argued, such petition must bear the signatures of all the petitioners. The members of the House were well aware that this was an impossibility because everyone knew that "the Freeholders and Inhabitants" of the six signatory colonies probably numbered in excess of 800,000.

Some members of the House took the position that the Congress that originated the petition appeared to be a Federal Union that had assembled without authority from the mother country. If the House were willing to act on an appeal submitted by His Majesty's colonists unconstitutionally assembled, it would be an implied admission that it had given countenance to an illegal legislative body.

Other members argued that the petitions questioned Parliament's right to impose internal and external taxes, and no petition could be accepted by the House that challenged a right that struck at the very heart of Parliament's legislative prerogatives. Furthermore, the illicit Congress and its bold actions "Strongly pointed at Independency upon the Mother Country."[29]

Despite logical refutation of these arguments by Cooke and others sympathetic to the colonies, Cooke was forced to withdraw the petition. It was ironical that the Rockingham Ministry, while favoring repeal, could not endorse the petition. To have done so would, in fact, have hindered their efforts for repeal, because it would be interpreted to mean that they were supporting a challenge of Parliament's legislative authority. When Lord Conway reported what had occurred to the King, the latter replied, "I am much surpris'd that after what had passed between You & Mr. Cooke, He still persisted in presenting the very extraordinary Petition of the Congress to the House of Commons & am glad for the Honour of Parliament it was obliged to be withdrawn."[30]

Like Conway, the King was concerned lest Parliament's honor be sullied if the impending modification or repeal of the Stamp Act were attributed to pressures exerted by his colonial subjects. Ten years later, when the Second Continental Congress sought reconciliation with the mother country, George III and his cabinet declined the so-called Olive Branch Petition for the same reason. The King was willing to deal with the colonies individually, but he persisted in refusing to recognize what he deemed an illegal Congress.

By using the parliamentary stratagem of moving to discuss "an order of the day," the House conveniently laid the petition of the Stamp Act Congress aside without acting on it. On January 28 the House went into a "Committee of the Whole House" to consider the affairs of the American colonies, their grievances, the powers of Parliament, the reimbursement of those who had suffered losses because of the Stamp Act, and other subjects of relevance, *except the petition*. The members sat on these discussions from eight to ten hours daily until February 21, listening to many witnesses, which left no opportunity for Cooke formally to reintroduce the petition.

During the discussions, Conway presented a series of resolutions stating that "tumults and insurrections of the most dangerous nature" had taken place in the colonies in open defiance of the laws passed by Parliament. These events, he said, had been "encouraged and enflamed by sundry votes and resolutions passed in the several of the assemblies of the said province," but he made no reference to the Stamp Act Congress.[31]

In actuality, the petition to Commons and the memorial to the Lords had little or no influence on Parliament's decision to repeal the Stamp Act. A situation had been reached in England where economic bans were more efficacious than addresses, memorials, resolves, or petitions. The Rockingham Ministry had been moving in the direction of repeal long before the petitions were received from the Stamp Act Congress, and economic developments accelerated repeal.

If the petitions sent to England were not directly responsible for the repeal of the Stamp Act, what was accomplished by the Stamp Act Congress? It cannot be said that the Congress inspired the formation of the Sons of Liberty, nor did it provoke the Stamp Act riots. It had nothing to do with provoking the resignations of the Stamp Distributors. These events took place before the delegates assembled in New York, and it was months later before the Declaration of Rights and transcripts of the petitions were published in colonial newspapers.

The event that triggered a chain reaction that finally led to the repeal of the Stamp Act took place in New York City less than a week after the Congress adjourned. The *New York Mercury* broke the news with a brief paragraph in its October 28, 1765, edition reading, "We hear that most of the Gentlemen in Town have entered into a Resolution not to buy any European Manufactures till their Trade is more opened, the Sugar Act altered and the Stamp Act repealed." The date of this item leaves no doubt that the matter must have been under discussion by the New York merchants *while the Congress was still in session,* and it is my belief that the merchant delegates to the Congress participated in these discussions. Actually a meeting had been called for Monday, October 28, according to the October 31 edition of the *New York Post Boy,* but because of the short notice, not enough merchants were able to attend to permit any action.

A second meeting was announced in the *Post Boy,* and on Thursday afternoon, October 31, at 4:00 P.M., about 70 of the city's leading merchants met in the "long room" in George Burns's City Arms Tavern, where they formally drew up a set of resolutions and agreements. These resolutions stated that the signers agreed to cancel all outstanding orders

on their suppliers in Great Britain, and that they would sell
no English goods shipped to them after January 1—until
the Stamp Act was repealed.[32]

Following the meeting, the cooperation of other New York
City businessmen who had not attended was solicited to join
the boycott. Eventually the resolutions were subscribed to
"by upwards of Two hundred principal Merchants." New
York retailers took their own separate action by signing
resolutions in which they also agreed not to "buy any Goods,
Wares or Merchandize of any Person or Persons whatsoever
that shall be shipped from Great Britain after the first day
of January next unless the Stamp Act shall be repealed."

Although New England consumers, in protesting the Act
of 1764, had made an attempt the previous year to boycott
English goods, what occurred in New York City was the first
concerted action by colonial businessmen to exert commercial
pressures on the mother country. If this boycott was hatched
in the Stamp Act Congress—and that is my contention—the
committee that censured the Journal was careful to allow no
reference to be made to it. But even if the idea did not take
root in the plenary sessions of the Congress, the subject of a
boycott must have been discussed when the merchant members were socializing with New York merchants. Four of the
most influential New York merchants—Cruger, Bayard,
Lispenard, and Philip Livingston—were members of the
Congress, and drastic action taken by the New York business
community immediately following the adjournment of a Congress held in their city to protest the Stamp Act was more
than a coincidence.

The Congress adjourned October 25, and the meeting of
the merchants was first called for October 28. Thus the delegates, more timorous than those in the First Continental
Congress, could not be accused of provoking action that might
be interpreted in England as disobedience to the authority of
King and Parliament. They were all officials in their respective colonies, and the safest course was to disassociate them-

selves from any action that might have the slightest resemblance to treason.

One hint that the members of the Congress felt that the technique of a boycott would be effective is found in a letter written by Robert R. Livingston shortly after the Congress adjourned. He wrote that the petitions drawn up at the Congress "will not have half so good an effect as the Resolutions of the Merchants."[33]

Although the evidence is purely circumstantial, it is possible that the delegates may have agreed that a general boycott throughout the colonies would be the best method to achieve repeal. If it were made to appear that the New York merchants took the first action on their own initiative, business leaders in the other colonies could be secretly encouraged to follow New York's example. From the viewpoint of British merchants, the season was the worst time of the year for a boycott, because American merchants normally placed their orders for spring shipment between October and January.

Whether or not the Pennsylvania delegates (especially Bryan, a merchant) worked behind the scenes on their return to inspire a similar nonimportation movement is a moot question, but it was reported from Philadelphia on November 7 that "An Agreement of the same Kind with that under the New York head relating to the Importation of Dry Goods &c from England is now on foot here." On November 14 Philadelphia merchants held a crowded meeting where they passed a series of resolutions signed by "above 400 traders." These resolutions, which extended the boycott to Philadelphia merchants, were patterned after the New York resolutions but contained much stronger language. For example, the fifth section provided for the appointment of a committee to make certain that all the signers held to their commitments. Because of the importance of these resolutions in view of the events that followed, they are quoted in full:

First. It is unanimously Resolved and Agreed, that in

all Orders, any of the Subscribers to this Paper may send
to Great-Britain for Goods they shall and will direct their
Correspondents not to ship them until the Stamp-Act is
repealed.

Secondly. That all those amongst the Subscribers that
have already sent Orders to Great-Britain for Goods shall
and will immediately countermand the same, until the
Stamp-Act is repealed. Except such Merchants as are
Owners of Vessels already gone or now cleared out for
Great-Britain, who are at Liberty to bring back in them,
on their own Accounts, Coals, Casks of Earthen-Ware,
Grindstones, Pipes, Iron-Pots, Empty Bottles, and such
other bulky Articles, as Owners usually fill up their Ships
with, but no Dry-Goods of any Kind, except such Kind of
Dye Stuffs and Utensils necessary for carrying on Manufactures, that may be ordered by any Person.

Thirdly. That none of the Subscribers hereto, shall or
will vend any Goods or Merchandizes whatever, that shall
be shipped them on Commission from Great-Britain, after
the first of January next, unless the Stamp-Act be repealed.

Fourthly. That these Resolves and Agreements shall
be binding on all and each of us the Subscribers who do
hereby, each and every Person for himself, upon his Word
of Honour, agree, that he will strictly and firmly adhere
to, and abide by, every Article from this Time, until the
First Day of May next, when a Meeting of the Subscribers
shall be called to consider whether the further Continuation of this Obligation be then necessary.

Fifthly. It is agreed, that if Goods of any Kind do arrive
from Great-Britain at such time, or under such circumstances, as to render any Signer of this Agreement suspected of having broken his Promises, the Committee now
appointed shall enquire into the Premises and if such suspected Person refuses, or cannot give them Satisfaction,
the Subscribers hereto will unanimously take all prudent
Measures to discountenance and prevent the Sale of such
Goods, until they are released from this Agreement by
mutual and general Consent.

Lastly. As it may be necessary that a Committee of the
Subscribers be appointed to wait on the Traders of this

City, to get this present Agreement generally subscribed, the following Gentlemen are appointed for that Purpose [the names of eleven merchants were given here].[34]

The retailers in Philadelphia, following the example of their New York brethren, also joined the boycott. Thus, the most populous city in the colonies, which ranked first in the consumption of imports, joined in the ban on English goods.

It was inevitable that Boston, the third largest city in the colonies, would follow the example set by New York and Philadelphia. On November 25 the *Boston Evening Post,* which had previously reported that a boycott had been agreed on by New York merchants, published a transcript of the resolutions and agreement signed in Philadelphia. This evidently was all that was needed to arouse the Boston business community to take action, and on Tuesday evening, December 3, a large number of merchants and traders assembled at the popular British Coffee House. There they passed a series of nonimportation, nonsale resolutions employing phraseology strikingly similar to that used in the resolutions agreed to by their commercial brethren in New York and Philadelphia. The December 16 issue of the *Evening Post,* which contained the full text of these resolutions, reported that they had been signed by 220 of the principal Boston merchants, and that traders at Salem and Marblehead had also agreed to affix their signatures.[35]

There is nothing new or startling today about economic pressures exerted on suppliers by trade or consumer groups, but in colonial America it was not yet a proven technique, and the outcome was by no means certain. In refusing to accept English imports, the merchants were taking an important commercial risk, because a decline in the sale of English goods was bound to affect their pocketbooks. Moreover, consumers would be directly affected, because many of the imported products were not manufactured in America, and substitutes were not available. Nevertheless, the mer-

chants were willing to take the risk, because the enforcement
of the Stamp Act was an intolerable alternative.

The news of the action taken by merchants and traders
in America's three major commercial cities spread throughout the colonies, and other merchants joined the boycott. As
the opposition became more widespread, the merchants also
decided to withhold payment of the outstanding bills of
about £4 million that they owed English manufacturers and
distributors. This was a paralyzing blow to English commerce.

Strangely enough, English merchants and manufacturers
bore no rancor against their colonial customers for the nonimportation and nonsale resolutions, but they blamed the
situation on Grenville, the former First Lord of the Treasury,
and his ill-advised fiscal policies.[38] Unlike the position taken
earlier by English squires, the merchants felt that taxing
the colonies was unwise to begin with because it would reduce colonial buying power and thus limit purchases of English commodities.

The Rockingham Ministry, fully aware of the riots in the
colonies, the resignations of the Stamp Distributors, the
resolves passed in the Assemblies, and deeply concerned
about the economic crisis imposed by the boycott, argued
that the Stamp Act was bringing economic ruin to Great
Britain. The ministry would not admit that the act was
unenforceable, nor were any arguments advanced that it
should be repealed because of its infringement of colonial
rights. Lord Rockingham avoided reference to political
pressures, concentrating his arguments on the economic
reasons for repeal. He argued that correcting his prede-
cessor's tragic mistake was solely a matter of protecting
Great Britain's economic self-interest.

The distress of the London business community provided
an opportunity to organize the opposition throughout England, and Rockingham allied himself with the London merchants. This is made clear in a letter that Grenville wrote

to Lord Botetourt on November 3, 1765, in which the following passage appears:

> I have this moment been informed that an attempt has been made by some of the Agents for the present [Rockingham] ministry to obtain some Petitions or memorials to be presented to them in relation to America & the West Indias to cast by that means some Reflections upon the late [Grenville] ministry & particularly upon your Humble Servant, & that a meeting at the Merchants Hall is ordered next Tuesday for that Purpose. Intimations of the like kind have otherwise been sent to Liverpoole & Lancaster by the same Persons.[37]

As a result of letters that London merchants circulated to businessmen in other English trading and manufacturing towns, petitions were drawn up demanding that Parliament repeal the Stamp Act. English businessmen needed little encouragement, because the American trade was a principal source of their profits, and the boycott and nonpayment of outstanding bills were causing a recession. Unless Parliament acted promptly to repeal the Stamp Act, they claimed, they would be facing economic disaster. Along with the petitions pouring into the House of Commons came rumors of impending riots and rebellion of the unemployed working class.[38] The King, who now had begun to favor some modification of the Act but not its repeal, was told by his advisers that he must take a position for either repeal or enforcement. He decided in favor of repeal, but it is extremely unlikely that the flattering address sent to him by the delegates of the Congress that he considered unlawful had anything to do with his decision.

Although the members of Parliament never yielded one inch in their declared right to tax the colonies, the vote in the House of Commons for repeal of the Stamp Act was 275 for and 167 against. In the House of Lords, 105 members voted for repeal and 71 against. The Act then received royal assent and was officially repealed March 18, 1766. Repeal was the result of expediency, not because Parliament was acceding to the right of the colonies to tax themselves. It was made to appear that English merchants, not the colonies, won a victory. The legislation stated that "the continuance of the said act would be attended with many inconveniences, and may be productive of consequences greatly detrimental to the commercial interests of these kingdoms. . . . "[39] Not one word in the statute made mention of colonial rights or referred to the Stamp Act Congress. Nevertheless, repeal was a victory for the colonies, and they rejoiced in it. There were celebrations in many American cities and towns, with parades and frolics. Gov. Samuel Ward of Rhode Island appointed Thursday, June 26, 1766, a day of Thanksgiving to celebrate the repeal. Addresses thanking the King were drafted by a number of the Assemblies, for, as a Boston minister declaimed from his pulpit, it "opened in all hearts the springs of joy."[40] The Stamp Act crisis was over.

About £4,000 in stamp taxes had been collected during the period the Act was in effect, which was far less than the administrative costs, and there still remained tons of unused stamped paper in storage throughout the colonies. There was nothing for the Stamp Commissioners to do but authorize the return of this stamped paper to England, as indicated by the letter in the Appendix written to John Hughes, the Pennsylvania Stamp Distributor.

The paper and parchment returned from the colonies was reused in England, either by cutting away the American stamped imprints and embossing the reduced sheets with English stamp impressions, or by overstriking the American imprints with English stamp dies. Today the original 1765 American stamp impressions are highly prized by stamp collectors, but the overstruck English stamps are extremely rare philatelic items.[41]

In examining the events of the pre-Revolutionary era, it becomes clear that a significant accomplishment of the Stamp Act Congress was in demonstrating that it was possible for the colonies to meet together and, having met, to decide on concerted action. An editorial in the *Boston Post Boy* on March 24, 1766 (which was reprinted from the *Providence Gazette*), expressed the general sentiment prevailing in the northeastern colonies:

> The Congress at New York, first planned by the house of representatives in the Massachusetts Bay, secured the desirable union of the colonies. This laudable step ought forever to be remembered and initiated as often as our common safety shall make it necessary.

The author was more prophetic than he realized. The Stamp Act Congress proved to be the first step along the road to unify the thirteen colonies, paving the way for the First and Second Continental Congress. As Dickinson expressed it, "By uniting We stand, by dividing We fall."[42]

The Stamp Act Congress also made the colonists aware that the thirteen mainland colonies, each of which had previously been preoccupied with its own problems, now shared issues in common. Prominent members of the colonial Assemblies were brought together in the forum of the Congress, and these relationships proved to be useful and valuable as future events unfolded.

Even though the petitions to King and Parliament originating in the Congress may not have been directly responsible for the repeal of the Stamp Act, they challenged the doctrine of the supremacy of Parliament. Despite the paradoxical references to "due subordination," in the petitions as well as in the Declaration of Rights, there was no doubt that the colonies would never quietly submit to taxation by Parliament.[43]

The Declaration of Rights enunciated principles that Dickinson later said "may be said to form the American bill of rights."[44] If one examines the later Declarations and Resolves drawn up October 14, 1774, in the First Continental Congress, he will find expressions therein relating to inherent rights and liberties; trial by jury; the unwillingness of the colonies to be represented in Parliament; the privilege to petition for grievances; and the right of self-taxation.[45] All of these can be found in the earlier Declaration of Rights that originated in the Stamp Act Congress. Moreover, two significant points in the 1765 Declaration of Rights were also emphasized in the Declaration of Independence of 1776; namely, that taxes should not be imposed without the consent of the taxpayer, and that trial by jury is an inherent right guaranteed to all free men.

It should not be forgotten that, as a by-product of the Stamp Act Congress, the boycott by colonial merchants in New York, Philadelphia, Boston, and elsewhere, supported by action taken by their respective Assemblies, struck at England's economic weakness. The success of this technique led colonial merchants to adopt nonimportation agreements again in 1768–69 to protest the enactment of the Townshend Duties. The nonimportation, nonexportation, nonconsumption agreements boldly passed by the First Continental Congress in 1774 were, in essence, enlargements of the same boycott measures that immediately followed adjournment of the Stamp Act Congress nine years before. It is important to note that the effectiveness of the boycotts was due to the joining of forces by private business and governmental agencies in protesting the objectionable actions taken by the mother country.

NOTES TO CHAPTER 5

1. The petition was published in the December 9, 1765, edition of the *Boston Evening Post*. The New York Assembly, in its petition to Commons October 18, 1764, was the "first unequivocal denial by any colonial assembly of Parliament's right to tax." Edmund S. Morgan, *The New York Declaration of 1764*, Old South Leaflets No. 224 (Boston, 1948).

2. *The Journal of the Votes and Proceedings of the General Assembly, November 8, 1743 to December 23, 1765* (New

York, 1766), 2: 795–802. In the discussions in the New York Assembly about selecting the proper agent to deliver the petitions, one suggestion offered was to send two of the members, William Smith, Jr., and Robert R. Livingston, but it was rejected. Livingston Papers, Bancroft Transcripts, New York Public Library, R. R. Livingston letter to John Sergeant dated Dec. 20, 1765.

3. *Journal of Votes and Proceedings* . . . , pp. 807–8. A transcript may also be found in *Prologue*, pp. 60–62.

4. William Samuel Johnson Papers, Historical Society of Connecticut Manuscripts, letter of November 4, 1765.

5. *Conn. Recs.*, 12: 420; see also *Conn. Hist. Colls.*, 18: 366–67; 370–73.

6. William Samuel Johnson Papers, letter of January 10, 1766.

7. Groce, *William Samuel Johnson*, p. 30.

8. A transcript appears in *Prologue*, pp. 54–56.

9. *Gibbes*, 1: 7; see also William Henry Dayton, *Memoir of the American Revolution, etc.* (Charleston, S. C., 1821), 1: 39. A transcript of the Resolves appears in *Prologue*, pp. 57–58.

10. *Georgia Gazette*, May 21, 1766.

11. *The Colonial Records of the State of Georgia*, compiled by Allen D. Candler (Atlanta, 1907), 14: 300–301, 315–18.

12. *N. H. Recs.*, 7: 92.

13. *The Colonial Records of North Carolina*, collected and ed. by William L. Saunders (Raleigh, N.C. 1890), 8: 347–48.

14. *Journals of the House of Burgesses (1766–1769)*, p. 12.

15. *Ibid.*

16. *Mass. Journals*, 42: 163–64; pp. 303–12. Massachusetts passed its own Resolves on Oct. 29, 1765; see *Prologue*, pp. 56–57.

17. *Pennsylvania Archives*, 8th s. 7: 5800–5810.

18. *Ibid.*, p. 5810. Joseph Galloway wrote Franklin that he felt that the language of the petitions drawn up at the Congress was not "Decent and Moderate," and would not be favorably received in Whitehall. *Papers of Franklin*, 12: 378.

19. *Maryland Archives*, 59: 139, 142, 180–81.

20. *NJCD*, 24: 682–83.

21. *Ibid.*, pp. 683–84. The Resolves are reprinted in *Prologue*, pp. 59–60.

22. *R.I. Recs.*, 6: 461–62; 474–75. On Dec. 13, 1765, Sherwood wrote to Samuel Smith stating that he had seen the petitions signed at New York and felt that "upon the whole they are modestly worded."

23. *Minutes Lower Counties,* p. 41. The amount allotted was £140; see *ibid.,* p. 51.
24. See DeBerdt's letters to Samuel White and George Wyllys, both dated February 15, 1766, *Transactions of the Colonial Society of Massachusetts Publications,* 13: 311, 315. DeBerdt was later the agent for the Lower Counties, given the assignment of delivering an address to the King and thanking him for the repeal of the Stamp Act. The Assembly presented him with a silver plate for his efforts in behalf of repeal. Massachusetts paid him £600 sterling for his services, *ibid.,* pp. 300–301.
25. *R.I. Recs.,* 6: 473.
26. See letter dated March 5, 1766, *Maryland Historical Magazine* (1911): 6, pp. 288–89. Except for Garth and DeBerdt, it is unlikely that the other agents acted formally on the petitions sent to them. They maintained good communications with each other, and were fully aware that the petitions signed by their "clients" had already been submitted. Rhode Island's agent Joseph Sherwood reported in a letter to Governor Ward that the House of Commons had all the papers relating to the opposition to the Act read before them, and it was obvious he did not feel it advisable to offer the identical petitions, *R.I. Recs.,* 6: 484. In another letter to Governor Ward dated March 13, 1766, Sherwood reported that the address to the King was delivered, and the petition to Commons was read, but not accepted, but "that which was Addressed for the Lords being called a Memorial, could not by the Rules of that House be Admitted, as nothing of that Sort can be presented to them, but under the Designation of an Humble Petition." *The Correspondence of the Colonial Governors of Rhode Island, 1723–1775,* ed. Gertrude Selwyn Kimball, 2 vols. (Cambridge, Mass., 1903), 1: 383.
27. *Adams Works,* 2: 175. As James Otis aptly appraised the situation in a letter to William Samuel Johnson dated Nov. 12, 1765, " 'tis much feared the Parliament will charge the Colonies with presenting petitions in one hand and a dagger in the other." William Samuel Johnson Papers, Connecticut Historical Society.
28. See Conway's letter to the King, *The Correspondence of King George III,* ed. Sir John W. Fortescue (London, 1927–1928), 1: 246.
29. Garth's letter, *Maryland Historical Magazine,* 6: 283–84.
30. *Correspondence of George III,* pp. 247–48. Official report of

the debate in Parliament is found in *The Parliamentary History of England,* ed. William Cobbett (London 1806–1820), 16: 96–163.

31. *Pitkin,* 1: 457. Cf. the protest in the House of Lords, *A Collection of Papers Relating to the Dispute between Great Britain and America, 1764–1775,* ed. John Almon (London 1777), pp. 81–85. See also Lawrence Henry Gipson, "The Great Debate in the Committee of the Whole House of Commons . . . ," *Pennsylvania Magazine of History and Biography* 86 (1962): 10–41.

32. *Boston Evening Post,* November 11, 1765, refers to seventy merchants having drawn up the resolution. The text of the resolution and other details are given in the November 7 edition of the *New York Post Boy.* See also *Prologue,* p. 106, for the same text as it appeared in the *Pennsylvania Gazette.* Albany merchants also joined the boycott (*New York Post Boy,* Nov. 7, 1765), and New York merchants organized a committee of five to solicit cooperation in the boycott from other seaport towns; see Mary Louise Booth, *History of the City of New York* (New York, 1866), p. 417.

33. Letter to his father, dated November 2, 1765, Bancroft Transcripts New York Public Library.

34. The text is found in the *Pennsylvania Gazette,* no. 1925, an undated four-page sheet headed "Remarkable Occurrences," with the masthead missing. During the crisis when no stamped paper was available, the editor resorted to this stratagem. Frank M. Etting, *The History of Independence Hall* (Boston, 1876), opposite p. 55 illustrates what is purported to be a facsimile of the merchants' resolutions, including all the signatories. However, this document is incorrectly dated October 25, 1765, which led Etting to conclude that the Philadelphia merchants took action first, followed by those in New York. The records are clear that the New York resolutions were passed on October 31, and those in Philadelphia on November 14.

On November 28, 1765, the *Pennsylvania Gazette* reported that Philadelphia merchants and traders prepared and signed a memorial addressed to merchants and manufacturers in Great Britain requesting them to influence Parliament to repeal the Stamp Act. This is a different document from the November 14 resolutions, and the text may be found in an undated printed brochure in the Jonah Thompson Collections, Manuscript Room, Historical Society of Pennsylvania (2: 111), entitled "To The Merchants And Manufacturers Of Great

Britain, The Memorial Of The Merchants and Traders Of The City Of Philadelphia." It not only called for repeal of the Stamp Act, but protested the Currency Act. It was signed by 281 merchants, including George Bryan.

35. The Boston resolutions permitted the importation of certain specified products used in local manufacturing, as well as products needed to carry on fishing.

36. *Crisis,* p. 264. In early December, the New York nonimportation resolutions were published in Bristol, England, and Bristol merchants took the initiative in petitioning Parliament for repeal of the Stamp Act. Walter E. Minchton, "The Stamp Act Crisis: Bristol and Virginia," *Virginia Magazine of History and Biography* 73 (1965): 145–55.

37. Grenville Letter Book, St-7, Henry E. Huntington Library, whose permission to quote the passage is gratefully acknowledged. There can be little doubt that American reaction to the Stamp Act, even prior to the Stamp Act Congress, especially the street riots, intimidated the relatively young and inexperienced Lord Rockingham, as is discussed by Jack M. Sosin, *Whitehall and the Wilderness* (Lincoln, 1961). Although political expediency, as Sosin maintains, played a part in repeal (p. 95), it was the economic factors that brought on the crisis in England. One can give no credence to Barry's remarks in *Mr. Rutledge of South Carolina* (p. 122) that repeal came about for the King's having been moved to action after he read the memorial sent to the House of Lords!

38. Miller, *Origins of the Amercian Revolution*, p. 155. Jack M. Sosin, *Agents and Merchants* (Lincoln, Neb., 1965), points out that Rockingham was ably assisted by Barlow Trecothick, a merchant and agent for New Hampshire, who helped organize the campaign to focus mercantile pressure on Parliament. Additional information on the activity of the colonial agents is found in Michael G. Kammen, *A Rope of Sand* (Ithaca, New York, 1968).

39. See *Prologue,* p. 155, for the statute. In one of his "Letters to the Inhabitants of the British Colonies," Dickinson bitterly complained that repeal resulted from commercial reasons, not as a consequence of depriving the colonists of their constitutional rights. *Dickinson,* pp. 479–80.

40. *Dr. Chauncy's Discourse on a Day of Thanks-Giving for the Repeal of the Stamp Act* (Boston, 1766). See other sermons listed in the bibliography.

41. Samuel Frank, "The Overstruck Stamps and the Altered Dies

of the Stamp Act of 1765," pp. 17–19 in *New Discovery from British Archives on the 1765 Tax Stamps for America*, ed. Adolph Koeppel, American Revenue Association (Boyertown, Pa., 1962).

42. *Dickinson*, p. 432.
43. In the Declaratory Act, passed immediately before the repeal of the Stamp Act, Parliament claimed authority over the colonies "in all cases whatsoever." This meant that by repealing the Stamp Act it was not giving up its right to tax the colonies, and it subsequently exercised that right with tragic results.
44. *The Political Writings of John Dickinson*, 2: 177.
45. *Journal of the Proceedings of the Congress Held at Philadelphia, Sept. 5, 1774*, facsimile ed., with introduction by Edwin Wolf 2nd (Library Company of Phila., 1974).

Appendix

Members of Stamp Act Congress

Bayard, William	N.Y.
Borden, Joseph	N.J.
Bowler, Metcalf	R.I.
Bryan, George	Pa.
Cruger, John	N.Y.
Dickinson, John	Pa.
Dyer, Eliphalet	Conn.
Fisher, Hendrick	N.J.
Gadsden, Christopher	S.C.
Johnson, William Samuel	Conn.
Lispenard, Leonard	N.Y.
Livingston, Philip	N.Y.
Livingston, Robert R.	N.Y.
Lynch, Thomas	S.C.
McKean, Thomas	Del.
Morton, John	Pa.
Murdock, William	Md.
Ogden, Robert	N.J.
Otis, James	Mass.
Partridge, Oliver	Mass.
Ringgold, Thomas	Md.
Rodney, Caesar	Del.
Rowland, David	Conn.
Ruggles, Timothy	Mass.
Rutledge, John	S.C.
Tilghman, Edward	Md.
Ward, Henry	R.I.

Excerpts from William Samuel Johnson's Diary
While Attending the Stamp Act Congress[1]

William Samuel Johnson's Memorandum Books and Diary,
covering the period from 1765 to 1802, contain important
historical data that have not yet been published. The following excerpts from his diary when he attended the Stamp Act
Congress in New York provide information not available in
other sources. I have extracted only those portions of the
diary which relate directly to the Congress; Johnson handled
a number of business and legal matters while he was in New
York, which are included in the diary but have nothing to
do with the Congress. Since I have lifted the pertinent pas-
sages out of context, I have supplied punctuation and normalized the spelling. I have also added the names of the days
alongside the dates appearing to the left in the diary.

Wed.	Oct. 2	Set out [from his home in Stratford, Conn.] at 10 o'clock with Van Dyck—At Fairfield took up Mr. [David] Rowland. . . . Dined at Norwalk, waited upon his Honor— Lodged at Stamford.
Thurs.	Oct. 3	Set out at 7. Breakfast at Knap's—Dined at Butler's. . . . Tea at 10 M. . . . Came in at 8 to Mrs. Stuy[vesant] [at New York] found Col. [Eliphalet] Dyer, Capt. Ledlie &c. there. All supped together.
Fri.	Oct. 4	. . . At 10 [A.M.] went to the Congress, and was introduced to the members.[2] Did no business but are waiting for Maryland and Jersey. Dined at home with Mr. Rowland and Col. Dyer. . . .[3] In evening at Coffee House till 8, supped at home.
Sat.	Oct. 5	. . . at 11 to Congress. Dined at Col. Stuy-vesant's . . . and spent the afternoon. In evening Rowland here.

Sun.	Oct.	6	[No reference to the Congress]
Mon.	Oct.	7	Opened the Congress. Formed [organized] and continued on business till half after two. Massachusetts, Rhode Island, Connecticut, New York, Pennsylvania, New Castle, Maryland & South Carolina appear by their Committees. At three went over the River to dine with Alderman [Philip] Livingston. In evening at Dr. Charlton's.
Tues.	Oct.	8	Congress opened at 9. Committees appointed.[4] Dined at the Mayor's [John Cruger]. . . . Committee met at 6—supped at 10 at Fisher's with Dyer & Rowland.
Wed.	Oct.	9	Met at 10—considered drafts [of Declaration of Rights] &c till 2. Dined at Mr. [William] Bayard's at Greenwich. Came in at 7. Spent the evening in walking.
Thurs.	Oct.	10	. . . At Congress ½ after 10. . . .
Fri.	Oct.	11	[Although the Congress met at 10:00 A.M., Johnson apparently did not attend. His diary entries refer to business matters that he handled.]
Sat.	Oct.	12.	All day at Congress writing &c. Dined at Burns's [City Arms Tavern]. Evening at Vander Burgh's, at Dyer's, and evening writing.
Sun.	Oct.	13	At old Church all day. . . . Wrote at night till 12.[5]
Mon.	Oct.	14	At 9 at Congress, dined and supped at Burn's. . . .
Tues.	Oct.	15	At Congress at 10. Dined with Court at Queen's Head. Evening walked. . . .
Wed.	Oct.	16	Rainy—dined at Mrs. Grant's—Afternoon & Evening at Congress. . . .
Thurs.	Oct.	17	At Congress at 9. This day we dined the Court and Bar.[6] In evening walking. . . .

Fri.	Oct. 18	. . . at Congress at 10. Dined with Judge [Robert R.] Livingston. Returned to Congress at 6—debated till 9 [on Declaration of Rights]. Supped and returned home at 11.
Sat.	Oct. 19	Congress at 9—Dined with the gentlemen of the town at Burn's.[7] At Mrs. Nicholls at 7. Came home at 8. Read till 12.
Sun.	Oct. 20	All day at Judge Livingston's. . . .[8]
Mon.	Oct. 21	. . . Dined at Burn's, afternoon at Congress. [On this day the Congress approved the address to the King, which Johnson had helped write.]
Tues.	Oct. 22	. . . at Congress 10. Dined Burns—afternoon at Congress.
Wed.	Oct. 23	. . . At Congress 10—Dined Lawyer Reade's—Afternoon at Holt's. Tea at Charlton's—evening at Congress and there till 12. [Petition to House of Commons approved at this session, apparently after an argumentative discussion that lasted until midnight.]
Thurs.	Oct. 24	. . . Dined John Watt's. . . . Evening [at] Congress.
Fri.	Oct. 25	. . . Broke up Congress at 3 o'clock. . . . Dined at 4 with [James] Otis, Patridge [Oliver Partridge] &c.[9]
Sat.	Oct. 26	Set out at 7 [for home]—Breakfast at Knap's. Dined Norwalk, left Dyer and Rowland at Fairfield—came home at 9 o'clock [P.M.] and found all well. . . .[10]

NOTES TO APPENDIX

1. The original diary is part of the William Samuel Johnson Memorandum Books and Diaries, 1765–1802, in the Special Manuscript Collections, Butler Library, Columbia University. I am grateful to the University for supplying me with a mi-

crofilm and for granting me permission to publish the excerpts. There is also a transcript of the diary for the period from October 2, 1765, to October 26 in the Bancroft Transcripts, New York Public Library. I have compared the transcript with the original and find that it is an accurate rendition.

2. If the Congress met in City Hall, as Stokes and others have indicated, the delegates must have gathered there prior to the official opening on October 7 in order to get acquainted and exchange views. The first informal meeting of September 30 was probably held here.

3. The delegates no doubt observed 4:00 as the dinner hour, following the custom in England during the reign of George III. (During the reign of George IV, dinner moved up to 6 o'clock, and later to 7 or 8.) Following dinner the delegates "supped" about 9:00 P.M. When Johnson refers to dining or supping "at home," he must mean his temporary lodgings in New York City.

4. According to the Journal of the Congress, the only committee elected on October 8 was the one to approve the minutes of the Congress. Apparently another committee was named to draft a Declaration of Rights, and this may have been the committee to which Johnson refers in the eleven-page manuscript report preserved in the Library of Congress. Regrettably, the names of the members of this committee were not recorded. Richard Barry in *Mr. Rutledge of South Carolina* (New York, 1942), p. 114, states that Rutledge, Dickinson, and Otis were members of a "Resolutions Committee" assigned to prepare the Declaration of Rights. I have not been able to confirm this, nor many other statements made by Barry, but he may have had access to manuscripts that I have failed to find, despite diligent search and with the cooperation of institutions cited in his book.

5. I interpret this entry to mean that he was working on the aforementioned eleven-page report, or on other reports having to do with the business of the Congress.

6. This must mean that the delegates were hosts to the presiding judges, and the lawyers who were members of the New York Court and Bar Association, thus reciprocating the dinner of October 15.

7. The "gentlemen of the town" may have referred only to the five New York delegates attending the Congress. On the other hand, it may also have included some of the local merchants. This could have been one of the numerous occasions when there was opportunity to discuss boycotting English imports.

8. On Saturday, October 19, according to the Journal, Robert R. Livingston, Johnson, and Murdock, were elected members of a committee to prepare the address to the King and lay it before the Congress on Monday the 21st. This may have been the business that caused Johnson to spend all day at Livingston's home. Unfortunately, he does not indicate whether or not Murdock was present.

9. This must have been an interesting dinner, with talk about the departure of Robert Ogden and General Ruggles after they had refused to sign the petitions.

10. On his trip from Stratford to New York on October 2 to attend the Congress, Johnson lodged overnight at Stamford. On the return trip, which required fourteen hours, he did not stop. The distance between City Hall and his residence in Stratford was perhaps no more than 75 or 80 miles via "the great road" between New York and Boston, which ran through Stratford. This was the route used by the stages.

Account of the Ships by Which the Stamps Were Transmitted to America and the Times of Putting Them on Board, 1765[1]

Distributors' Names	Ships' Names	Captains' Names	When Stamps Were Shipped
Archib[al]d Hinchelwood [Henchedwood?][2] *Nova Scotia*[3]	Rainbow	Philip Westcot	29th June, 1765
	Polly	Henry Wilson	10 July
	Boston Packett	John Marchall	16 Septr.
Colin Drummond *Quebec*	Ranger	James Cooper	4 July
	Glory	Wm. Haberjamb	11 Do[Ditto]
	John & Sukey	James Bruce	18 Septr.
John Mackenzie *Montreal & Trois Rivieres*	Ranger	James Cooper	4 July
	Glory	Wm. Haberjamb	11 Do
	John & Sukey	James Bruce	18 Septr.
John [George?] Meserve *New Hampshire*	Thomas & Sally	Wm. Deverson	28 June
	John Galley	Thomas Hulme	22 July
	Devonshire	Hugh Hunter	7 August
Andrew Oliver *Massachusetts*	John Galley	Thos. Hulme	22 July
	Devonshire	Hugh Hunter	7 August
	John & Sukey	James Bruce	5 Septr.

	Ships	Masters	Dates
Augustus Johnson *Rhode Island*	John Galley Devonshire John & Sukey	Thomas Hulme Hugh Hunter James Bruce	22 July 7 August 5 Septr.
Jared Ingersol *Connecticut*	Edward Polly Minerva John & Sukey	William Davis Joseph Haviland Thos. Tillet James Bruce	29 July 5 August 15 Do 18 Septr.
James Mc Evers *New York*	Edward Polly Minerva York	Wm. Davis Jos. Haviland Thos. Tillet Peter Barton	29 July 5 August 15 Do 20 Septr.
William Cox *New Jersey*	Royal Charlotte Philadelphia Packett Prince George	Benja. Holland Richd. Budden Jas. Robinson	16 July[4] 7 August 5 Septr.
John Hughes *Penna. and Three Lower Counties*	Royal Charlotte Philadelphia Packett Prince George	Benja. Holland Richd. Budden James Robinson	16 July 7 August 5 Septr.
Zachariah Hood *Maryland*	Leeds Royal Charlotte Mary & Elizabeth	John Anderson Benja. Holland James Sparks	16 July Do 30 Septr.

	Ship	Captain	Date
George Mercer *Virginia*	Leeds Matty Theodorick	John Anderson Henry Fox John McNab	16 July Do 30 Septr.
William Houston *North Carolina*	Leeds Matty Theodorick	John Anderson Henry Fox John McNab	July Do 30 Septr.
Caleb Lloyd *South Carolina*	Planters Adventure Carolina Packet Portland	Miles Lowley William White Geo. Higgins	1 August 26 Do 19 Septr.[5]
George Angus *Georgia*	Planters Adventure Carolina Packet Portland	Miles Lowley William White Geo. Higgins	1 August 26 Do 19 Septr.
Thomas Graham *East Florida*	Planters Adventure Carolina Packet Portland	Miles Lowley William White Geo. Higgins	5 August 26 Do 19 Septr.
Jacob Blackwell *West Florida*	Grenville Packet Carolina Packet Portland	Chs. Edwards William White Geo. Higgins	August 26 Do 19 Septr.
John Slater *Bermudas*	Mercury	Nathl. Butterfield	24 August

		Planters Adventure	Miles Lowley	1 Do
Governor of Bahama	*Bahama*	Carolina Packet	William White	26 Do
		Portland	Geo. Higgins	19 Do
		Countess of Dumfries	John Gordon	25 July
John Howell	*Jamaica*	Catherine	Hector Rose	26 August
		Lively	John Pringle	10 Septr.
		Duke of Marlborough	Saml. Auther	1 August
William Tuckett	*St. Kitts*	Union	Anthony Hooper	15 Do
		Nevis Planter	John Beach	27 Septr.
William Otley		Prince of Wales	Roderick Wilson	5 August
[Ottley, Jr.]	*Leeward Islands,*	New Elizabeth	John Smith	31 Do
	except St. Kitts	William & Elizabeth	David Young	12 Septr.
		Harriot	T. Blackburn	1 August
William Whitehead	*Barbados*	Catherine	Henry Carter	19 Septr.
[Whitefield?]		Payne	John Lee	16 Do
		Grenville Packet	Charles Edwards	August
Robert Seaman	*Granada*	Bellona	Thos. Parkinson	23 Do
		Grenada Frigate	Richd. Whitehead	13 Septr.
Colin Drummond	*Quebec*	Ellis	Saml. Richd. Egdon	20 Novr.

James [John?] Mackenzie	Do	Do	Do[6]
Archibald Hinchelwood	Do	Do	Do
George Meserve	Do	Do	Do
Andrew Oliver	Do	Do	Do
Augustus Johnson	Do	Do	Do
Jared Ingersoll	Waddel	James Chambers	22 Octr.
James McEvers	Do	Do	16 Do
William Cox	Ellis	Saml. Richd. Egdon	2 Novr.
John Hughes	Do	Do	2 Do
Zachariah Hood	Do	Do	2 Do
George Mercer	Do	Do	2 Do
William Houston	Do	Do	2 Do
Caleb Lloyd	London	Stracham [Strachan?]	2 Do
George Angus	Do	Do	2 Do
Thomas Graham	Do	Do	2 Do
Jacob Blackwell	Do	Do	2 Do
John Slater	Ellis	Saml. Richd. Egdon	20 Novr.

Governor of Bahama	London	Strachan	20 Do
William Tuckett	Rowley	J. Kiddall	15 Do
William Otley	St. Kitts Planter	John Young	11 Do
William Whitehead	Fanny	Alexr. Hamilton	11 Do
Robert Seaman	Hankey	John Tobin	13 Novr.

1. This list is taken verbatim from the Fisher Transcripts, Manuscript No. 360, Maryland Historical Society. The assistance of Richard J. Cox, Curator of Manuscripts, and the Society's permission to reprint the list are both gratefully acknowledged.
2. The names given in brackets are taken from Gipson's *The Coming of the Revolution* (New York, 1954), pp. 82–83, based upon data Gipson found in transcripts of the Treasury Papers, Public Records Office, London.
3. I have added in italics the name of the colony where each stamp Distributor was located. The term *Stamp Master* was also used to describe this position.
4. On October 10, 1765, the *Pennsylvania Gazette* published an article describing the arrival of the *Royal Charlotte* in Philadelphia on Saturday, October 5. The article stated that she carried stamped paper for Maryland, New Jersey, and Pennsylvania, which confirms the above. The vessel remained for awhile at anchor off New Castle, sailed up the Delaware River protected by the warship *H.M.S. Sardine*. On its first appearance around Gloucester Point, the vessels lying in the harbor hoisted their colors at half mast, and the bells were tolled in Philadelphia.
5. According to the November 21, 1765, edition of the *Georgia Gazette,* the *Portland,* under command of Captain Higgins, arrived at Charleston, S.C., after a six-week voyage from London with stamped paper for Georgia, South Carolina, Bermuda, and the Bahamas.
6. This shipment delivered to MacKenzie by the *Ellis* was the fourth consigned to him; as the list indicates, the earlier shipments were made on the *Ranger,* the *Glory,* and the *John & Sukey.* The other distributors whose names are listed below his also received subsequent shipments, which left England on the dates indicated. It is apparent that careful planning was required in the London Stamp Office to schedule the shipments in order to minimize shipping costs and to avoid building up an unwieldy inventory in the warehouses of the American Stamp Distributors. The repeal of the Stamp Act disrupted the entire operation.

Complete List of 44 Vessels Carrying Stamped Paper
June to November, 1765*

Bellona

Boston Packet

Carolina Packet

Catherine

Countess of Dumfries

Devonshire

Duke of Marlborough

Edward

Ellis

Fanny

Grenada Frigate

Grenville Packet

Glory

Harriot

Hankey

John Galley

John & Sukey

Leeds

Lively

London

Mary & Elizabeth

Matty

Mercury

Minerva

Nevis Planter

New Elizabeth

Payne

Philadelphia Packet

Planters Adventure

Polly

Portland

Prince George

Prince of Wales

Rainbow

Ranger

Rowley

Royal Charlotte

St. Kitts Planter

Theodorick

Thomas & Sally

Union

Waddel

William & Elizabeth

York

* Most of the vessels carried stamped paper to more than one Stamp Distributor. For example, the *Carolina Packet* brought consignments to the Bahamas, East Florida, West Florida, Georgia, and South Carolina.

Stamp Office. Lincoln Inn
London May 10th 1766*

Sir

    I am ordered by the Commissioners to acquaint you, it is the direction of the Lords Commissioners of His Majesty's Treasury to have all the stamped parchment and paper Consigned to you, sent back to this Office and the Commissioners will endeavour to get directions from the Admiralty for the ships of War returning to England to bring all the Stamps home. Therefore if you have any stamps in your Custody or power, you will please to apply to the Commanders of such ships to take the stamps, on Board in order that they may be brought to England by them.

I am
Your humble servt.
John Brettett [Secretary]

[to] John Hughes, Esqr.

---

* Copied from a photograph of the original document in the Miscellaneous Collections, Stamp Act Congress, Manuscript Room, Historical Society of Pennsylvania. The Society's permission to reprint the document is gratefully acknowledged. Apparently the same letter was sent to all the Stamp Distributors, but this is the only copy that has been found to date. However, Grey Cooper wrote Governor Stephen Hopkins of Rhode Island on May 5, 1776, requesting the return to London of all stamped paper that remained in the colonies, *R.I. Recs.*, 6: 491, although Hopkins was no longer in office, having been succeeded by Samuel Ward. Undoubtedly similar communications were sent to the other colonial governors, or to the former Stamp Distributors, or both.

Select Bibliography

PERTAINING ONLY TO STAMP ACT

Although it is more than twenty years old, one of the best comprehensive bibliographies of the period preceding the American Revolution is given by Lawrence Henry Gipson *The Coming of the Revolution* (New York, 1954), pp. 235–78. Another, with later titles, is found in Bernhard Knollenberg, *Origin of the American Revolution* (New York, 1961), pp. 277–317, and still another in John C. Miller, *Origins of the American Revolution*, rev. ed. (Stanford, Calif., 1966), pp. 508–17. More recently, Bernard Bailyn, *The Ideological Origins of the American Revolution* (Cambridge, Mass., 1967), discusses in his first two chapters the pamphlets published prior to the war. Finally, an excellent bibliography of economic history references is found in Joseph Albert Ernst, *Money and Politics in America* (Chapel Hill, N.C., 1973), pp. 379–93.

Since these volumes are readily available, it seems unnecessary to duplicate the titles that have been used in the footnotes in the present volume. In fact, to make a separate bibliography of the references cited in the footnotes would serve no useful purpose. It seemed more valuable and useful to compile a select bibliography, limited to published books, pamphlets, articles, and printed sermons related specifically to the Stamp Act. Such a listing is not now available and students should be able to use this to advantage. Omitted are theses and dissertations; titles of books containing chapters or sections discussing the Stamp Act (such as Edmund S. Morgan, *The Birth of the Republic, 1763–1789* (Chicago, 1956) ; and textbooks, papers, and articles that contain only incidental reference to the Stamp Act. The list contains only those works, all of which I have consulted, which deal exclusively, or primarily with the subject.

Anderson, George P. "Ebenezer MacIntosh, Stamp Act Rioter," Colonial Society of Massachusetts Publications 26. *Transactions, 1924–1926.* Boston, 1927.

Appleton, The Rev. Nathaniel. *Thanksgiving Sermon on the Total Repeal of the Stamp Act.* Boston, 1766.

Chauncy, [Charles]. *Dr. Chauncy's Discourse on a Day of Thanks-Giving for the Repeal of the Stamp Act.* Boston, 1766.

Church, Benjamin. *Liberty and Property Vindicated and the ST--P --N Burnt.* New London, Conn., 1765. [The "STAMP MAN" refers to Jared Ingersoll, Connecticut Stamp Distributor.]

Conduct of Cadwallader Colden, Esq., Late Lieut-Governor of New York (Relating to the judge's commission, appeals to the King and the Stamp Duty). London, 1767.

Connolly, James C. "The Stamp Act and New Jersey's Opposition to It." *Proceedings,* New Jersey Historical Society, n.s. 9 (1924) : 137–50.

Considerations on the American Stamp Act and on the Conduct of the Minister Who Planned It. London, 1766.

Crane, Verner W. "Benjamin Franklin and the Stamp Act." Colonial Society of Massachusetts Publications 32. *Transactions, 1937.* Boston, 1937.

Crisis, Or a Full Defence of the Colonies. Printed for W. Griffin, London, 1766.

Crouse, Maurice A. "Cautious Rebellion: South Carolina's Opposition to the Stamp Act." *South Carolina Historical Magazine* 73 (1972) : 59–71.

Davidson, Philip G. "Sons of Liberty and Stamp Men." *North Carolina Historical Review* 9 (1932) : 38–56.

Dickinson, Alice. *The Stamp Act, a Focus Book.* New York, 1970.

Dowell, Stephen. *A History and Explanation of Stamp Duties.* London, 1873.

Ellefson, C. Ashley. "The Stamp Act in Georgia." *Georgia Historical Quarterly* 46 (1962) : 1–19.

Emerson, Joseph, *A Thanksgiving-Sermon Preach'd at Pepperell, July 24, 1766,* Boston, 1766.

Engelman, F. L. "Cadwallader Colden and the New York

Stamp Act Riots." *William and Mary Quarterly*, 3d s. 10 (1953) : 560–78.

Ericson, Fred J. "The Contemporary British Opposition to the Stamp Act." *Michigan Academy of Science, Arts and Letters, Papers* 29 (1943) : 489–505.

Examination of Doctor Benjamin Franklin . . . Relative to the Repeal of the Stamp Act in 1766. London, 1766.

Fish, Elisha. *Joy and Gladness: A Thanksgiving Discourse Preached in Upton, May 28, 1766.* Providence, R.I., 1767.

General Opposition of the Colonies to the Payment of the Stamp Duty. London, 1766.

Giddens, Paul H. "Maryland and the Stamp Act Controversy." *Maryland Historical Magazine* 27 (1932) : 79–98.

Gipson, Lawrence Henry "The Great Debate in the Committee of the Whole House of Commons on the Stamp Act, 1766." *Pennsylvania Magazine of History and Biography* 86 (1962) : 10–41.

Greene, Jack P., ed. "Not to be Governed or Taxed, But by . . . Our Representatives" (four essays by Col. Landon Carter opposing the Stamp Act). *Virginia Magazine of History and Biography* 76 (1968) : 259–300.

Haywood, C. Robert. "The Mind of the North Carolina Opponents of the Stamp Act." *North Carolina Historical Review* 29 (1952) : 317–43.

High, James. "Henry McCulloh: Progenitor of the Stamp Act." *North Carolina Historical Review* 29 (1952) : 24–38.

Hildeburn, Charles R. "Notes on the Stamp Act in New York and Virginia." *Pennsylvania Magazine of History and Biography* 2 (1878) : 296–302.

Hodge, Helen M. "The Repeal of the Stamp Act." *Political Science Quarterly* 19 (1904) : 252–76.

Hughes, Edward. "The English Stamp Duties, 1664–1764." *English Historical Review* 56 (1941) : 234–59.

Hull, C. H., and Temperley, H. W. V. "Debates on the Declaratory Act and the Repeal of the Stamp Act, 1766." *American Historical Review* 17 (1912) : 563–86.

Johnson, Allen S. "British Politics and the Repeal of the Stamp Act." *South Atlantic Quarterly* 62 (1963) : 169–88.

Kemmerer, Donald L. "New Material on the Stamp Act in New Jersey." *New Jersey Historical Society Proceedings* 56 (1938) : 220–25.

Kerr, Wilfred B. "The Stamp Act in Quebec." *English Historical Review* 47 (1932) : 648–51.

———. "The Stamp Act in Nova Scotia." *New England Quarterly* 6 (1933) : 552–66.

———. "The Stamp Act in the Floridas." *Mississippi Valley Historical Review* 21 (1935) : 463–70.

Koeppel, Adolph, ed., *New Discovery from the British Archives on the 1765 Tax Stamps for America.* Boyertown, Penna., 1962. [This excellent work contains five papers dealing with philately and a select annotated bibliography of philatelic literature relating to the stamped paper used in America.]

LaPrade, William T. "The Stamp Act in British Politics." *American Historical Review* 35 (1930) : 735–57.

"London Merchants on the Stamp Act Repeal." Letters of Feb. 28, 1766; March 18, 1766; and June 13, 1766, Massachusetts Historical Society *Proceedings* 55 (Oct. 1921–June 1922) : 215–23.

Mc Anear, Beverly. "The Albany Stamp Act Riots." *William and Mary Quarterly*, 3d s. 4 (1947) : 486–89.

Mayhew, Jonathan. *The Snare Is Broken.* Boston, 1766. (Sermon preached in Boston May 23, 1766, following repeal of the Stamp Act.)

Minchton, Walter E. "The Stamp Act Crisis: Bristol and Virginia." *Virginia Magazine of History and Biography* 73 (1965) : 145–55.

Miller, E. J. "The Virginia Legislature and the Stamp Act." *William and Mary Quarterly* 21 (1913) : 233–48.

Morgan, Edmund S. *Stamp Act Congress Declarations and Petitions.* Old South Leaflets, no. 223, Boston, 1948.

———. "Thomas Hutchinson and the Stamp Act." *New England Quarterly* 21 (1948) : 459–92.

———."The Postponement of the Stamp Act." *William and Mary Quarterly*, 3d s. 7 (1950) : 353–92.

———, and Morgan, Helen M. *The Stamp Act Crisis.* Chapel Hill, N.C., 1953.

———, ed. *Prologue to Revolution.* Chapel Hill, N.C., 1959.

Necessity of Repealing the America Stamp Act Demonstrated. London. 1766.

Newcomb, Benjamin H. "Effects of the Stamp Act on Colonial

Pennsylvania Politics." *William and Mary Quarterly*, 3d s. 23 (1966) : 257–72.

Patten, William. *Discourse . . . on the day of Thanksgiving to Almighty God . . . for the Repeal of the Stamp Act.* (Sermon preached at Halifax, Mass., July 24, 1766.) Boston, 1766.

"Resistance to Stamp Act." *Maryland Historical Magazine* 4 (1909) : 134–39.

Richardson, E. P. "Stamp Act Cartoons in the Colonies." *Pennsylvania Magazine of History and Biography* 96 (1972) : 275–97.

Ritcheson, Charles R. "The Preparation of the Stamp Act." *William and Mary Quarterly*, 3d s. 10 (1953) : 543–59. (See comments by Edmund S. Morgan on Ritcheson's paper in *William and Mary Quarterly* 11 (1954) : 157–60.)

Rowland, David Sherman, *Divine Providence Illustrated. . . .* (Sermon preached June 24, 1766, after repeal of Stamp Act.) Providence, 1766.

Schlesinger, Arthur M. "The Colonial Newspapers and the Stamp Act." *New England Quarterly* 8 (1935) : 63–83.

Short History of the Conduct of the Present Ministry with Regard to the American Stamp Act. Printed for J. Almon, London, 1766.

Sosin, J. M. "A Postscript to the Stamp Act, George Grenville's Revenue Measures. A Drain on Colonial Specie?" *American Historical Review* 63 (1958) : 918–23.

"Stamp Act Activities in New York, 1765." New York Historical Society *Quarterly Bulletin* 5 (1921) : 45–47.

"Stamp Act Papers." *Maryland Historical Magazine* 6 (1911) : 282–305.

Stillman, *Good News from a Far Country.* (Sermon preached at Boston, May 17, 1766.) Boston, 1766.

Stout, Neil R. "Captain Kennedy and the Stamp Act." *New York History* 45 (1964) : 44–58.

Troop, Benjamin. *A Thanksgiving Sermon Upon The Occasion of the Glorious Newes of the Repeal of the Stamp Act.* (Sermon preached July 26, 1766.) New London, 1766.

Turner, Sydney R. *Some Notes on the Stamps of the Stamp Act, 1765–1766.* Privately printed at Cheam, Surrey, England, 1945.

————. *Caricatures of the Newspaper Tax Stamps of Great Britain and America, 1765–1842.* Privately printed at Cheam, Surrey, England, 1941.

Waddell, Colonel A. M. *The Stamp Act on the Cape Frear.* North Carolina Booklet 1, no. 3 (July 10, 1901). (Published in Raleigh by the North Carolina Society of the Daughters of the American Revolution.)

Wolf, Edwin II, "Benjamin Franklin's Stamp Act Cartoon," American Philosophical Society *Proceedings* 99 (1955): 388–90.

Woody, Robert H. "Christopher Gadsden and the Stamp Act." South Carolina Historical Association *Proceedings* (1939), pp. 3–12.

Zubly, John Joachim. *The Stamp Act Repealed.* Savannah, Ga., 1766. (Sermon at Savannah, June 25, 1766.)

Index

(Illustrations are in boldface)